WHAT IS AMERICA?

Also by
RONALD WRIGHT

———

Fiction
A Scientific Romance
Henderson's Spear

History
A Short History of Progress
Stolen Continents

Travel
Time Among the Maya
On Fiji Islands
Cut Stones and Crossroads

Essays
Home and Away

WHAT IS
AMERICA?

A Short
History *of*
the New
World Order

RONALD WRIGHT

 VINTAGE CANADA

VINTAGE CANADA EDITION, 2009

Published in Canada by Vintage Canada, a division of Random House of Canada Limited, in 2009. Originally published in hardcover in Canada by Alfred A. Knopf Canada, a division of Random House of Canada Limited, in 2008. Distributed by Random House of Canada Limited, Toronto.

Vintage Canada and colophon are trademarks of Random House of Canada Limited.

www.randomhouse.ca

LIBRARY AND ARCHIVES CANADA CATALOGUING IN PUBLICATION

Wright, Ronald
    What is America? : a short history of the new world
order / Ronald Wright.

Includes bibliographical references and index.

ISBN 978-0-676-97983-1

    1. United States—History. 2. United States—Social
conditions. I. Title.

E178.W95 2009   973   C2009-900367-8

Book design by Kelly Hill

Printed and bound in the United States of America

10 9 8 7 6 5 4 3 2 1

For Diane

Contents

Author's Foreword

What then is the American, this new man?

—Hector St. John de Crèvecoeur, ca. 1776[1]

Whither goest thou, America, in thy shiny car in the night?

—Jack Kerouac, 1957[2]

T HE ARGUMENT AT THE HEART of this book—that the New World made the modern world and now threatens to undo it—came to me from the final chapter of my last one, *A Short History of Progress,* which outlined the long record of collisions between Nature and human nature. Much of *What Is America?* seeks to understand the rise of the United States from small colony to world power, but I raise the question within a larger context that has been neglected. Modern America—and modern civilization in general—are the culmination of a half-millennium we might call the Columbian Age. For Europe and its offshoots, the Americas really were Eldorado, a source of unprecedented wealth and growth. Our political and economic culture, especially its North American variant, has been built on a goldrush mentality of "more tomorrow."

The American dream of new frontiers and endless plenty has seduced the world—even Communist China. Yet this seduction has triumphed just as the Columbian Age shows many signs of ending, having exhausted the Earth and aroused appetites it can no longer feed. In short, the future isn't what it used to be.

When Stanley Kubrick made the film *2001: A Space Odyssey* forty years ago, it did not seem far-fetched to imagine that by the start of this millennium Americans might have a base on the moon and be flying manned craft to Jupiter. After all, only five decades had passed from the first aeroplane to the first space flight. But by the real 2001 there had been no man on the moon since 1972, elderly space shuttles were falling out of the sky, and the defining event of that year—and perhaps of the new century—was not a voyage to outer planets but the flying of airliners into skyscrapers by fanatics.

⸱⟫◉⟪⸱

The question "What is America?" could fill a library and a lifetime. At the beginning of his *Eminent Victorians,* published in 1918, the eminent modernist Lytton Strachey declared: "The history of the Victorian age will never be written: we know too much about it."[3] The wise explorer of the well-papered past, he advised, "will attack his subject in unexpected places . . . he will shoot a sudden, revealing searchlight into obscure recesses, hitherto undivined." I have tried to follow Strachey's advice. If history was already choked with data ninety years ago, how much more so now.

So this is an eccentric book, seeking the centre by its edges. I spend less time on the broad highways to the Founding Fathers, slavery, the Civil War—already glutted with a thousand books—and more on backroads to Mexico, Peru, the Pequots, the Five Civilized Tribes, the Mormons and the Philippines.

All who delve into American history have to contend with a language of misnomer and condescension: whites are soldiers, Indians are warriors; whites live in towns, Indians in villages; whites have states, Indians have tribes. As the Grand Council Fire of American Indians told the mayor of Chicago in 1927, the school histories "call all white victories, battles, and all Indian victories, massacres. . . . White men who rise to protect their property are called patriots—Indians who do the same are called murderers."[4]

Then there is the term *Indian* itself, which some indigenous Americans accept and others dislike. The word seems to commemorate Columbus's mistaken idea of where he went. America found Columbus. The unknown continents got in the way of his back route to China, and the admiral died in 1506 still believing he had been to islands off the coast of Asia—or, in his less rational moments, of which there were quite a few, to the shores of the Earthly Paradise (a venue revealed to him by its resemblance to a woman's breast).[5] Not for a generation did European visitors begin to grasp the scale and complexity of the new hemisphere stretching north and south to both polar seas. In yet another mistake, they then named it after the unworthy Amerigo Vespucci, described by his latest biographer as a pimp and confidence man.[6]

It is also true that European notions of "India" and "the Indies" were so vague that "Indian" could mean almost anyone who wasn't white, black or Chinese; Polynesians, for example, were also called Indians. Most of the current alternatives are flawed, unclear or difficult to use. "Native American" is seldom used outside the United States and, confusingly, was also the name of a white political movement of the nineteenth century. "Aboriginal" has long been associated with Australia. "First Nations" is little known outside Canada and does not work well as an adjective. However, the word *nation* has rightly been used for (and by) indigenous peoples since early colonial times—in the senses of both ethnic group and polity.

In English, American Indians should really be called "Americans"—as they often were until the eighteenth century. The wholesale takeover of that word by white settlers is a measure of the demographic catastrophe that gave rise to the United States. In this book, when the context is clear, I have restored the term *American* to its original meaning before the Revolution of 1776. Thereafter I find it impossible to avoid using *Indian*— especially as the word is embedded in historical sources, treaties and Acts of Congress. I apologize to readers who find the term objectionable.

⊹⇒○⇐⊹

Any outsider writing about the United States does so in the shadow of a twenty-five-year-old French aristocrat, Alexis de Tocqueville, the self-styled "bird of passage" whose *Democracy in America* has never been bettered as a broad analysis of the American character and promise.[7] I have also drawn on his private travel notes and interviews, published as *Journey to America,* which are less well known than *Democracy* but often more revealing.[8]

In 1831–32 Tocqueville toured the United States on a commission from the French government to study the young nation's prison system, a duty to which he by no means confined himself. He praised the modern "idea of reforming as well as of punishing the delinquent" but added that he also saw "dungeons . . . which reminded the visitor of the barbarity of the Middle Ages."⁹ That this observation might stand today for Guantánamo, Abu Ghraib or a number of stateside penitentiaries is typical of the unfading relevance of Tocqueville's work.

Though a keen observer and inspired extrapolator, Tocqueville was no historian. I mention this now, not to dwell on his flaws but to dispose of them. The Americans, he wrote, "have no neighbours, and consequently they have no great wars, or financial crises, or inroads, or conquest to dread; they . . . have nothing to fear from a scourge which is more formidable to republics than all these evils combined, namely, military glory. . . . Nothing is more opposed to the well-being and the freedom of man than vast empires."¹⁰

No neighbours? Tocqueville meant, of course, no *white* neighbours. By the lights of his time and class, only white men of standing were true actors in world events. Because he did not see the first Americans, or "Indians," as protagonists in American history, he failed to grasp that America already *was* an empire—armed, aggressive, expanding before his eyes and presided over by a militarist, General Andrew Jackson."¹ President Jackson was the George W. Bush of his day, loved by the gullible, hated by the intelligentsia and dismissed by Tocqueville himself as "a very mediocre man." The young Frenchman was a cautious optimist, and he hoped the presidency of the uncouth and violent general would be an aberration. He therefore failed to look very far into Jackson's career as an Indian killer and a practitioner of what is now called ethnic cleansing, the Indian Removal of the 1830s.¹²

Tocqueville's neglect of the past can also be put down to his youth: like the new republic itself, he fixed his gaze on the future.[13] For him, America had begun with its independence from Britain, barely fifty years before his visit. His interest in the formative colonial period went no deeper than skimming a few "histories" written by early Puritan settlers in New England and later books based on those accounts, which were also the reading of Americans he talked to. Like other extreme Protestants in Ulster and South Africa, the Puritans viewed their colonial migration through the lens of the Old Testament, seeing themselves as a chosen people in a Promised Land.[14] Tocqueville took those writings at face value, unaware they were religious and racial propaganda obscuring the truth about native societies and native-white relations.[15]

He therefore missed the importance of the frontier—a westering zone of warfare and cultural exchange since the 1600s—in shaping the settler nation. That insight would await the great American historian Frederick Jackson Turner, who saw that the frontier, which "strips off the garments of civilization," is the key to understanding American cultural patterns that have drifted away from the European mainstream.[16] "The wilderness masters the colonist," Turner announced in a lecture at the Chicago World's Fair in 1893, "Before long he has gone to planting Indian corn and plowing with a sharp stick; he shouts the war cry and takes the scalp in orthodox Indian fashion."[17]

Although Tocqueville missed Turner's insight, he did wonder how white America seemed to be having her cake and eating it too: conquering her hinterland yet doing so with her reputation unbesmirched. The Spanish conquerors of Mexico and Peru, he noted tartly, had failed to exterminate the indigenous race or even fully quash its rights, yet the Americans had "accomplished this twofold purpose . . . without violating a single great principle of morality in the eyes of the world."[18]

Then as now, such sleight of hand was done by invoking lofty hopes and ideals to hide unsightly truths. America is the country of the future, shriven from the past, including its own: a land paved with good intentions. As Lewis Lapham wrote sardonically in a *Harper's* essay called "Terror Alerts": "We're the good guys, released from the prison of history and therefore free to imagine that our era will never pass."[19]

1.

THE NEW WORLD ORDER

The American Empire . . . bids fair, by the blessing of God,
to be the most glorious of any upon Record.

—William Henry Drayton, 1776[1]

I tremble for my country when I reflect that God is just.

—Thomas Jefferson, 1784[2]

I never apologize for the United States of America. I don't
care what the facts are.　　　　—George H. Bush, 1988[3]

"WE ARE ALL AMERICANS NOW!" the front page of
Le Monde cried in sympathy in September 2001,
after airliners became missiles over New York and
Washington. Besides solidarity and outrage, the headline held
a broader truth, intended or not, that has been slowly dawning
for the past one hundred years: through military might, big
business, popular culture, covert operations and above all
through social example and the shining promise of modernity,
the United States has Americanized the world.

This process was just beginning when President Woodrow
Wilson idealistically called for "a new world order" after the

First World War.[4] At that time the phrase had nothing to do with empire. Quite the reverse. Wilson was promoting his plan for a League of Nations, an international body that would safeguard each country's sovereignty and settle disputes by arbitration. More than 10 million had died in four years of slaughter set off by a terrorist attack, the shooting of the heir to the throne of Austria-Hungary by a Serbian extremist. Or rather, the war had begun with the *reaction* to that attack—the invasion of a small country that had not sponsored the terrorism by an empire thirsting for revenge.

The United States never did join the League of Nations: not enough of Wilson's countrymen shared his ideals. And it would take another great war before Europe learned the lessons of its past. The phrase "new world order" was not much heard again until the collapse of the Soviet Union in 1989, leaving one nation mightier than all the others. An ironic reversal of Wilson's internationalism came in 2002, when President George W. Bush did all he could to sabotage the founding of the International Criminal Court (ICC). Bush feared that American nationals might be brought to book overseas—a realistic worry, given that his administration was breaking international law on the treatment of war prisoners. In March 2008, with only months left in office, he vetoed a Congressional bill that would have stopped American interrogators from torturing their suspects.[5]

⋅→⟛◉⟛←⋅

The United States is now the world's lone superpower—a successor to Britain, Spain and ancient Rome—an empire whose deeds could make or break this century.[6] Both within and beyond America, people are asking themselves what sort of imperium this might be. Will the new Rome, like the old, see its democracy wither as its power grows? Will it be ruled by a Senate, a Caesar or a Nero? Will its dominion be benign and inclusive, offering benefits as well as duties to its subjects, as in Rome and Britain at their best? Or will it be a rapacious overlordship, a robber empire extorting tribute and obedience, like the unloved reign of the Aztecs or the client-state networks of both Cold War superpowers at their worst?

After the flawed presidential election of 2000, the new Bush regime took the United States further to the political right than any other major western country since 1945, a shift that began *before* the terrorist attacks of September 11, 2001.[7] Washington's reaction to that tragedy—trampling its own Constitution and the Geneva Conventions in an unjust "war on terror"—has squandered solidarity at home and goodwill abroad, provoking a re-examination of the nation's essence: Is America what it thinks it is? Is America what the world has long believed it to be?

I hold that the recent difficulties run much deeper than a stolen election and an overreaction to a terrorist assault. The political culture and identity crisis of the United States are best understood as products of the country's past—the real past, not the imaginary one of national myth. The United States did not grow in a vacuum by the power of its ideals: it is not so much a new Europe across the Atlantic as a unique organism engendered by history's "Big Bang"—the collision of worlds that began in 1492. The new world order did not begin in 1919 with the League of Nations, nor in 1989 with the fall of the Soviet Union. It flows from Europe's takeover of the entire New World, or Western Hemisphere: the Spanish conquests of Mexico and Peru, which triggered five centuries of European expansion, and the British-American conquest of what is now the United States. So the America of my title has two meanings: the great republic most of the world simply calls "America" and the American landmass as a whole. My question "What is America?" applies to both. The answers have long roots, reaching far beyond the familiar tale—the rise of one nation to predominance.

The year 1492 wasn't very long ago. If you're past fifty, as I am, you've seen for yourself at least a tenth of the time since Columbus sailed. We are all still living with the consequences, good and bad. Our world descends from the American "surprise" that stopped Columbus on his way to Asia.[8] Within a few decades of that momentous contact, the wealth, crops and land of half a planet—a half that had been developing in isolation for at least fifteen thousand years—were suddenly laid open to the whole. The seed that would become the United States was planted then. The new order is indeed a *New World* order, and modern America more truly American than we know.

As the historian Frederick Jackson Turner first recognized in 1893, the United States was forged "in the crucible of the frontier."[9] In the mythology created by romantic novels and Hollywood westerns, the frontier is a virgin wilderness tamed by heroic pioneers. The real frontier was a rolling three-century war zone, from 1607 to 1890, in which the continent violently changed hands. As white migrants both displaced and absorbed the original Americans, a new culture came into being: a rapacious hybrid dependent on expansion—part European, part indigenous, yet neither. Elements of the old European civilization withered or got left behind; other elements grew rank in new ways. Isolated and unschooled, the frontier became a breeding ground for militarism and religious extremism—the two aspects of American culture that outsiders, and many Americans, find most alarming today, especially when they converge in government policy as they did under Ronald Reagan and again, more strongly, under George W. Bush.[10]

Even before the Indian wars ended in 1890 at Wounded Knee, the United States had begun projecting its power across the Pacific and into Latin America. The nation did not wake up one morning and find that it was suddenly imperial; it always has been so. Its founding president, George Washington, was right when he called the United States "a rising empire" back in 1783.[11] Nearly two centuries later, President John F. Kennedy proclaimed: "Our frontiers today are on every continent [stretching] ten thousand miles across the Pacific, and three and four thousand miles across the Atlantic, and thousands of miles to the south."[12] When American Marines sing "From the halls of Montezuma / To the shores of Tripoli," they are not boasting idly but recalling their conquest of Mexico in 1847 and a war with Libya as early as 1801.[13]

The new republic was also a bold and worthy experiment, an attempt to remake western civilization along utopian ideals of freedom, democracy and opportunity—"the world's best hope" as Thomas Jefferson, its third president, famously said.[14] But the practice of those ideals relied on a unique historical circumstance: the opening up of a new territory, with new means, in which to try them. Seen from inside by free citizens, the young United States was indeed a thriving democracy in a land of plenty; seen from below by slaves, it was a cruel tyranny; and seen from outside by free Indians, it was a ruthlessly expanding empire. All these stories are true, but if we know only one without the others, what we know is not history but myth. And such myths are dangerous.

Today's world, some argue, changes so quickly that the past is no longer much help to us. But I agree with the Australian historian Inga Clendinnen, who writes in a 2006 essay, "It is precisely because change is so swift that we need history."[15] From the personal to the international level, humans understand one another by watching behaviour through time. History is the best guide we have for threading our way through the frenetic video game of current events.[16] As the game speeds up, with runaway technological and social change, the great risk is that both the old and the young become isolated, in different ways, by the parochialism of the present: one generation gets marooned, the next swept along without a ship's log or a rudder.

To understand what forces shaped the United States and how the lone superpower may now play on the world stage, we must follow its record of expansion—for three centuries across its continent and for another century beyond. And we must begin with a clear sight of its American origins: of what awaited the European invaders in the Western Hemisphere. Any account that begins at the usual departure—the white-settler revolt against Britain in 1776—is starting halfway through the story.

Much of the first half is also the history of the English, my own nationality, who, like most human beings, have shown themselves capable of almost anything. Just as English schoolchildren don't hear much about their ancestors' colonial outrages in Ireland or how the Mutiny in India was avenged by binding rebels to cannon and blowing them apart, so American youngsters are not taught about the conquest and "removal" of the original Americans or the events that made Benjamin

Franklin denounce his compatriots as "Christian white savages."[17] To sleep well in their beds, nations, like individuals, rely on the art of forgetting.

It is said that indigenous Americans can live with themselves only by remembering the past, and white Americans only by forgetting it. The United States may not have committed more crimes than most other imperial nations, but it forgets them more quickly and more thoroughly. From the earliest days, the country has been built on the belief that it is an exception to history and an example to the world. Each failure of its ideals is therefore seen as an anomaly, not a pattern.

When the realities of power do intrude on the national consciousness, Americans undergo a "loss of innocence." This seems to happen about once a generation—as in the Mexican War, the Civil War, the Philippine War, the World Wars, Korea, Vietnam and now Afghanistan and Iraq. At least six of these nine were started mainly by Americans. Innocence grows back in defiance of truth like a self-restoring hymen, only to be lost again and again, with surprise and consoling resolutions of reform. Innocence is saved by ignorance, by not caring what the facts are—and therefore not learning from them. The elder George Bush made the remark quoted at the head of this chapter after a U.S. warship shot down an Iranian Airbus (said to have been mistaken for an F-14 fighter) in 1988, killing all 290 on board. It is hard to imagine a leading citizen of any other leading nation making such a remark in such circumstances or, if he did, receiving so little public censure. Only four months later, Mr. Bush was elected president. That his words did not wreck, or even hinder, his political career raises questions about American culture that the country and the world must address.

The United States regards itself, and has long been regarded, as the most "modern" country on Earth. Yet it is also archaic, a redoubt of Victorian beliefs in endless growth, untamed capitalism, unabashed nationalism and a universal mission. Such ideas may have been truly modern a century ago, but they have since fallen under suspicion elsewhere in the west, a rethinking driven by two world wars.

The United States is also home to a deep religious archaism, descended from the early Puritans and eerily similar to the belief system of today's Islamic terrorists. (After the September 11 attacks, the televangelist Jerry Falwell, a key matchmaker of Christian extremism with the Republican right since Ronald Reagan's day, said that America's tolerance for atheists, gays, civil-rights workers and the like had angered God and "helped this happen.")[18] One in two Americans rejects the evidence for evolution; the rest of Christendom gave up fighting Darwin a century ago. From biblical literalism flows a distrust of science and learning, and even of mere intellect in politicians. Half the nation tends to vote on the basis of narrowly defined religious views and moral "values"—an electorate easily gulled by folksy demagogues fronting for powerful interests.

In his latest book, called *The Assault on Reason*, former vice-president Al Gore, who lost the 2000 general election (though not the popular vote) to the younger George Bush, castigates the "persistent and sustained reliance on falsehoods as the basis of policy." The facts do matter. "Reason," Gore underlines, "is the true sovereign in the American system. Our self-government is based on the ability of individual citizens to use reason in holding their elected representatives . . . accountable. When reason itself comes under assault, American democracy is put at risk."[19]

Not only democracy but the future; not only America but the world. Historical amnesia may be a balm for patriots, but it can have no place in the twenty-first century's increasingly precarious world order.

2.

Loot, Labour and Land

Since the discovery of America, the greater part of Europe
has been much improved. England, Holland, France, and
Germany; even Sweden, Denmark, and Russia have all
advanced . . . both in agriculture and in manufactures.

—Adam Smith, 1776[1]

The Indians . . . seem to have been placed by Providence
amidst the riches of the New World to enjoy them for a season, and then surrender them.

—Alexis de Tocqueville, 1835[2]

The genius of American democracy comes not from any
special virtue of the American people but from the
unprecedented opportunities of this continent and from
a peculiar and unrepeatable combination of historical
circumstances.   —Daniel Boorstin, 1953[3]

IN THE 1830S THE YOUNG FRENCHMAN Alexis de
Tocqueville, making his way around the fledgling United
States by horse and steamboat, briefly discussed the mys-
tery of prehistoric American buildings with Sam Houston, who

had lived among the Cherokees and later became famous as the president of Texas.[4] At that time the ancient towns and earthen pyramids found along the Mississippi and elsewhere were a mystery, but Tocqueville (ever the futurist) took them as evidence of America's potential, rather than its past. "The whole continent," he mused prophetically, "seemed prepared to be the abode of a great nation, yet unborn."[5]

The New World had indeed been ripe for takeover by the Old, if not quite in the way Tocqueville imagined. Besides the land itself, the modern American empire would get most of its makings from two ancient American empires further south—albeit by way of Europe. Ever since the Aztecs of Mexico and the Incas of Peru had fallen to Spain in the sixteenth century, their treasures had been transforming the world.

The Aztecs and Incas have become marginal figures in our winners' history, exotic bit-players in the pageant of Europe's rise. Their only well-known role—as victims on a world stage stalked by the conquistadors—was indeed brief, a dozen years' tragedy from contact to collapse. But their legacy (and that of their forerunners) has been vast and enduring. In life the ancient American civilizations were unknown to the outside world. In death they became the key drivers behind the population boom of the last five centuries, the slave trade and, perhaps most surprisingly, the Industrial Revolution—a connection first noted by Karl Marx.[6] With the conquests of Mexico and Peru began the accumulation of loot, labour and land that would build the Columbian Age, at first in Europe and then in North America.

In the year 1500, there were some 400 million humans on Earth, of whom a fifth, or maybe a fourth—80 to 100 million—were living in the Americas. About half these Americans were subjects of the Aztec and Inca empires, each of which ruled 20 million people, more or less. (All such figures are merely informed guesswork; what matters here is their relative weight.[7]) Today, about one in twenty people is a citizen of the United States. In 1500 one in twenty was either an Aztec or an Inca subject. Taken together, the Mexican and Peruvian empires held one-tenth of humankind.

But that was at their height. They have since been sidelined by history—and for the same reason that they fell so swiftly. Within decades of first contact with Europeans, the populations of Mexico and Peru collapsed by more than 90 percent, abruptly reducing their presence in the world to less than one-hundredth of the human race. The demographer George Lovell has called this decline "the greatest destruction of lives in history."[8]

The Spaniards were doubtless efficient killers in those days, but no human agency of the time could have slaughtered anything like so many and so fast. It was the work of fate or, as the Europeans saw it, the will of God. For several thousand years, fate had been stacking biological weapons against America: smallpox, measles, influenza, bubonic plague, yellow fever, cholera, malaria and more—all unknown in the Western Hemisphere before 1492. Unlike Africa, whose tropical diseases kept whites at bay for centuries, America lacked mass killers of her own.

If we picture the 5 or 6 million years since humans and other apes parted company as a single day, we have achieved civilization in the last minute and a half. And industrial civilization—which is not much older than the United States itself—arose only in the last five seconds.[9]

By civilization, I mean the settled way of life that slowly took hold after the discovery of agriculture transformed the food supply, a chain of events called the Neolithic or Farming Revolution.[10] The Farming Revolution began around ten thousand years ago, and the earliest societies complex enough to be called civilizations appeared about five thousand years ago—in Mesopotamia, Egypt and Peru.[11]

For the industrial stage, we have only one primary example: northern Europe and its offshoots. But for all the previous stages—from hunting and gathering to plant breeding and animal husbandry, and on from there to the growth of cities, states and empires—we have two independent examples, two cultural laboratories coincidentally running similar experiments on opposite sides of the Atlantic.[12]

By about fifteen thousand years ago, many big animals across Eurasia were sliding toward extinction, mainly because of human hunting pressure. Around the same time, or before, hunters made their way from Asia to the Americas—either across a Bering land bridge or down the coasts, or both.[13] Whatever the exact route and date of their arrival, these first people were also the first apes of any kind to set foot in the Western Hemisphere (though monkeys already lived there). This absence of near kin made the Americas exceptionally welcoming: the game had no fear of murderous bipeds, and there were few local diseases that might leap from prey to man.[14]

The incomers fanned out, eating their way through most of the big game from the Arctic to the Amazon. Like modern humans, ancient ones could be reckless overconsumers. The first Americans then faced the same problem as their cousins left behind in the Old World; they had to find new ways to make a living. And they came up with similar solutions: plant gathering became gardening; gardening became farming. Animals were tamed: llamas, alpacas, dogs, guinea pigs, ducks, turkeys. But the ancestral hunters had left the American faunal cupboard rather bare, having killed all the mammoths and horses in the hemisphere and all camels north of Panama; deer proved untameable (as elsewhere), and so did the lone survivor of the bison family, who was too wild and wily to become a cow.[15]

Luckily, the New World was exceptionally rich in obliging plants: foods, pharmaceuticals, fibres and rubber. Like the first true cities in the Old World, the first in the Americas grew with the invention of irrigation, and at about the same time. In Peruvian desert valleys beside rich Pacific fishing grounds, archaeologists have recently found towns with large temple platforms and stone houses dating from five thousand years ago—a time when the only comparable buildings on Earth were in Mesopotamia.[16]

Within another thousand years, agrarian civilization had got under way throughout the Andean region (or Greater Peru) and Mesoamerica (or Greater Mexico). In the process a number of efficient food staples were developed—maize, the potato, the sweet potato, manioc, beans and squash. Most of these crops were more productive than those of the Old World, making up for the dearth of animals.[17]

From this agrarian footing, the full edifice of civilization arose in the Americas: towns, roads, governments, priesthoods, armies, art and architecture, books and archives. The New World's path was enough like the Old World's that, by 1519, when Hernán Cortés first saw the capital of Aztec Mexico, the Spaniard could describe the alien city—the end result of fifteen thousand years of independent growth—by comparing it to European ones. It had forty "towers" (steep pyramid-temples),

the tallest "higher than that of the cathedral of Seville";[18] the
central square was so great that within it "a town of some five
hundred inhabitants could easily be built"; the commercial
plaza was so extensive that even those Spaniards who had been
to Constantinople "had never seen a market so well laid out, so
large, so orderly, and so full of people."[19]

On the eve of its destruction, Aztec Mexico City had some
quarter million inhabitants—about the same as contemporary
Constantinople, or London, Paris and Seville combined. Then
(as now) it was the biggest city in the Americas and among the
top half dozen in the world.

⋆⇒◎⇐⋆

Like the modern Americans, the Aztecs and Incas were late-
comers to fortune in their day, merely the most recent empire
builders in a long succession reaching back thousands of
years.[20] Mesoamerica (a name for both Mexico and the adjoining Maya region of Central America) and Greater Peru (the
Andean region of South America from Colombia to Chile) had
been the two heartlands of American civilization from the very
beginning. They had much in common but were also quite distinct culturally, economically and politically. Mesoamerica was
the more teeming, mercantile and urban world—a welter of
competing city-states. With its jungles, mountains and flood-
plains jumbled together, the land itself seemed to stimulate
diversity, warfare, trade and edgy brilliance. From time to
time, one city would rise above the others, much like Florence
or Venice in medieval Italy.

When the Spaniards arrived, by far the most powerful
Mesoamerican state was Mexico, also a general name for the
Aztec capital, a twin city built on largely manmade islands in a

great mountain lake surrounded by volcanoes.[21] Mexico's core alliance comprised several neighbouring cities, though the hard power lay with Tenochtitlan, whose main square and street grid survive as downtown Mexico City. Tenochtitlan did not try to integrate its domains; it simply extorted wealth from vassals, both by outright levies and through the high-handed trading of merchant-princes backed by the Aztec war machine. The great city also meddled in the affairs of tributaries, toppling rulers and installing puppets. Ritualized militarism held the system together, expressed, as in Rome and so many other places, by grand displays of mass slaughter—in this case the sacrifice of war captives at the top of stepped pyramids two hundred feet high.[22] Such political and commercial practices were normal in Mesoamerica; the Aztecs were hated by rivals not for what they did but for doing it best. As Inga Clendinnen has written, "Tenochtitlan was a beautiful parasite, feeding on the lives and labour of other peoples and casting its shadow over all their arrangements."[23]

⋅→⟦○⟧←⋅

Around the world, in both ancient and modern times, there have been two main kinds of imperial system: tribute (or hegemonic) empires, in which client states are dominated but not integrated by an overlord, and centralized (or territorial) empires, which aim to incorporate their subjects into a greater whole, with a single economy, government, official language and religion.[24]

Tribute empires are protection rackets: exploitive, unstable, usually short-lived. So long as wealth and loyalty flow upward, client states are left to run their home affairs, which means squeezing their own people to pay the overlord. Subject peoples receive no benefits beyond survival and are kept in line

by fear of a military harrying or a palace coup if the flow of tribute falters. Like a top dog, a hegemon is only as good as his last
fight. Centralized empires, on the other hand, see themselves
as civilizing and benevolent, extending public works, education and citizenship to what Rudyard Kipling called "lesser
breeds without the law."[25]

Some empires have combined elements of both kinds or
evolved from one into the other. Rome and Britain began as
tribute gatherers but later became centralized. During the Cold
War, both the United States and the Soviet Union behaved as
tribute empires beyond their heartlands, manipulating quasi-
independent states in Europe, Latin America and the rest of
the Third World (a matter I shall return to in Chapters 7 and 8
when discussing American power today).

If the Aztec Empire was a textbook case of a tribute system,
things were very different in the Inca Empire, which called
itself Tawantinsuyu, the "United Four Quarters," and had its
capital at Cusco in the highlands of southern Peru.[26] The Incas
were great organizers and builders, the Romans of the New
World. They had spread their rule up and down the Andean
backbone of South America and from the desert Pacific coast to
the Amazon jungle, controlling all of what are now Peru,
Ecuador and Bolivia plus half of Chile and parts of Argentina.[27]
This is a hard and sprawling land: three thousand miles long,
hundreds of miles wide, with treeless steppes more than
twelve thousand feet high and snow-capped ranges nearly
twice that height, broken by passes through icefields. To support human life in any abundance and security, the Andean
region demanded massive public works: irrigation on the
coast, terracing in the mountains, raised fields and drainage
canals in the jungles and good roads to bind all together and

distribute food. In a land where one in three harvests was likely to be lost in any zone, the incentives for spreading risk by central management were high.[28]

Although many of the ethnic groups who had been conquered or persuaded to join the Inca realm were not fully absorbed by the 1520s, the United Four Quarters was well on its way to becoming an integrated territorial empire like Han China or Augustan Rome, with imperial administrative hubs linked by well-built roads and bridges.[29] There was no cult of militarism or mass human sacrifice; Inca warfare was certainly ruthless, but it was politics by other means, not an end in itself. Andean political prestige depended on a ruler's ability to impose order, redistribute wealth, and control a network of reciprocal exchanges. These were not equal exchanges—the rulers lived more grandly than their subjects—but there was no slavery, hunger or grinding poverty.[30] "In each head province," wrote the Spanish soldier and chronicler Cieza de León, "there were great numbers of warehouses full of supplies and provisions . . . and if there was no war all these supplies were distributed among the poor and widows, the very old, the lame [and] the blind and the sick."[31] In Mexico, by contrast, one of the familiar features noted by Cortés was that "the poor begged from the rich in city streets . . . just as they did in Spain."[32] And just as they do now in the wealthiest nations of all time.

→⇒◉⇐←

There is no need to retell here the Spanish conquest of Mexico in 1519–21, but I do want to underline one important fact that is too often overlooked. Despite the technology gap between Mexico and Europe, and the large Spanish army assembled at Mexico City by Hernán Cortés—1,200 Europeans and thousands of local allies—the Aztecs *won*. On a rainy summer night in 1520, remembered by the Spaniards as the Night of Sorrow, Mexican forces killed at least two-thirds of the Europeans and a similar number of their native allies.[33] It was an utter rout.

That should have been the end of the invasion for many years—years during which Mexico could have readied its defences. The Europeans' technological and psychological advantages were a one-shot weapon, now spent; subsequent attempts at colonization would have been more gradual, more difficult and ultimately reversible, more like the British career in India.[34] But just then, "when the Christians were exhausted from war," a Spaniard wrote, "God saw fit to send the Indians smallpox."[35]

Smallpox (eradicated in 1978) was probably the deadliest mass killer to afflict humanity. Europeans had known it for centuries; they often caught it in childhood and, if they lived, held both acquired and some genetic immunity. But the plague that hit Mexico in the fall of 1520 was the first outbreak ever on the American mainland—a true "virgin soil" pandemic—and its virulence was catastrophic. In a matter of weeks, it killed the Aztec ruler and at least half the population, utterly transforming the balance of power.[36] In the chaotic aftermath, Cortés was able to resupply, return, rebuild his alliance with Tenochtitlan's foes and besiege the stricken city, which still took nearly three months to fall. Even that was far from the end for the luckless Mexicans: wave after wave of pestilence scythed through their population for decades, reducing them to less than a tenth of their original strength.[37]

The main credit for establishing beyond doubt that the New World's true conquerors were microbes must go to the American bio-historian Alfred Crosby. "Had there been no epidemic," he wrote in 1972, "Cortés might have ended his life spread-eagled beneath the obsidian blade of [an Aztec] priest."[38] The truth is that the Spaniards did not succeed in conquering *any* major state on the American mainland until *after* a smallpox plague had struck. When they tried, they lost. Cortés's Night of Sorrow was not unique: in 1517 and 1518, first Francisco Hernández and then Juan de Grijalva were defeated by Maya on the Yucatán and Gulf coasts; in 1521 a Floridian arrow put an end to Juan Ponce de León's quest for the Fountain of Youth; and around 1524 Alejo García's attack on the south-eastern flank of the Inca Empire from Paraguay ended with its leader's death. "The miraculous triumphs" of the Spanish conquistadors, Crosby underlines, "were in large part the triumphs of the virus of smallpox."[39]

The same virgin-soil outbreak that gave victory to Cortés then ran ahead of the Spaniards for several years: a pan-American wildfire, burning north beyond the Aztec Empire, south through the Maya city-states to the Spanish base at Panama, and deep into South America. This first pandemic may have ranged from the Great Lakes to the pampas—the full gamut of advanced societies in the New World—before running out of tinder.[40]

⊷⟰⊶

Meanwhile, Francisco Pizarro and other would-be conquistadors in Panama had begun a long search for a golden kingdom to the south, rumours of which had been tantalizing them for years.[41] Rumour gained substance on an exploratory voyage in 1526. Reaching the equator off what is now Ecuador, one of Pizarro's ships met an Inca ship heading north. The Spaniards at first mistook the native craft for a rival caravel, noting it had "masts and yards of very fine wood, and cotton sails in the same shape and manner as on our own ships."[42] The strange vessel was a *balsa*, a great raft similar to the famous *Kon-Tiki*, reconstructed from old drawings by Thor Heyerdahl in the 1940s, but much bigger and more sophisticated. On board were twenty seamen and thirty tons of freight for export, including worked gold, pottery and fine clothing. For about a thousand years, Peruvians had been sailing the Pacific Ocean, not only along the coast but as far west as the Galápagos—a feat comparable to reaching the Canaries and Azores from Europe.[43]

Guided by men he seized from the Peruvian ship, Pizarro scouted the coast, going ashore and meeting Inca officials at Tumbes and other seaports. The Spaniards found a thriving empire, apparently still under the firm yet benign hand of the Inca Huayna Capac, said to have been a great beer drinker and "much beloved by all his subjects."[44] Smallpox had not yet struck.[45] Pizarro passed himself off as a friendly envoy from a distant lord, then sailed back to Panama and on to Spain for royal backing and reinforcements.

When he returned to Peru with a bigger force four years later, everything had changed, as perhaps Pizarro knew.[46] Smallpox had burst upon the Incas in 1527–28; the port of Tumbes had become an eerie ruin. The plague had killed Huayna Capac, his chosen heir, at least half the Inca court and general population as well as government and military personnel throughout the empire.[47] An ensuing power vacuum had led to wars of secession and succession. High up, along the spine of the Andes, minor sons of the dead Inca (in this sense, the word means "emperor") were waging a bitter civil war. The white intruders were largely ignored, left to do as they liked in the lowlands for a year and a half; they even began building a Spanish town.[48]

Wittingly or not, Francisco Pizarro had avoided fighting a native American kingdom in its prime. Smallpox had set up the conditions that would make his conquest possible. His cousin Pedro later wrote: "Had Huayna Capac been alive when we Spaniards invaded this land, it would have been impossible for us to win . . . not even if more than a thousand Spaniards had come at once."[49] As in Mexico, the great plagues struck for decades, until Peru had lost at least 93 percent of its people.[50]

In November 1532, at some hot springs outside a highland city called Cajamarca, the winner among Huayna Capac's sons— a man in his early thirties named Atahuallpa—received a visit from Pizarro's lieutenant, Hernando de Soto (who would die beside the Mississippi ten years later). Despite being preoccupied with his dynastic war, Atahuallpa had already sent spies to investigate the Spaniards at their camp on the coast.[51] They had reported that the intruders were barbarians and thieves, disorderly in their ways and so lazy that they rode on "big llamas." "With this, Atahuallpa was reassured," wrote Pedro Pizarro, "and he took [us] for nothing."[52]

In a display characteristic of each culture, Soto reared his horse so that its breath stirred the crimson fringe of vicuña wool across the Inca's brow. Atahuallpa, who had never seen a horse or a Spaniard before, sat perfectly still; it was said that he executed any of his men who flinched. Certainly, he later admitted that he'd planned to kill most of the Spaniards, make the rest into household eunuchs, and breed the horses.[53] Inca officials had kept a tally of the outlanders' crimes: theft, torture, murder, rape and more. The spies had correctly informed

Atahuallpa that the barbarians were few, not quite two hundred men, with about a third on horse. The Peruvians had examined the intruders' swords and may even have seen gunfire, but they had not watched the Spaniards in battle.[54] Fasting, nursing a war wound and arrogant from recent victories, the young Inca seriously underestimated the Europeans.

According to a memoir written by Atahuallpa's nephew, insults were exchanged at the first meeting.[55] The Inca then told the Spaniards to go into the city and wait in the open public halls surrounding the plaza. They were left there until late the following afternoon, taunted by passersby: "We thought our lives were finished," one of Pizarro's men wrote home.[56] At last the Inca entered the square, borne on a golden throne and accompanied by thousands of retainers who had not bothered to bring weapons "because they thought so little of the Spaniards."[57] Unaware that he was deep inside a trap of his own making, Atahuallpa confronted the foreigners with their crimes. When a Spanish priest handed him a Bible, he haughtily cast it down.[58]

The rest of the story takes its well-known shape. Mounted Spaniards charged from the tall doorways of the halls and slaughtered the unarmed Peruvians. "We killed eight thousand men in about two and a half hours," one boasted.[59] Atahuallpa was pulled from his palanquin and thrown in chains.

The crestfallen Inca soon took better measure of his captors. "Do you *eat* gold?" he asked sarcastically, and the strangers answered yes, they did.[60] (In Mexico, Cortés had said much the same, telling Moctezuma that Spaniards suffered from "a disease of the heart for which gold is the only cure."[61]) So Atahuallpa offered to call off his armies and pay a king's ransom for his life: a room full of gold and two of silver. For six months, llama trains brought tons of gold stripped from all the great buildings of Peru: architectural bands from walls and rooftops; thrones, altars, statues, urns, dishes.[62] The ransom bought Atahuallpa time, but time was not on his side. Spanish reinforcements came from Panama, doubling his captors' strength.[63] Pizarro forced the Peruvian goldsmiths to melt their own work into bullion, then killed Atahuallpa anyway.[64]

◦→≡◎⊂═→◦

So, how much did the Spaniards really get, and what was it worth at the time? The haul from Cajamarca, as declared to the Spanish king, was 13,420 pounds of 22.5 carat gold—nearly 7 tons—and about 13 tons of silver. Later that year Pizarro stripped 3 more tons of gold (and many more of silver) from Cusco, the Inca capital.[65] It is fair to assume that further "saint-seducing gold" escaped the eye of the royal taxman, who, as usual, was sent along with the invasion. The Inca's subjects also defied their ruler, burying items they deemed too precious or too holy to be lost, though hoards were later uncovered by Inquisitional techniques. In safe round figures, as officially declared, Pizarro and his men seized 10 tons of gold from the two cities. It sounds like a lot. Yet at today's bullion price, it would fetch only $300 million—small change in a world of a thousand billionaires. Bill Gates alone is worth more than $50 billion.[66]

That said, current gold prices tell us very little—because the world economy and money supply have exploded since the 1530s. Indeed, the buying power of gold and silver dropped through the centuries mainly *because* of the New World treasure, as the political economist Adam Smith explained in his 1776 *Wealth of Nations*.[67] Since Smith's day the picture has changed again: industrial mining has vastly increased the bullion stock, but the really big money has only a ghost's life nowadays, in electronic files.

William Prescott, the great historian of the Spanish conquests, said that few European monarchs of that day possessed anything like such a sum. He reckoned that Atahuallpa's gold would have been worth more than £5 million sterling, or US$22 million, when he was writing in the 1840s.[68] At that time, the Bank of England's gold reserves were about £8 million.[69] In 1867 the United States bought Alaska from Russia for $7.2 million. Clearly, Pizarro's band of thugs seized a treasure of national proportions, equivalent to many billions, perhaps trillions, today.

Like a gravitational mass warping space and time, the great pile of heavy metal distorted everything around it. As soon as each conqueror got his share, hyperinflation broke out in Peru: horses fetched astronomical sums, and their hooves were shod in silver.[70] Peru became a goldrush land, the Eldorado of all time.[71]

Years later, dictating his will on his deathbed, the last of Pizarro's men unburdened his conscience to King Philip:

> His Catholic Majesty must know that we found these countries in such a condition that there were no thieves, no vicious men, no idlers. . . . We have transformed these natives, who had so much wisdom. . . . There was then no evil thing, but today there is no good.[72]

⊶⊷

Some modern writers have seen Peru's tragedy as a Manichaean fight between individualism and community, wealth and commonwealth. For the left, the United Four Quarters was a "socialist" empire, overthrown by robber barons. For the right, it was a grim, totalitarian state. Both views are naïve anachronisms, examples of posterity's "enormous condescension" to the past.[73] The real link between ancient Peru and modern capitalism is more substantial than any political or moral point.

Karl Marx may not be America's favourite philosopher, and his utopian project, like that of the Incas, lies in ruins, yet he remains one of the best economic historians and analysts. In 1847 he drew a direct link between the Industrial Revolution and Atahuallpa's gold: "An indispensable condition for the establishment of manufacturing industry," Marx wrote, "was the accumulation of capital facilitated by the discovery of America and the importation of its precious metals."[74]

Ever since money began, gold and silver had been in tight supply in pre-Columbian Europe.[75] Precious metals tended to migrate toward the Orient in exchange for silk, spices and ceramics. Like the trade imbalance between today's America and China, the Silk Road was a one-way street; the Chinese wanted nothing from the west but cash. This had been going on since Roman times. Toward the end of the first century A.D., Pliny the Younger estimated that half of Rome's bullion was flowing to Asia. At about that time, the empire began debasing its coinage, and the "silver" denarius slowly became worthless.

Medieval kings were also notorious debtors and debasers. The only way Edward I of England could escape bankruptcy was by expelling his Jewish creditors. And in 1516—just before the big payoff from America—Ferdinand of Spain, another ejector of Jews and the founder of the Inquisition, left barely enough in

his treasury to cover his own funeral.[76] Today, after five centuries of European triumph, it is easy to forget just how marginal Europe was until she stumbled on the New World jackpot.
For all the dash and brilliance of the Italian Renaissance, it was
China that had the world's greatest economy and most
advanced technology.[77]

In 1534 a Seville official wrote deliriously to King Charles:
"The quantity of gold that arrives every day from the Indies,
and especially from Peru, is quite incredible. . . . This city will
become the richest in the world."[78] A few conquistadors
invested wisely and settled down, but most wasted their treasure and died young. The important thing is that the gold went
into circulation. Like Pizarro himself, Europe leapt from
poverty to wealth and power almost overnight.

⊷⇒◉⇐⊷

Consider how things might have gone if the Americas had
been uncivilized or uninhabited when the Europeans turned
up half-dead from months at sea. There would have been no
towns, roads and bridges, no stores of food and clothing, and
no labour pool—let alone cities of gold to repay investors
promptly and recruit new men. One of the first things the
Spaniards did in Mexico and Peru was interrogate native officials, miners and smiths. If the hemisphere had been a
wilderness, there would have been no local knowledge of
where gold and silver might be found.

Despite the pandemics, enough subjects of America's pre-
Columbian empires survived to make wealth for their new
masters. Most colonial mines were expansions of ancient ones,
and the miners were raised from existing tribute and taxation
networks. In Mexico, the Aztec tribute books were minutely

studied by the Spanish viceroys.[79] In Peru, the work tax, the *mit'a*, was perverted into forced labour with none of the food, clothing or other benefits of the Inca system. As the shafts wormed ever deeper into the Andes, the work became harder and deadlier. Often the journey to the mines was a one-way trip. In 1586 an eyewitness wrote that of the healthy Indians who went underground each Monday, "half may emerge crippled on Saturday."[80] During the three centuries of Spanish rule, more than a million Quechua and Aymara lives may have been devoured by the great "mountain of silver" at Potosí and its even more evil twin, the mercury mine at Huancavelica.[81] "Oh, Peru!" wrote García Lorca, "Land of metal and of melancholy!"

By the late 1570s, Potosí's production had soared to more than 3 million pesos—equivalent to Atahuallpa's treasure every year.[82] By the mid-eighteenth century, 500 tons of silver and 25 tons of gold were crossing the Atlantic annually. Adam Smith reckoned this influx to be worth "about six millions sterling," adding that American mines were by far the most productive in the world.[83] More recent studies have borne him out: for two and a half centuries, Spain's American empire mined more than four-fifths of the world's silver and nearly three-quarters of its gold.[84]

Just as work overtakes the time allowed for it, so political ambitions consume the funds at hand. We might think that Spain would have become the wealthiest country on Earth. But the Emperor Charles and his heir, Philip II, spent their fortune trying to conquer everyone in sight: the French, the Turks, the Portuguese, the English, various Italian city-states and not least the Netherlanders, many of whom were rebelling and sliding into Protestant heresy.[85] Spain's dream was nothing less than to carry out God's work by crushing infidels and bringing

Christian civilization to the world. The mood of the day—its "full-spectrum dominance"—was summed up by a Spanish friar: "Potosí lives in order to . . . humble the Moor, make Flanders tremble and terrify England."[86]

After taking over the New World's kingdoms and crossing the Pacific, Spain at last reached a point where west met east. The Spaniards had only limited influence on the real Asia, however, giving an idea of how Europe's impact on the Americas might have looked had there been no demographic collapse. The Far East was part of the Old World; its people did not conveniently sicken and die on contact. Spain had to content herself with making the Philippines the western border of her empire—as her successor there, the United States, would do three centuries later.[87]

For all its corruption, chaos and sclerosis, the Spanish Empire still holds the record as the longest-lived world superpower to date—exactly three hundred years from the conquest of Mexico to Mexican independence. But its military ambitions beggared it.[88] By the mid-seventeenth century, Spain had lost most of her money, her European possessions and her prestige. As William Prescott dourly observed after reckoning the worth of Atahuallpa's gold: "The wealth thus suddenly acquired, by diverting [the Spaniards] from . . . more permanent sources of national prosperity, has in the end glided from their grasp, and left them among the poorest of the nations of Christendom."[89]

Spain's loss was others' gain. The wealth went north, becoming venture capital for weaponry, shipbuilding, supplies—all the manufacturing and innovative foment that thrives on a diet of warfare. Foundries and ironworks that began by making guns would soon go on to produce mine pumps, mills and machines. As I have written elsewhere, "In a way Mao Zedong didn't intend . . . power would indeed grow from the barrel of a gun: from the cannon's 'reeking tube' descends the cylinder of the steam and petrol engines."[90] The Industrial Revolution was young when Adam Smith was writing his *Wealth of Nations* in the 1770s, but his nose for following money had sniffed out the new home of Atahuallpa's gold—Britain, already well on its way to becoming the workshop of the world.[91] By 1775, James Watt was building the first efficient steam engines, at the engineering works of Matthew Boulton, "a man of energy and capital."[92]

In the end Peru's metal would again become a metaphor: bricks glistering in bank vaults, of no more practical use than the bands of gold on Cusco's walls. As the dragon remarks to Grendel in John Gardner's retelling of the Beowulf tale: "My advice to you, my violent friend, is to seek out gold and sit on it."[93]

-+≡○⊂=+-

The Industrial Revolution was not, of course, made by money alone. It also required technical and scientific knowledge—and it is this aspect that has always been emphasized in the west's admiring account of its own leap forward. But science alone won't make a revolution either. Without both needs and means, inventions fall on stony ground. The many ingenious devices of Classical times, the Renaissance and China all failed to realize their potential. Something was lacking in the mix.

Besides an innovative spirit, heavy industry needed four key ingredients for success: capital to fund it; efficient farming to feed it; labour to work it; and growing demand to sustain it. As both Adam Smith and Karl Marx understood, the first of these ingredients came from the New World. But what about the other three? Manufacturing requires a large workforce released from the need to grow food. For this to happen, the people who do grow food must be able to raise a dependable surplus year after year. These conditions are common nowadays—half the world lives in cities and towns—but they were rare before modern times.

For two thousand years, China suffered serious famine in at least one province nearly every year.[94] The same was true of most ancient civilizations: they could barely feed themselves. In fat times there would indeed be a surplus, and it was then that great military campaigns and building projects were undertaken. But the palmy days seldom lasted; either good harvests were soon followed by bad ones or, as the early demographer Thomas Malthus observed, the people outgrew the food. Either way, farmers lived on the edge of hunger. Towns were tiny by present-day standards. Of every ten people alive, eight or nine worked the land.[95] The only big labour surpluses were seasonal: a few months between sowing, reaping and ploughing. Seasonal workers can do great things—they built the pyramids of Egypt and the cathedrals of Europe—but they won't run a railroad.

For industrialization to take off, a difficult horse-and-cart trick must be performed: a food surplus *and* a labour surplus must be raised at the same time. And both have to be sustained until technological feedback can occur—until industry can make enough farming machines to free yet more hands from the land.[96] And the world's *first* Industrial Revolution had to take root and grow by chance—because nobody foresaw where it might lead.

It is hardly surprising that no civilization, no matter how technically ingenious, had managed to pull off this trick before. So, what was different about Europe in the eighteenth and early nineteenth centuries? The traditional answer is that

Europe was blessed by genius.[97] But the revolution of coal, iron and steam was not launched by scientists; it was made by shrewd investors and grimy practical men—fitters, mechanics, ironworkers—men such as Thomas Newcomen with his condensing steam engine, James Watt with his improved design, Richard Arkwright with his spinning mills and Isambard Brunel with his bridges, railways and steamships.[98]

⊷⇒◯⇐⊷

We come to the second ingredient: food. Gold is valuable only because people think it is. Its worth is a form of magic, not utility, as Atahuallpa sardonically implied when he asked the Spaniards if they ate it. Perhaps he knew that America's greatest treasure—in the long run—would be her crops.[99] It's hard to imagine Italians without tomatoes, Asians without chiles, the Belgians without chocolate, Christmas with no turkeys and Hawaii with no pineapples. But for demographic impact, the really significant introductions were the boring, starchy staples: the "miracle crops" of maize, potato, sweet potato and manioc (or cassava).[100] The last two are tropical, the potato temperate, and maize, in its many varieties, can be either.

One may well ask why the arrival of these crops made any difference beyond wider choice. Wouldn't a field given over to maize instead of wheat simply swap one food for another? But it wasn't a zero-sum game. Maize and potatoes give twice the food value of wheat; manioc yields more in volume than any other tropical plant.[101] Also, the new crops seldom competed with the old ones. Maize would thrive on land too dry for rice and too wet for wheat. Manioc, potatoes and sweet potatoes were easy to grow, needing little work and tolerating a wide range of soils. Marginal and exhausted land could be brought into production with these crops—as with peanuts and beans, which fix nitrogen in the soil.[102] The American root crops were also good keepers, taken on board by sea captains and spread promiscuously around the world. One particular virtue of the potato was its hardiness in wartime. It was one thing to torch an enemy stand of wheat; quite another to uproot a muddy field of tubers.

European and Asian governments promoted the American foods, especially during famines. In the last days of France's *ancien régime,* potatoes were dished up at Versailles, and Marie-Antoinette wore potato flowers on her breast.[103] Sir Walter Raleigh first brought the plant to Ireland in the 1580s, and the Irish had become "mighty lovers of potatoes" by 1700.[104] Ireland's landlords were delighted to find that a peasant family could live on an acre or two of tubers, freeing the rest of their estates for cash crops. The new food was wholesome: in the ninety years from 1754 to 1845, the Irish population grew from 3 million to 10. Then came the potato blight, when many who had "lived by the potato died by the potato," and many more fled to the New World. (The disaster was no fault of the Peruvian plant but of the way it had been misused.[105])

In the Middle East, Africa and Asia, maize caught on with astonishing speed. By 1574, large stands of it were growing in Mesopotamia, the very birthplace of wheat and barley. From there it spread into southeastern Europe, Egypt and India. At about the same time, maize reached Asia direct from the Americas, probably on Spanish galleons plying between Acapulco and Manila.[106]

❖⟹C⟸❖

The *de*population of the New World has ended in the *over*population of the whole. While human numbers in the Americas went into a dive after 1492, those in Europe, Africa and Asia began to soar on the back of the Americas' vegetal wealth.[107] Within four centuries of Columbus and Cortés, humanity had quadrupled—to 1.6 billion by 1900. We have since quadrupled again.[108]

The later phase of this boom can be attributed to better sanitation, public health and farming, as the industrialization of land and town took hold. But those improvements had scarcely begun before Victorian times. It was not until 1854 that John Snow famously stopped a cholera outbreak by taking the handle off the Broad Street pump in Soho.[109] London and Paris were so unhealthy that their populations would not have grown at all without a constant flood of migrants from the land. There can be little doubt that the human boom is a direct consequence of the worldwide adoption of American crops: the third ingredient for the Industrial Revolution—labour—flowed from the second.

As the productive new plants took root on Britain's farms, fewer workers were needed. Under the old manorial system, the country squire had been the head of a community, with almost as many obligations as privileges. Now he became a businessman, a champion of heartless efficiency. "When farmers become *gentlemen*," William Cobbett wrote acidly, "their labourers become *slaves*."[110] The poor protested that the landlords "keep us here like potatoes in a pit, and only take us out for use when they can no longer do without us."[111] This treatment, plus the land enclosures and the Highland clearances—the privatization of public farmland from the sixteenth to the eighteenth centuries—drove the peasantry to the towns. Some found work in mills and factories; others went on to North America and Australia.

By 1830, technological feedback also began to kick in as threshing machines and other equipment put ever more farmhands out of work. For those left on the land, the machinery itself became the enemy. The *Times* reported the following year: "At Norwich, fifty-five prisoners convicted of machine-breaking and rioting . . . at Petworth, twenty-six for machine-breaking and rioting; at Gloucester, upwards of thirty." Luddites were hanged.

The trick was done. Northern Europe had a steady surplus of people *and* of food. The industrialists had all the workers they could want, at bargain wages. Meanwhile, another source of labour had been proliferating in the tropics. Like Europeans and Asians, Africans multiplied dramatically on American crops. Africa had not been rich in home-grown staples. Maize and manioc caught on so quickly that they were soon believed to be native plants.

White seafarers did not introduce the new staples to Africa for philanthropic reasons; rather, they sowed them along the coast as fodder for human cargoes. Slaver captains were already familiar with these foods, having at first taken slaves the other way. Even Columbus himself had dabbled in the trade— shipping American Indians across the Atlantic—only to find it unprofitable because his merchandise died from Old World disease just as readily in Europe as in America.

Africa had been a source of slaves for both Arabs and Europeans since ancient times, though never on the scale that began after the sixteenth century. With the growth in population, the continent suddenly had surplus people, whom local rulers did not shrink from using as foreign exchange, sold across the water for guns, metal and luxury goods.

In most of Mexico and Peru, enough local people survived

to work the Spanish mines and haciendas. But the Caribbean islands were almost utterly depopulated within twenty years of 1492, and much the same happened along the mainland coasts. Even before Columbus, the Spaniards and Portuguese had been seizing West Coast Africans to work sugar plantations on Madeira, the Canaries and the Azores. So Spain and Portugal repeated in the Americas what they had done in those Atlantic islands, but on a far greater scale, filling the sultry parts of the Caribbean and Brazil with sugar cane and Africans to work it.

In the seventeenth century, the British, French and Dutch took up the slave economy, adding two American products— tobacco and cotton—to the sugar, molasses and rum of the West Indies. The three solaces of the British sailor were said to be "rum, baccy and bum." Bum was nothing new, but rum and tobacco were the first exportable wealth produced in the New World by imported slaves. So began the modern trade in agricultural commodities. By 1840 world sugar shipments exceeded 1 million tons a year.[12] Most of this supply went to European and North American cities, providing cheap, high-energy food and drink for factory workers.[13]

In short, Europeans took Africans to America to replace dead Americans and made them grow food, clothing and luxuries for Europeans and the world market.[14] The economic engine of loot, labour and land had built up steam.

Until the turn of the nineteenth century, the demand—the fourth and last requirement for industrialization to sustain itself—lay mainly in Europe. But as the Old World's extra people spilled across the Atlantic, the ultimate bonanza opened up: the idea and possibility of a second Europe building itself on the vastness of the New World's widowed land. There, on a seemingly inexhaustible frontier westering (by Tocqueville's reckoning) at seventeen miles per year, a vision of endless prosperity was bequeathed down the centuries to white settlers by Atahuallpa's gold."[15]

3.

VERY WELL PEOPLED AND TOWNED

They have ruined [these provinces] by wandering in
search . . . of Eldorado or a new Atahuallpa; thus they
wasted their time and destroyed whatever was there.

—Martín de Urué, 1573[1]

American history is . . . the history of our drive into
abundance.   —Leland D. Baldwin, 1981[2]

There is no clearer fact in American history than the fact of
conquest. . . . It is perfectly clear who started this fight.

—Patricia Nelson Limerick, 2000[3]

AMONG THE TOOTHY AMERICAN CARS of the 1950s was
a large and primitive sedan (now extinct) with De
Soto written on its tailfins, a chrome memorial to a
man better known as a "discoverer" of the Mississippi than
a conqueror of Peru. No doubt more than one De Soto made a
trip from the Cartier Bridge in Canada to Raleigh, North
Carolina, and many must have chugged across the Verrazzano
Bridge in New York City. All four famous names—the Italian
Verrazzano, the Frenchman Cartier, the Spaniard Soto and the

Englishman Raleigh, to put them in chronological order—tried to open up the unknown continent north of Mexico in the sixteenth century. And all failed, as did others whose deeds are too obscure to be immortalized on maps and tailfins. But the information they (or their men) brought back reveals what eastern North America was really like before being changed forever by the European onslaught.

The mythic history we have all soaked up describes the land as a "virgin wilderness" or "primaeval forest" inhabited only by a handful of "wild men" or "savages." In a typical (and still influential) popular history published in 1931, James Truslow Adams declared that "a squirrel might have leapt from bough to bough for a thousand miles and never have seen a flicker of sunshine on the ground."[4] This idea of an empty, sylvan America has always had unshakably strong appeal for both the early British invaders and their American descendants— because it brushes aside awkward questions of indigenous ownership and sovereignty. Virginia may have been named for a questionably virgin Queen Elizabeth, but the pun on her nickname was soon used to sell the idea of an untouched land awaiting the white man's seed. Even the canny Tocqueville, researching his great book on the settler republic in the 1830s, would fall for the notion that the original Americans were nomadic hunters flitting about in the woods, people without sovereign rights to their homeland because "the Indians occupied, without possessing. . . . It is by agricultural labour that man appropriates the soil."[5]

The true state of affairs was very different—as the first eyewitnesses make clear.[6]

◦◦◦▻═◖═◅◦◦◦

In the spring of 1524 Giovanni da Verrazzano, a Florentine navigator working for the French king, reconnoitred the eastern seaboard of what is now the United States.[7] This was still early in the clash of worlds: soon after the fall of Aztec Mexico and eight years before the conquest of Peru.

Verrazzano sailed up the coast from the Carolinas to Canada—probably the first European to do so and certainly the first to leave a good account. For much of the way, his ship was held off by the Outer Banks, but he went ashore at several spots, including a wooded hill he named Arcadia, now known to have been Kitty Hawk, North Carolina—more famous for a later pioneering trip, the Wright brothers' flight in 1903.[8]

Whenever he sighted good land, Verrazzano found it thickly inhabited by farmers, whose fires were "burning continually along the shore."[9] He became the first white visitor to New York, anchoring off Staten Island in what are now the Verrazzano Narrows. From there he took a small boat into Upper Bay and glimpsed Manhattan, which was also densely populated: "Running back and forth across the water were about thirty of their boats with an infinite number of people aboard."[10] These Americans greeted the strangers with curiosity and laughter; indeed, they sound rather like later New Yorkers—noisy, bustling, loudly dressed, scooting about in fleets of big canoes where ferryboats now take tourists to the Statue of Liberty.

At this engaging moment, when Europeans and Americans were about to meet, contrary winds forced the strangers to make for open sea. Verrazzano had better luck at Narragansett Bay, Rhode Island, where he anchored for two weeks, establishing good relations with the locals and making several trips inland. He found the people here "confident . . . beautiful

[with] the most civil customs [and] taller than we are." They had polished stone tools, sheets of worked copper, seagoing boats that could hold fifteen men, and large round houses in which up to thirty people lived together."¹ Verrazzano makes it clear that these folk were farmers, like everyone he'd seen along the seaboard. The Rhode Islanders' fields stretched inland, he reckoned, for "25 to 30 leagues¹² [80 to 100 miles] . . . open and free of any obstacles and trees." He adds intriguingly that the people followed an astronomical calendar: "When sowing they observe the influence of the moon, the rising of the Pleiades, and many other customs derived from the ancients."¹³

On his way back to France, Verrazzano sailed past Bacalaia ("Cod-land"), or Newfoundland, which didn't delay him. He knew it had been "found a long time ago by the Portuguese" and then claimed by John Cabot for England.

⋆⇌◎⇋⋆

Verrazzano made his report to the French king and returned to the New World two years later, only to be killed by aggrieved natives in the Caribbean. In the mid-1530s, the French tried again, sending the Breton Jacques Cartier up the St. Lawrence River. There he found two large towns that would one day become the chief cities of New France: Stadacona (Quebec City) and Hochelaga (Montreal). Cartier gathered words at both towns—enough for present-day scholars to identify the language family as Iroquoian, which includes Huron and Mohawk among its members.¹⁴ On his first trip, he kidnapped two boys and took them to Europe as proof of his discoveries. These two, who were sons of the Quebec leader, he brought back unharmed, but when he shanghaied ten more Quebeckers in 1535, nine of them died overseas—grim evidence of the vulnerability of New World people to Old World sickness.

On a sunlit autumn day in 1535, Cartier reached what is now Montreal and was then Hochelaga—or "Great Rapids"—for the first time. (Thinking he might be in Asia, or at least well on his way there, he named the rapids *La Chine,* China.) "More than a thousand people," he wrote, had gathered at the landing, "welcoming us as warmly as a father greets a son." The Hochelaga ladies showered the Frenchmen with fish and cornbread, "which they threw into our boats in such a way that food seemed to rain from the sky." After this greeting, the strangers went ashore:

> We came to their tilled land and beautiful open fields
> full of the grain of that country, which is like Brazilian
> millet, about as big or bigger than a pea, and on which
> they live as we do on wheat. And in the midst of these
> open fields stands the town of Hochelaga, beside a
> mountain whose slopes are farmed and very fertile and
> from whose top one can see a long way. We named this
> hill Mount Royal.[15]

Cartier's description of the strongly fortified town is equally interesting and reliable—his details borne out by later accounts of similar Iroquois towns, which the English called "castles." Hochelaga had a triple stockade and parapet enclosing fifty multifamily longhouses, "each about fifty or more paces in length and twelve or fifteen in width, built completely of wood." The houses were arranged on a grid plan around a broad central square.[16] Reckoning fifty residents per longhouse (which may be on the low side), several thousand must have lived within Hochelaga's walls.

For reasons Cartier does not explain, he left for Stadacona (Quebec) the next day, never to return to Hochelaga. When other Frenchmen went far enough upriver to reach Hochelaga in the early 1600s, the towns on the St. Lawrence and most of the people had disappeared.[17]

⋘⊙⊙⋙

The early French glimpses of a thickly settled, agricultural North America are confirmed in much greater detail by a three-year "expedition"—*rampage* is a better word—through the southeastern United States, led by Hernando de Soto and bankrolled by his share of Atahuallpa's gold.

Although he had become one of the world's richest men overnight, Soto wanted an Eldorado all to himself, another golden empire like the one he had found with Pizarro in Peru. So, not seven years since the grassy breath of his horse had stirred the crimson fringe on Atahuallpa's brow, he outfitted a substantial private army and invaded Florida, landing at Tampa Bay in 1539 with about six hundred men, two hundred horses, dozens of war dogs (armoured mastiffs routinely fed on Indians) and a large drove of swine. Things did not go well. The people of Florida vividly recalled meeting other Spaniards in the 1520s and put up a sharp resistance, their archery proving a good match for cumbersome crossbows and crude guns. Spaniards were shot through chinks in their armour; horses, through the heart.[18]

On his way through what are now South Carolina and Georgia, and then westward through Alabama to the Mississippi, Soto saw farming polities advanced enough to sustain his dream that an imperial city, another Cusco, lay somewhere within reach. In reality, the societies he saw were not provinces of an empire but independent states and small kingdoms, heirs of the Mississippian Temple Mound culture that had built the great city of Cahokia, near modern St. Louis, a few centuries before. These peoples had trading and political alliances, but the power of Cahokia had waned. In any case, their wealth was in copper, mica and pearls; there was no Cusco of the north with stone temples sheathed in gold. Since plunder was Soto's only goal, his search was doomed.[19]

The European army had to live off the land—which meant finding towns, seizing corn from their granaries and enslaving the citizens to carry it—so the records of Soto's march give useful data on the population and economy. Thousands were rounded up and snapped into iron collars; horses and hogs devoured the growing crops. Local guides who disappointed the Spaniards were tortured, mutilated, thrown to the dogs or burned alive. Anyone who began as a friend soon became a foe.

The way of life the Spaniards saw was indirectly influenced by Mexico, where the triad of maize, beans and squash—the famous "three sisters" who together give sustainable tilth and a balanced diet—had developed between seven thousand and ten thousand years ago.[20] North America also had its own domesticates, including the sunflower and several grains of the chenopodium, or goosefoot, family. The maize economy had slowly spread onto all suitable soils and climate zones of the future United States and southern Canada, moving north and east as plant breeders achieved more cold-resistant varieties.[21] Whenever Soto and his men drew near a major settlement, they described riding for miles beside great fields of corn.

The main towns of the South were considerably bigger and more elaborate than Hochelaga. Some had hundreds of dwellings around ceremonial plazas, from which rose tall, earthen platforms supporting temples, public halls and houses for chiefs. Most of these mounds were later levelled by white Americans building their own towns in the same agreeable spots (to say nothing of dams and highways), but enough survive to show they were like Mexican pyramids in shape: rectangular, often tiered, with flat tops reached by flights of stairs. The greatest, at the city of Cahokia itself, has a base larger than that of Egypt's Great Pyramid and is still more than a hundred feet high—the biggest building in the United States until the twentieth century.[22] Several other temple platforms approach Cahokia's size, including Etowah (or "Hightower"), a 64-foot mound near Atlanta, Georgia, which Soto may have seen. Architecture on such a scale can only have been the work of sophisticated, stratified, farming societies, just as Soto's records describe.

The three eyewitness chronicles (and a fourth by the half-Inca historian Garcilaso, who wrote in Spain after interviewing survivors) differ in detail but agree on substance.[23] Names in these documents are tantalizingly familiar to anyone who knows the South of later years: *Tazcaluza* (Tuscaloosa), *Chalaque* (Cherokee), *Chicaza* (Chickasaw), *Mabila* (Mobile), *Alibamu* (Alabama) and so forth. Scholars have been able to trace the general swath of the Spanish invasion, though the exact path, the whereabouts of many ancient towns and the borders of polities are still moot.

⊷⇌◉⇋⊶

In May 1540 the Spaniards entered a realm called Cofitachiqui, which controlled most of South Carolina and parts of the Smoky Mountains from a capital, Talimeco, whose remains may well lie buried in silt beneath the modern city of Columbia.[24] The ruler was an elegant woman, dressed in fine white linen and carried like an Inca princess on a palanquin. "She spoke to the Governor with much grace and self-assurance," wrote Soto's secretary. "She was young and of fine appearance, and she removed a string of pearls that she wore ... and put it on the Governor's neck."[25]

The Spaniards promptly found more pearls in a charnel house and stole two hundred pounds of them. Perhaps understanding her own helplessness in the circumstances, the Lady of Cofitachiqui told the invaders to go to her capital, where they would find so many pearls that the horses wouldn't be able to carry them.[26] Soto's secretary described Talimeco as "a town of great importance," with a commanding "mosque" on a high mound. Garcilaso adds detail:

> It had five hundred houses, all large and of the best workmanship and materials . . . so that it indeed looked like the seat and court of a mighty lord, built with more finery and adornment than the common towns. The halls of the ruler could be seen from far away because they were in the highest place. . . . In the middle of the town, opposite the ruler's houses, was the temple or burial house. . . . Around the temple were eight halls . . . filled with weapons . . . very well made with bronze blades gleaming so brightly that they looked like gold.[27]

Thinking the shiny bronze might at least be alloyed with gold, Soto set out for the Smoky Mountains, where he hoped to find the real thing.[28] Some idea of the indigenous political structure can be gleaned from the Spaniards' observation that they rode through the Lady of Cofitachiqui's lands "for a hundred

leagues [330 miles], in which . . . she was very well obeyed"
and that people beyond Cofitachiqui regarded themselves
as her vassals.[29] By this time, however, the locals had begun
to rise up against the marauding strangers.[30] Soto decided to
resort to the standard conquistador technique of taking
the ruler hostage, but the Lady slipped from his grasp in the
mountains.

From the Smokies, the Spaniards turned southwest, driven
by hunger—and lured by rumours of gold that had been planted
to get rid of them. At Guaxule, desperate for meat, they ate
three hundred of the Indians' dogs.[31] The next important town,
Chiaha, had stores enough to feed the European army for two
weeks and provide five hundred bearers to carry off what was
left. Relations must have been unusually cordial, for Soto
allowed these carriers to work without "collars and chains."[32]

In October 1540 the Spanish vanguard turned up at Mabila,
or Mobile, Alabama.[33] By this time their reputation had pre-
ceded them, and the locals were less obliging. The town's leaders lured Soto and some of his officers inside the elaborate
fortifications. After a show of hospitality, a great many armed
men (some sources say five thousand, but this may be an exaggeration) sprang from hiding. They killed half the Spaniards
on the spot and wounded the rest, including Soto and Rodrigo
Rangel, his secretary and chronicler.

The Europeans got out and regrouped. The Americans
readied their defences, and the battle raged until dusk. It was
an unequal fight, with native deaths running a hundred to one
against the armoured whites. Mobile's walls and bastions were
of wood, mortared and coated with clay, which made them hard
to burn, but eventually the Spaniards managed to set the town
ablaze. Thousands died in both the fighting and the flames,

including an unknown number of women, some of whom took up Spanish weapons and fought to the death.[34]

According to Rangel, the people of Mobile killed 22 Spaniards and wounded 148. Though not huge losses in themselves, they proved to be the turning point in Soto's fortunes. Since setting out from Tampa, more than a hundred men had died—a sixth of his army. Many horses and most of the baggage had been lost. The would-be conqueror slid into depression—moody, aggressive, more careless than ever of others' lives. His men began to murmur about building boats and fleeing to Mexico.

But Soto kept up his mad search for more than a year, harrying Alabama, Arkansas and the Mississippi Valley. Everywhere that corn would grow, the Spaniards saw similar cultures: populous, hierarchical, ruled by haughty lords who lived on pyramids, rode on palanquins and claimed a special relationship with heaven.[35] When Soto tried to overawe one ruler by claiming to be the "Son of the Sun," the chief (who likely claimed that title himself) replied that if the white man would dry up the Mississippi, he might believe him.[36]

At last, in 1542, Soto fell ill and died. The survivors of his army—now only half the number who'd set out—straggled back to Mexico in disgrace, shoeless, dressed in rags and starving, having salted and eaten the few horses not killed or taken by Indians. The only treasure they brought out is the information in their chronicles, a final view of the South's pre-Columbian way of life. For, even as his men trod the streets of Talimeco and other towns, the citizens were dead or dying, less from Spanish steel than from the tiny weapons in the Europeans' breath, blood and bowels.

The Lady of Cofitachiqui may have deferred to Soto because she had few fighters left to wield her arsenal of bronze. Near her temple the Spaniards saw four longhouses with the dead stacked up inside like firewood. "About the place," wrote one eyewitness, "were large empty towns, grown up in grass. . . . the Indians said that, two years before, there had been a great plague in the land." Even the capital itself was already a ghost town: "The Castilians found the town of Talimeco without any people at all."[37]

In the United States, as in Mexico and South America, plague was already running ahead of the whites themselves, smoothing the invaders' way. America was no virgin; she was a widow.[38]

The English got off to a late start in the scramble for America, and their first effort was as fruitless as Hernando de Soto's. In the mid-1580s, Sir Walter Raleigh (who never set foot in North America himself) sent kinsmen and followers to secure an outpost in "Virginia," at that time as vague and elastic a name as Spain's "Florida," with which it overlapped.[39]

Anyone mentioning Sir Walter Raleigh in later ages is likely to be deafened by applause. But in his day, though dashing and brilliant, he was thought cruel and devious, as adept at making enemies as making myths.[40] His Englishmen were much like Soto's Spaniards—adventurers seeking gold, slaves and plunder, often in the form of Spanish treasure ships. (Europeans who couldn't find an Eldorado of their own were not above poaching from those who had, committing piracy on the high seas as "privateers.") In 1585 the expedition disembarked at the low island of Roanoke, near Kitty Hawk, North Carolina, the "Arcadia" Verrazzano had seen sixty years before. Raleigh's colony was little more than a garrison. Of the five hundred sent out, most were fighting men; only 108 were settlers, none were women and there was no priest—which shows up the professed mission of bringing God to the heathen for what it was, a mere fig leaf over worldly desires.[41]

In promoting the venture, the London lawyer Richard Hakluyt had listed three reasons for sailing to Virginia: "to plant Christian religion . . . to trafficke . . . to conquer; or, to doe all three."[42] His list makes it clear that the place was already spoken for—you can't convert, conquer or trade with people who aren't there. Hakluyt's friend Ralph Lane, writing back to him from Roanoke, described the region as "very well peopled and towned . . . Savages possesse the land."[43] In one town, the English counted more than seven hundred locals at a feast.[44] Either the great plagues of the early 1500s had missed this backwater of swamps and islands or the population had recovered in the meantime. At this date, "savages" (from a Latin word for "woodland dwellers") was not necessarily an insult; it was more a general term for non-Christians interchangeable with "natives," "naturals" and "Indians." The English described the people as "very handsome, and goodly . . . and in their behaviour as mannerly, and civill, as any of Europe."[45]

At first these "goodly" folk welcomed the newcomers and showered them with gifts, hoping to draw them into a network of reciprocal exchange. The Americans even tried to teach the English how to grow maize and build fish weirs, lessons that went unlearned. Meanwhile, hogs and cattle brought by the whites ran amok in unfenced native fields. Come winter, the intruders grew hungry and tried to buy, beg or steal the locals' supplies, even (like Soto) barbecuing their dogs.[46] In return, the Americans stole metal tools and other European goods. Outraged by these losses and fearful of an attack—or perhaps seeking an excuse to take everything by force—the English struck first.

History records two such incidents in the Roanoke area: one in July 1585, when Raleigh's cousin Sir Richard Grenville burned the Indians' homes and "spoiled their corne"; and another, much worse, at the Roanoke people's head town a few months later.[47] There Ralph Lane gunned down the friendly chief Wingina to a battle cry worthy of Pizarro: "Christ our victory!" It was white America's first preventive war.[48]

Christ's victory was short-lived. In 1586 Francis Drake had to rescue the starving settlers and take most of them back to England. About this time, the native people "began to die very fast" of an Old World plague. When Raleigh's ships returned for the rest in 1590 (after being delayed by the Spanish Armada's attack on England), they found Roanoke empty and in ruins. Letters carved on a tree suggested that the survivors had fled to a friendly town called Croatoan near Cape Hatteras, but the weather did not allow a search. The Lost Colony, as it became known, was never found.[49]

Nearly a whole century had passed since Columbus's first voyage, yet the peoples of North America—though bloodied by Europeans and devastated by their plagues—were still free and independent. In the following century, the whites would come to stay.

4.

RELIGION AND PROFIT JUMP TOGETHER

Thou . . . hast washed thy feet in the blood of those native
unnatural Traitors, and now becomest a pure English virgin; a new other Britain, in that new other World: and let all
English say and pray, GOD BLESS VIRGINIA.

—Samuel Purchas, 1623[1]

Indian-hating still exists; and, no doubt, will continue to
exist, so long as Indians do.   —Herman Melville, 1857[2]

The conquest of the earth . . . is not a pretty thing when you
look into it too much. What redeems it is the idea only . . .
something you can set up, and bow down before.

—Joseph Conrad, 1899[3]

EMPIRES ARE BY NATURE PARASITIC. Anglo-America was no
exception.[4] The European invasion of North America
was reminiscent of events to the south, though with
important differences: instead of a single great conquest,
there were many small ones.[5] Yet "conquest" is a word seldom
used to describe what happened north of Mexico. The
national myth of the United States is built on softer words:

"settlement, pioneering, opening up." When Theodore Roosevelt wrote his epic of American expansion, he called it *The Winning of the West,* as if the country changed hands in a tough yet gentlemanly poker game. However, a century after Roosevelt, the American historian Patricia Limerick states: "There is no clearer fact in American history than the fact of conquest. In North America, just as much as in South America, Africa, Asia, and Australia, Europeans invaded a land fully occupied by natives."[6]

Throughout the three centuries of Spanish rule in Mexico and Peru, Europeans kept the whip hand yet never outnumbered the descendants of the conquered.[7] But in North America, native peoples became so weakened by disease and warfare, and so many newcomers poured in from Europe and multiplied, that the English invaders' form of parasitism became the kind that kills the host.

In 1867 Francis Parkman, America's popular historian of the mid-nineteenth century, wrote, "The Indians melted away, not because civilization destroyed them, but because their own ferocity and intractable indolence made it impossible that they should exist in its presence."[8] In other words, Indians were not merely unlucky enough to be run over by civilization's advance but, by being both savage and lazy, were actually to blame for their own extermination. Echoes of this blame-the-victim rhetoric would be heard a century later in Vietnam—with the argument that it was necessary to destroy the village, or even the country, in order to pacify it. As Limerick adds: "It is no easy matter to distinguish the lessons of the Indian wars from the lessons of Vietnam."[9]

⤙⟹◯⟸⤚

The first successful British attempt to settle in North America began in May 1607, in what is now Virginia, on the Powhatan River, renamed the James River in honour of the king who had recently succeeded the Virgin Queen.[10] The hundred English who landed there had some earlier intelligence, wrung from Americans who had been taken to London on previous voyages.[11] Even so, things got off to a bad start. The site chosen for Jamestown, about 40 miles upstream from the south end of Chesapeake Bay, was marshy, unhealthy and unlikely to fulfill the investors' aim of finding "all Manner of Mines of Gold, Silver, and Copper."[12]

During the first summer, half the English died (perhaps from malaria, an Old World sickness spreading north from the Caribbean). More settlers came, only to suffer hideously in the "starving time" of 1609–10, when some were reduced to cannibalism, eating "the very Hides of their Horses and the Bodies of the Indians they had killed."[13] One man, caught hoarding the salted flesh of his wife, was burned alive for his crime. The survivors decided to abandon the colony, but on the very day they were leaving, ships turned up with reinforcements—a timely deliverance attributed to God.

The local Americans belonged to the Powhatan Confederacy, a recent alliance or conquest-state of some thirty tribes living in two hundred towns and villages.[14] Their capital, Powhatan, was eighty miles further upriver, by the falls where Richmond, Virginia, now stands. Some 250 years later, this place would become the capital of a much bigger but much shorter-lived confederacy: the Confederate States of America.

The Powhatans were not entirely naïve about Europeans. In the 1570s they had obliterated a Spanish fort and mission on Chesapeake Bay, and it is even possible that their leader,

Wahunsonacock—a man in his sixties whom the English called "King Powhatan"—had had a hand in the demise of Roanoke. He could easily have wiped out the struggling Jamestown colony on several occasions. But he chose not to, most likely because he sought European weapons and goods for his own political ends.

Although the Powhatan Confederacy did not reach far beyond the tidewater lands of Chesapeake Bay, it seems to have been influenced by the larger polities Soto had seen on his rampage further inland. At the head town, the English visited a cluster of lordly buildings on top of a steep hill or mound they called "Powhatan's Tower," where the king, flanked by a retinue of tattooed men and women, sat in "a great robe made of raccoon skins." At another town, the English saw a hilltop temple nearly a hundred feet long.[15] The economy, as elsewhere, was based mainly on maize. The newcomers acknowledged that without local supplies of "Bread, Corne, Fish, and Flesh in great plentie which was the setting up of our feeble men . . . we had all perished."[16]

King Powhatan and John Smith, Jamestown's most famous and possibly most able leader, were two of a kind: headstrong and wily, with a mutual regard based on self-interest. Powhatan's spirited daughter Pocahontas—still a girl when the strangers arrived—spent much of her time with the English, picking up their language and performing cartwheels in the fort. The old tale of her saving Smith's life may be apocryphal, but she did marry his fellow settler John Rolfe in 1614. The couple and several leading Powhatans visited King James in England, where Pocahontas bore a son before she sickened and died near London in 1617. This bedroom alliance helped stave off open race warfare for several years, though there was often trouble over the colonists' raids for food. John Smith called his unruly settlers "ten times more fit to spoil a commonwealth . . . than to begin one."[17] In the harsh winter of 1609–10, an exasperated King Powhatan told him: "I know the difference between peace and war better than any man in my country. . . . Why will you take by force what you may quietly have by love? Why will you destroy us who supply you with food? What can you get by war?"[18] Some Englishmen were given a practical warning: left dead beside the road, their mouths "stopped full of Bread . . . as it seemeth in Contempt."[19]

Over the fifteen years between 1607 and 1622, as many as ten thousand colonists may have landed, of whom up to eight thousand died from hunger, illness and violence, worsened by bad leadership, embezzlement and oppression. The settlement's death rate was deemed shocking even at a time when lives were hard and short. "Instead of a Plantation," one resident protested, Virginia "will shortly get the name of a slaughterhouse."[20] Others defected to the Powhatans, risking the penalties of treason. "Many fled for relief to the savages," said a contemporary report, "but were taken again, and hung, shot, or broken upon the wheel."[21]

The colony survived because of sustained, if not steady, backing from London and a stream of hopeful incomers, not so much drawn as driven across the Atlantic by wars and worsening conditions at home, especially the enclosure (the appropriation by landlords) of common lands. The ultimate success of Jamestown was determined by a new and lucrative addiction— the famous "Sot-Weed," or tobacco, later immortalized by the poet Ebenezer Cooke in the 1700s and the novelist John Barth in the 1960s.[22] The colonists had shown little interest in growing maize, but tobacco was another matter. Like opium in

Victorian times and cocaine in ours, the weed made its own way to the purse through the brain.

In 1612, a couple of years before he married Pocahontas, John Rolfe began to plant a mild Caribbean variety that was already in demand in London from Spanish sources. In 1616 Jamestowners sent more than a ton of this new crop to England; three years later, when they shipped ten tons, the colony showed its first real return on investment, at last turning "smoke into gold," as Queen Elizabeth had once joked with her wily courtier Sir Walter Raleigh.[23] The tonnage soon soared into the hundreds and thousands. By the outbreak of the American Revolution, about one-sixth of the Thirteen Colonies' exports (by value) would be tobacco.[24]

Unlike the initial trade in furs, which had required cooperation between the old Americans and the new, tobacco demanded land—and docile hands. Most of the early workers were indentured whites from the London slums and Indians who had been hired or enslaved. The forgotten story of thralldom in America is that many early slaves were indigenous Americans, usually war prisoners sold by their captors in return for guns, copper and other trade goods. Another sinister precedent was set in 1619, when the privateer *White Lyon* brought some twenty Africans to the colony—the first known shipment of the millions who would be sold in North America over the next two hundred years.[25]

At about this time, the colony ended landholding in common, a practice that had blunted competition with the Powhatans and among the whites themselves. When Jamestown's leaders converted the prime land into private estates, lesser fry and newcomers had to fan out into the backcountry and take what they could from the Indians.[26] The self-replicating machinery of encroachment and conquest that would gnaw its way across the continent had been installed.

⋅⇒◎⇐⋅

The white migrants of this period were not yet "Americans" except in a geographical sense. They were British (and a few other Europeans), largely unchanged by their new home, behaving with all the desperation, superstition and showy violence of early post-Medieval Europe. (Sir Walter Raleigh's half-brother Sir Humphrey Gilbert, for example, had been well known in Ireland for lining the way to his field tent with a Kurtz-like avenue of trophy heads.[27])

The old Americans were certainly not pacifists either. Like Europe, America had been bloodied for centuries by war among its nations. Neither race had a monopoly on violence or on virtue; both practised massacre, torture and differing forms of slavery. The moral distinction between them is simply that Europe invaded America, not the reverse.[28] Even under the rudimentary international law of that time, the indigenous people of the Americas held a right to self-defence.[29]

In 1618 old King Powhatan died and was succeeded by his brother Opechancanough. With rising encroachment, sickness and interracial crime, the shaky peace between locals and intruders at last began to break down. A charismatic "prophet" arose, calling for a return to the happy days before the English, telling Opechancanough that the pristine world could be restored by a mix of military and sacred power—a message much like Joan of Arc's in fifteenth-century France. Such movements, called "crisis cults" by anthropologists, often arise in desperate times; this was the first of many that would inspire native resistance in America for the next three centuries, ending in the famous Ghost Dance on the Great Plains in the 1880s.[30]

The Jamestown authorities struck first: in March 1622 they killed the agitator on a trumped-up murder charge.[31] Days later Opechancanough launched his well-planned attack. About 350 colonists, one-fourth of the total, died as Powhatan's fighters swept through outlying plantations. But the whites regrouped, held the fort at Jamestown and fought back with everything they had. They even poisoned two hundred Powhatans at a peace conference while toasting "eternal friendship"—a deed that may well be the first but would not be the last of its kind.[32]

The Powhatan War was put to good use by those who had been seeking an excuse to dispense with diplomacy and the faraway Crown's good name.[33] Under European concepts of Natural Law, another people's sovereignty could be abolished by treaty, by conquest or by declaring them to be subhuman barbarians (the standard excuse for slavery). While American peoples stayed at peace or allied with the English, there was no lawful way to extinguish their title without their agreement, which the Powhatans had been careful not to give. When John Smith had used language suggesting that the English monarch was King Powhatan's "father" (meaning overlord), the "subtile Salvage" answered, "I am also a king, and this my land . . . neither will I bite at such a baite."[34]

But now, with victory, the colonist Edward Waterhouse could gloat:

> We, who hitherto have had possession of no more
> ground than their waste . . . may now by right of Warre,
> and law of Nations, invade the Country, and destroy
> them who sought to destroy us: whereby wee shall

> enjoy their cultivated places, turning the laborious
> Mattocke into the victorious Sword . . . and possessing
> the fruits of others' labours. Now their cleared grounds
> in all their villages (which are situate in the fruitfullest
> places of the land) shall be inhabited by us.[35]

This is one of the clearest statements in American history of how the land was won. Here, at that history's dawn, Waterhouse lays bare the business end of the conquest machine: the new Americans assault and encroach on the old Americans until they provoke a counterattack, which is sometimes planned by the native leadership and at other times carried out by a radical splinter group. The white authorities then express outrage at what bloodthirsty "barbarians" have done to God-fearing tillers of the earth. A punitive war is then launched with overwhelming force—a war of "civilization" against "savagery," in which the first Americans are driven further into the "wilderness" or exterminated on the spot.[36]

Such rhetoric is not, of course, exclusive to America. It is heard wherever rival peoples fight for the same turf—the Middle East and Northern Ireland come immediately to mind. In American expansion, such talk outlived the Indian Wars. It was heard in the Philippines, in Korea, in Vietnam and most recently from both George Bushes when speaking of Iraq and Afghanistan.

Waterhouse's statement also confirms that the best land was fully cultivated by the original Americans and that they built in the "fruitfullest" spots. Like Powhatan's capital, most native towns soon became white ones—a transition that explains why archaeologists find relatively few remains of ancient American settlements, especially in the East. Absence of evidence is not necessarily evidence of absence.

But absence was exactly what the whites now wanted. The historian Francis Jennings has shown how English attitudes toward indigenous Americans underwent a profound change after the Powhatan War. Until 1622 the English had acknowledged the native peoples to be settled agriculturalists in organized societies with towns, leaders, customary laws and, therefore, inherent rights of sovereignty and ownership. King Powhatan was fulsomely described as "a great emperour," his subjects having "their own Magistrates for good commanding . . . that would be counted very civill."[37] But after the war, the Indians (whom Smith himself had called "poore innocent soules" misused by his colonists) suddenly became demonized as "Outlawes of Humanity." Their beliefs were condemned as devil-worship and the word *savages* now took on its full pejorative freight.

Demonization happens in all wars, but this propaganda lived on and solidified into a cornerstone of white entitlement. Myths usually enjoy a certain obscurity around their birth, and it is not often that historians can trace a political fiction back to the instant when it pecks its shell. Yet this one can be securely placed in the years 1622–25 and within the influential writings of the Essex clergyman Samuel Purchas. He never saw the New World for himself but drew freely on information from his friend John Smith and others who did. Purchas knew very well "that the Virginia Indians were sedentary and agricultural and that the Jamestown colonists had been preserved from total starvation by Indian farm produce."[38] In his earliest writings, published in 1613 (shortly before the wedding of John Rolphe and Pocahontas), Purchas had emphasized the importance of fair dealing according to "the milde Law of nature, not that violent law of Armes."[39]

But after the war, Samuel Purchas quickly hatched a Big Lie. America became, in his words, an "unmanned wild Countrey" that the Indians "range rather than inhabite."[40] At a stroke, settled farmers were magicked into rootless nomads, and from there it was a short step to conclude that such people, especially when guilty of "disloyal treason" (as he redundantly put it), had no right to the land. "Future dangers," Purchas went on, should "be prevented by the extirpation of the more dangerous, and commodities also raised out of the servileness and serviceablenesse of the rest."[41] In other words, Indians who posed a threat should be exterminated and docile ones, enslaved. Either way, all could lawfully be dispossessed.[42]

The lie grew long legs, and it is still widely believed today. Two centuries after Purchas, President Jackson would use it to justify his "removal" of the Five Civilized Tribes from the South in the 1830s, describing Cherokees, Creeks and others—corn farmers descended from the pyramid builders who had seen off Hernando de Soto—as having "traversed but not occupied" the land.[43]

-◦─◦═◦═◦-

The history of white America runs down through time in two gathering streams that eventually collide in the Civil War of 1861–65. The slave-owning South flows from the Virginia plantations, while the entrepreneurial North rises from Plymouth and other colonies founded in New England a few years later by Puritans and profiteers. The latter categories weren't mutually exclusive: "religion and profit jump together," wrote one of New England's leaders.[44]

In December 1620 the Pilgrim Fathers alighted from the *Mayflower* at Plymouth Rock. Every American schoolchild learns this nation-founding fact. What they seldom learn is that the Pilgrims were soon accosted there in fluent English by a lonely, grief-stricken Wampanoag—a member of the same people whom Verrazzano had visited at Rhode Island nearly a century before. On the face of it, this man, whose name was Squanto, had little reason to be friendly.[45] About 1615 he had been kidnapped in a slave raid on the Massachusetts coast— probably by an associate of John Smith—taken to Spain and sold in a Málaga slave market.[46] Somehow he escaped, made his way to England and returned via Newfoundland to Massachusetts, an amazing journey that took him four years.

When Squanto got back, he found his hometown, Patuxet, inhabited only by the dead, "a new found Golgotha" strewn with human bones.[47] A plague or mix of plagues (likely including smallpox) had struck the New England coast, killing nine out of ten in many places and everyone at Patuxet. Smallpox was terrible enough for Europeans, but because native Americans had no immunity, they caught it far more easily and suffered more severely: "They lie on their hard mats, the pox breaking and mattering and running. [And] when they turn them, a whole side will flay off at once as it were, and will be all of a gore blood, most fearful to behold . . . they die like rotten sheep."[48]

Word of Squanto's town—with empty houses, worked fields and cribs full of corn—had reached the Pilgrims during a landfall at Cape Cod. They sailed on to Patuxet, renamed it Plymouth and moved in. "The good hand of God favoured our beginnings [by] sweeping away great multitudes of the natives," their leader wrote, "that he might make room for us."[49]

Despite the Almighty's favour, about half the would-be settlers died that winter of hunger and scurvy. Like the Jamestowners, the Plymouth colonists were mostly fighters, traders and townsfolk, unskilled on the land. Late December was a bad time to turn up in North America anyway, especially after a long crossing. Once they'd eaten everything in the ghost town of Patuxet-Plymouth, the Pilgrims began raiding the country for miles around. The decimated Wampanoags were not a rich source of supply, even at gunpoint. Meanwhile, their western neighbours and traditional foe, the Narragansetts, had avoided the worst of the plague and were threatening the Patuxet region. Probably for this reason, Squanto and other survivors decided to help the newcomers. In the spring, they made peace with the English, teaching them how to grow maize and other American crops and later how to repay the Earth with the autumn festival of Thanksgiving.

The Pilgrims thanked their God for saving them in a "wilderness," but the feast speaks for itself: turkey, corn, beans, pumpkin, cranberries, potatoes and the rest came from thousands of years of New World civilization.[50] It was the heathen, not the Lord, who saved them. Without Squanto and Patuxet, the Plymouth colony might have gone the way of Roanoke.

Although the English had at first been reluctant to grow American corn, hunger proved the best spice. Nowadays, most maize in the United States is processed or fed to livestock, but for the early white farmers it became the staff of life, eaten as cornbread, succotash and hominy, or "hasty pudding."[51] Corn, the Iroquois ethnologist Arthur Parker wrote in the 1920s, became "the bridge over which English civilization crept . . . to a foothold and a permanent occupation of America."[52] Alexis de Tocqueville saw this process for himself when he visited the edge of white settlement in 1831, a tiny hamlet called Pontiac in the Michigan woods beyond an "American village" called Detroit. "Corn is providential in the wilds," a settler told him.

"It grows in the water of our marshes and pushes up under the foliage of the forests. . . . It is corn that saves the emigrant's family from inevitable destruction."[53]

The Pilgrims of Patuxet repaid their native hosts in two ways. In 1622 Squanto and other Wampanoags died in yet another wave of European disease. That was accidental. The second way was clearly intentional. About 1630 William Bradford, a leader of Plymouth, began writing a polemical history of his flock. Although only a decade had passed since the Pilgrims' arrival—and the help given by the Wampanoags must still have been fresh in their minds—Bradford didn't care about the facts. What mattered was the myth:

> [They had] no friends to welcome them . . . no houses or much less towns to repair to, to seek for succour [and] these savage barbarians, when they met with them . . . were readier to fill their sides full of arrows than otherwise. What could they see but a hideous and desolate wilderness, full of wild beasts and wild men. . . . What could now sustain them but the Spirit of God and His Grace?[54]

This New England contribution to Purchas's Big Lie isn't even internally consistent. How can a "desolate wilderness" supposedly without houses or fields be "full of wild men"? Yet Bradford's work made its way through the centuries into other books and has shaped white America's perception of itself for a dozen generations. Tocqueville himself reproduced whole pages from a history of New England published in 1826, unaware that the author had lifted much of it from Bradford verbatim, including the passage quoted above.[55]

Although Pilgrims controlled the Plymouth colony, only about a third of the hundred migrants aboard the *Mayflower* had been card-carrying members of the Pilgrim sect. Also known as Separatists, these people differed from Puritans in general by withdrawing from the Church of England instead of hoping to reform it.[56] The main Puritan colony of Massachusetts Bay was founded at Boston in 1630. Further north, up the coast at Naumkeag, or Salem (later famous for its so-called witches), a mixed group of settlers arrived at the end of the 1620s. In all these places, recent plagues had greatly reduced, though not eliminated, the original inhabitants.[57]

⚬══◉══⚬

Both mainstream Puritans and Pilgrims saw themselves as modern Saints migrating from the Old World to the New (a belief system that would eventually spawn the Latter-Day Saints, or Mormons, in the 1830s). They were the new Israelites, a chosen people on a divine "errand" to transform a supposed wilderness into a promised land, as commanded by the Lord in the Book of Genesis: "Get thee out of thy country, and from thy kindred, and from thy father's house, unto a land that I will show thee: And I will make of thee a great nation."[58] As a Puritan town meeting was said to have voted in 1640 after becoming troubled in conscience about taking Indian land: "1. The Earth is the Lord's and the fullness thereof. 2. The Lord can dispose of the Earth to his Saints. 3. We are his Saints."[59]

If America was a second Canaan, turned over to the Saints by God, it was also occupied by "Canaanites"—dusky descendants of Ham, with whom racial mixing was forbidden. The Puritans' attitude toward American Indians was therefore deeply conflicted from the start: on the one hand, they saw it as their duty to win the "heathen" to the God of Love; on the other they rejoiced when Jehovah reverted to Old Testament form and smote the heathen with plagues or intervened in battle on the invaders' behalf. The oval seal of the Governor and Company of Massachusetts Bay, struck in 1629, has a Latin inscription surrounding a crude image of a naked Indian, from whose mouth issues a speech-bubble with the words "Come over and help us."[60] It is perhaps the first product of the American advertising industry and by no means the least disingenuous.

In the end the Puritans had it both ways: they were not above slaughtering Indians and selling them into slavery; yet they later established small communities of "Praying Indians," whose descendants were among the few native Easterners not driven west by warfare or "removed" in ethnic cleansing by the early United States.

Both cultures became deeply changed through contact, a process that would continue along the rolling frontier for centuries, creating (as the historian Frederick Jackson Turner recognized in 1893) a hybrid society wherever native and white America traded blows, goods and ideas. The well-known exchange was of vices, the new Americans taking up tobacco and giving the old Americans liquor in return.[61] Less well known is the degree to which white settlers became Americanized in subtler ways. Of the hundreds of words that passed into English, some—such as the Algonquian "caucus"— express abstractions as well as things. At the time of the Revolution, the native language was still widely spoken, even by whites, on the islands of Martha's Vineyard and Nantucket, where Praying Wampanoags dominated the early whale fishery.[62] Massachusetts Bay used wampum, the indigenous shell currency, as legal tender for decades. And that colony's law forbidding whites from building wigwams instead of English-style houses gives a strikingly fresh picture of what early Boston must have looked like. It also reveals white fears of "going native." When Thomas Morton, a settler who enjoyed genial relations with his Indian neighbours, invited them to a Maypole Dance at his farm near Plymouth "to see the manner of our Revels," the scandalized Pilgrims condemned him as a Lord of Misrule and deported him.[63]

The greatest Puritan fears, however, lay in the spiritual realm. In 1642 a young man named Thomas Granger was caught having sex with a horse, admitting further pleasures with "a cow, two goats, five sheep, two calves and a turkey." The judges wanted to know whether he had acquired his tastes in Old England or New—fearing the latter, because "Satan hath more power in these heathen lands."[64] Relieved to learn that Granger's habits hailed from the mother country, they executed him along with all the four-footed sinners who could be identified.

There's little doubt that the Salem witch hunt of the early 1690s owed much of its ferocity to the Puritans' feelings of isolation on the edge of a dark continent and their dread that Satan was out for revenge on those who had killed or converted so many of his native subjects. "The devil was exceedingly disturbed," wrote the Puritan divine and prolific author Cotton Mather in his *Wonders of the Invisible World*, "and is now making one more attempt upon us."[65]

⟶⟵

The political events in early New England were complex, with constant strife among the various English and American players.

The Plymouth colony eventually became absorbed by the Puritan Massachusetts Bay Company, which was much bigger and better funded.[66] Connecticut began early in the 1630s as a dissident offshoot of Massachusetts Bay. There were also Puritans in the South (the law books of Jamestown were full of moral strictures), but the dominant feeling there was "Damn your souls! Make tobacco!"[67] Mainstream Puritans treated other sects—Quakers, Baptists, Antinomians and the like—as heretics and outcasts, forcing them to make their own colonies in Rhode Island.

One of the shabbier intercolonial fights was Plymouth's overthrow of Wessagusset, a small Anglican colony at peace with local Indians and therefore a rival in both religion and the fur trade. On the pretext of "saving" Wessagusset from a non-existent Indian plot, a Plymouth force murdered some of the colony's native allies in cold blood and made the deed stick to the Anglicans—who then *did* come under Indian attack and fled back to England. "The trick," wrote Francis Jennings, was "diverting the blame to the 'savages.'"[68] It was a trick that would be played again many times, most famously in 1773 at the Boston Tea Party, and most bloodily in 1857 at Mountain Meadows, Utah, where more than a hundred California-bound migrants were slaughtered by "Indians" who were mainly Mormons in fancy dress and greasepaint.[69]

"In our enchantment with the ideal of democracy," wrote Leland Dewitt Baldwin in his masterly *American Quest for the City of God,* "we have [asserted] the myth that the American colonies were settled to ensure political and religious liberty. Doubtless some of the colonizers did have this aim, but in by far the most cases they refused liberty to others. . . . Baptists were scourged and Quakers hanged."[70]

The power of faith, especially of a fundamentalist turn, in the life and politics of the United States is unique among major modern countries. "No Western nation is as religion-soaked as ours," writes the cultural critic Harold Bloom, adding that this "demands some understanding, if our doom-eager society is to be understood at all."[71] Many a conversation between an American and a European founders on the rock of piety. In short, most Americans believe that God takes a direct hand in human affairs; most other westerners do not. And many in the United States, like their Puritan forebears, are so certain they are privy to the Almighty's intentions that they are willing to help him carry them out: some in the positive ways of altruism; others in bigotry and on the battlefield. With their sense of being actors in a war between good and evil fought on Earth but directed from Heaven, such Christians have more in common ideologically with the hardliners of Islam than with the mainstream secular west.

⊷⟝⊚⟞⊷

To understand how this cultural gulf has developed, we must make a brief detour to medieval Europe and its aftermath. The Christian soldiers who fetched up in the New World were blown across the Atlantic by the tempests of the Reformation. When Martin Luther made a bonfire of papal decrees at Wittenberg in 1520, he ignited a great heap of ideological and social tinder that had been building up since the high Middle Ages.[72] Catholics and Protestants then descended into a pan-European conflict that lasted nearly two hundred years, its fury and madness foreshadowing the twentieth century's hot and cold wars between right and left. In Britain, the storms would not die down until the end of the Civil War in 1660.

Catholicism had wielded exclusive sway over the souls of Western Europe for a thousand years. Reform movements had arisen from time to time, but they were either absorbed as new religious orders (as the Franciscans were) or brutally crushed as heresies.[73] There was no agreed separation of Church and State. Religious dissent was therefore akin to treason, a challenge to the religio-political hierarchy.[74]

The medieval popes claimed to hold not only spiritual but also temporal power—to be the inheritors of Roman imperial might, or at least the arbiters of who should wield that power as Holy Roman Emperor.[75] This claim, both courted and thwarted by barbarian leaders from Charlemagne onward, took a mortal blow when its founding document, the *Donation of Constantine*—supposedly transferring the Western Empire to the papacy—was shown by a shrewd fifteenth-century scholar to be a fake.[76]

Donation or not, the pope was still spiritual emperor over the One True Faith. He and his officials anointed all Christian kings. Catholic dogma upheld the social pyramid. Yet the pyramid was being undermined on all sides: by the scandalous behaviour of popes and antipopes; by the harm done to Christendom's self-confidence by the Black Death in the mid-fourteenth century; by the rise of national governments; by intellectual contact with Islam and the rediscovery of Classical knowledge; by the invention of printing and the spread of literacy; and by the shock of the New World, which God had neglected to mention in the Bible.

Even so, Protestantism was a risky business. On what basis could the law apply to folk who did not accept the holy foundation of state power? On what moral footing could their relations with society be built? And if they rejected interpretations of Christian doctrine handed down by the learned doctors of the Church, how would they know *what* to believe? How would they even tell right from wrong?

As the Church Fathers knew, the Bible was explosive—a contradictory and subversive body of writings that needed careful handling and interpretation. Having arisen as a radical sect of Judaism, Christianity carried within it, like a dormant virus, the seeds of chaos. When ordinary citizens began reading Holy Writ for themselves, they found that the early Christian community of fishermen, misfits and outcasts portrayed in the New Testament bore little resemblance to the vast, wealthy and gorgeous edifice of the Catholic Church. With the revival of Classical learning, it also became clear that the Roman Church was more Roman than anyone had thought. Indeed, the popes' title Pontifex Maximus had formerly belonged to the high priests of pagan Rome.[77]

There is much to admire in the Protestant challenge to the old order. It was taken up mainly by the lower and middle classes: by peasants, artisans, freeholders and small business-folk seeking freedom from a top-heavy hierarchy, demanding the right to read and think for themselves. But while some were content to ponder the Bible quietly, others were not. Fanaticism and intolerance soon sprang up like weeds in the liberated acres of the Lord's garden. (As Mr. Dooley put it, "a fanatic is a man who does what he thinks the Lord would do if He knew the facts."[78]) Too many people found that it was all so simple: God was speaking to them personally, telling them what to do. Nowadays, when individuals think that God is speaking to them, that they have been chosen for a great purpose, that they are unquestionably right while everyone else is mistaken or evil, they are likely to be removed from society and treated for mental illness.

But when delusions of persecution and grandeur seize a whole group, the illness is less easily dealt with. If many are affected, who can say what is normal? At what point does one group's religious mission become a threat to other groups? It seems to me that the acid test for determining when a religious community has become a peril to itself and others is when it starts killing people on God's orders. The 1978 massacre at Jonestown in Guyana and the 1995 Aum Shinrikyo gassing of the Tokyo Underground are but two examples of mass psychosis—one suicidal, the other murderous. But today's standards of collective sanity aren't easily imposed on the past. The Catholic Church itself had been involved in mass murder for centuries—against heretics and infidels, and later through the Inquisition.

When religious violence occurs on such a scale, there is usually a substantial dose of earthly politics behind the spiritual imperative. This is true of the Crusades, the Aztec sacrifices, the Reformation wars, the al Qaeda attacks and sectarian troubles in Northern Ireland and the Middle East. One thread that runs through all these cases, from the First Crusade to the World Trade Center, is a conviction of supreme moral and metaphysical right (or a facsimile thereof, bearing in mind that fanaticism is often overcompensation for doubt[79]).

The atrocities of the medieval popes and kings had been committed under an overarching theology formidable enough to persuade most people that Christ allowed his delegates on Earth to practise war, torture and ingeniously painful executions on His behalf. Protestants knew that was bunk, but were soon doing much the same themselves. By its nature, Protestantism was fissiparous, spawning dissidents who hived off to form rival sects. Some were relatively harmless; others became the fascists, Maoists and terrorists of their time. Many came to regard themselves as Saints, above the moral run of humanity, or even as the Elect—the only people God would save on Doomsday. One recent embellishment, very popular in evangelical America, is the curious notion of the Rapture, when God will beam the "saved" up to heaven before unleashing the horrors of the Last Days on Earth.

It is no coincidence that the unravelling of the Catholic tapestry released a host of witches and demons, descended in part from the old heathen beliefs of pre-Christian times. One person's God became another's Satan. Europe was gripped by holy paranoia, exploited by rabble rousers and authorities alike. Tens of thousands of "witches" (three-fourths of them women) were tortured and killed, often by being burned alive.[80]

Despite warfare and poverty, Europe's population was rising sharply at this time. The increase was partly due to the impact of American crops (which was just beginning) but mainly to a general rebound from the effects of the Black Death, when a third of the population had died, shaking up old patterns of landholding, labour and social consensus.

By weakening the papacy and its Holy Roman Empire, the Reformation also strengthened nation-states—especially Britain. When Henry VIII broke with the Vatican in the 1530s (for worldly reasons, above all to divorce Catherine of Aragon and marry his lover Anne Boleyn), the Church of England he set up was less a Protestant body than a nationalized branch of Catholicism. He, and his daughter the Virgin Queen Elizabeth, managed to shoo pragmatic Catholics and Protestants (known as "High" and "Low" Church) into one big top, with the English sovereign as ringmaster instead of the pope.

While most people allowed this broad but flimsy tent to erect itself over their observances, a few did not. Militant Catholics (such as Sir Thomas More, who contested the king's right to divorce) were liable to arrest for treason. Militant Protestants—the Puritans—denounced High Church "superstition," wrecking splendid stained-glass windows, statues, rood screens and other church finery—even whitewashing over the great Doom paintings which had cowed and titillated the peasantry with Bosch-like scenes of God's wrath.

The political temperature rose steeply after a foiled act of terrorism: the Gunpowder Plot to blow up Parliament and Elizabeth's successor, the Stuart King James, in 1605. This may have been the work of *agents provocateurs*. Rightly or not, it was blamed on Roman Catholics, and, like the show trials run by Stalin and McCarthy, became the pretext for a purge of "traitors" and a hardening of state power.

Ironically, the plot's targets—king and Parliament—soon began fighting each other. Throughout the first half of the seventeenth century, James and his son Charles I were in a position similar to that of President Bush after the 2006 midterm elections: the king had the executive, but Parliament had the funds. Fiscal problems were worsened by inflation caused by the flood of silver and gold from Spanish America.[81]

The tussle soon spread far beyond money matters. Most Catholics threw in their lot with the nobles and the king, supporting his claim to rule by Divine Right, while the Puritans sided with Parliament and claimed to uphold the common law that had come down from Saxon England and the Magna Carta.[82] But the Puritans' egalitarianism was undercut by their many hates and forbiddings—no dancing, no acting, no sports on Sundays. Their project to make England a Low Church theocracy was no more

democratic, at bottom, than Lenin's dictatorship of the proletariat. In 1633 William Prynne, a hardline Puritan lawyer, wrote
against sinful habits such as people drinking toasts, men with
long hair and women on stage—things that King Charles and his
young queen, who herself dabbled in theatre, were well known
to enjoy. For this Prynne had his ears cut off, was fined £5,000
and later jailed for life by order of the Star Chamber, the king's
special tribunal, which, like the arbitrary justice reappearing
today in the so-called war on terror, was beyond the law.[83]

Open civil war broke out in 1642. From their styles of dress
and hair, the two sides were nicknamed Roundheads and
Cavaliers. The flamboyant Cavaliers, with their long hair and
richly feathered hats, were politically conservative but culturally liberal. They supported kingship, nobility and privilege but
were easygoing in moral and religious matters.[84] The short-
cropped Roundheads were Parliamentarians and generally
Low Church, from many sects and social factions. The radical
Levellers, for example, demanded abolition of the monarchy, a
written constitution, land reform, one-man-one-vote and
other ideas that had been simmering since the 1381 Peasants'
Revolt, with its protosocialist ditty, "When Adam delved and
Eve span, / Who was *then* a gentleman?"[85]

The fight between king and Parliament ended, for a time,
with the beheading of Charles I and the making of the
Commonwealth by the Puritan warlord Oliver Cromwell, who
took the Orwellian title Lord Protector.[86] Personally honest yet
politically ruthless, Cromwell tried to build a war machine
strong enough to stop world Catholicism and the return of the
Stuart kings.[87] A few years later, in the mock epic *Hudibras*,
Samuel Butler would make wicked fun of "Such as do build
their Faith upon / The holy Text of pike and gun."

Cromwell's dictatorship came undone soon after his death in 1658. With Charles II returning in triumph to the throne two years later, England awoke from the Puritan nightmare. Theatres reopened, writers and thinkers filled their lungs, and the new king set an example of loose living (thousands today believe themselves, with cause, to be descended from him). The wrangling between king and Parliament resumed for a while, to be settled by the Bloodless Revolution of 1688, when royal power was at last tamed by the Bill of Rights.[88]

The day of the hardline Puritans was done. Most were eventually drawn back into the Anglican mainstream; others would take the more moderate path of Methodism. The wider society reabsorbed the extremes, slowly growing more tolerant and varied in the process. England would yet undergo many stumbles on the way to modern democracy, but God withdrew to Heaven and forsook taking sides on Earth.

⋯⇒◎⇐⋯

So it went in the mother country. Not so in her colonies. In its New World haven, Puritan zealotry not only lingered but grew rank. The religious migrations to America had been a divorce of convenience—the sects seeking room in which to thrive; London happy to see them go. Low Church radicals therefore had a much higher profile in the American population than they had at home.[89]

As the Puritans' hopes for Britain died along with Cromwell's Commonwealth, their dreams for the New World became grander and more obsessive, inspired as much by the Book of Revelation as by Augustine's *City of God*. In his *Wonder-working Providence of Sion's Saviour in New England* (the title really says it all), one of Boston's leading settlers prophesied that in

America "the Lord will create a new Heaven and a new Earth, new Churches, and a new Commonwealth. . . . Who would not be a Soldier on Christ's side, where there is such a certainty of victory?"[90] Virginal America would be "the holy city, New Jerusalem, coming down from God out of heaven, prepared as a bride adorned for her husband."[91]

John Winthrop, the founder of the Boston colony, had preached in this vein even before his ship had raised the muddy shore of Massachusetts.[92] "We shall be as a city set upon a hill," he foretold, "the eyes of all people are upon us." Winthrop's words are now lodged so deeply in the American soul that Ronald Reagan may not have known whom (or what) he was quoting when they flowed smoothly from his tongue three and a half centuries later.

In the Puritan view, America would purify England, Europe and the world—a concept that "in secularized form [has] become the vaunt of the United States."[93] By fulfilling biblical prophecy, the New World was hastening the end of time itself— a notion that would rattle down the centuries until Francis Fukuyama naïvely declared that history had "ended" with America's winning of the Cold War.[94]

Beyond the Puritans' colonial redoubt, such ideas seemed increasingly absurd. By the end of the seventeenth century, the European Enlightenment was dawning and Old Englanders still outnumbered New Englanders by a hundred to one. Small, isolated populations can evolve quickly in new directions; they also tend to retain archaic features that fade from the larger gene pool. In biology this process is called genetic drift; in human culture it is called provincialism.

The English Civil War has yet to end in two places: Northern Ireland, where it was still being fought with "pike and gun" until yesterday, and America, where its opposing theologies spread with the white invader across the continent.[95] The first case lies outside this book, and the two have grown very different over time, but what they share is an archaic parochialism. In Ulster the war against "popery" thrived in the old style for ethnic reasons. In America it found new bones of contention, transforming itself from a fight among Christians into a cultural war between fundamentalism and humanism, faith and evidence, Jehovah and Darwin. "The narrow conservatism and religious bigotry of the Bible Belt," Leland Baldwin pointed out in 1981, "are the creation of forces that emerged from the decaying corpse of Puritanism."[96]

Modern America's *kulturkampf,* like seventeenth-century Britain's, is a war between regions and classes: between the sophisticated internationalism of the seaboard and the parochial extremism of the inland "backwoods." Ironically, Harvard College, founded by Puritans in 1636, has become one of the world's great seats of learning, while peculiar institutions such as Jerry Falwell's Liberty University of Lynchburg, Virginia, nourish a mindset that the ghost of Cotton Mather might applaud.[97]

⤙═◉═⤚

At first, America had been only a refuge for the Puritans, a faraway place in which to follow their beliefs in isolation. But the "Soldiers on Christ's side" were nothing if not fighters, and they soon took the chance to expand at the cost of non-Christian neighbours ill-equipped to resist. "Ask of me, and I shall give thee the heathen for thine inheritance," sang the Psalmist, "and the uttermost parts of the earth for thy possession. Thou shalt break them with a rod of iron."[98]

Break them they did. New England's version of the Powhatan War was the destruction of the Pequots, whom Herman Melville described in *Moby Dick* as "a celebrated tribe . . . now extinct as the ancient Medes." Little celebrated as a people today, they live on in Melville's great novel as the whaling ship *Pequod,* his microcosm of America—a "cannibal of a craft" containing multitudes.[99]

The Pequots' homeland was southern Connecticut from Saybrook to Rhode Island, and their head town was on the Pequot River, now the Thames. Disliked by the English because they traded with the Dutch, the Pequots were also at odds with their fellow Americans, the Mohicans and Narragansetts.[100]

The number of white settlers was rising steeply as thousands fled the build-up to the English Civil War. The widowed acres around Plymouth and Boston were no longer enough.[101] Opportunity came in the mid-1630s, when smallpox hit Pequot and Narragansett towns that had somehow escaped the earlier outbreak. "God hath hereby cleared our title to this place," exulted Governor Winthrop, who had earlier described the region as "full of Indians."[102]

Trouble of all sorts came to a head, not only between but within the races. Massachusetts hoped to bag Connecticut for itself and shut out Plymouth, other English, and the Dutch colonies along the Hudson from New Amsterdam (now New York City) to Fort Orange (now Albany). The Pequots' native enemies also mobilized. Traders and settlers began to swarm onto Pequot territory, sparking the usual round of strife and vendetta.

War broke out after some people—who may not, in fact, have been Pequots—killed two fur traders, starting with John Stone, a West Indian pirate who had tried to hijack a Plymouth ship and was later "caught in Boston rolling in bed with another man's wife."[103] While fleeing Puritan wrath for his wild night, Stone was unwise enough to kidnap some Connecticut Indians, who broke free and killed him. Few mourned his passing until a more respectable Englishman was slain on Block Island two years later. Again, this murder was probably not the Pequots' work. But Massachusetts used both killings as an excuse to crush the Pequot nation before it could recover from the pox.

By some accounts, the English slaughtered the Block Islanders and sold the survivors into slavery; others say the expedition was a fiasco. Either way, the Pequots besieged Fort Saybrook and tried to negotiate a truce, inquiring whether it was the English practice to kill women and children—something the Dutch on their western border had been doing, but the native peoples normally did not. When told they should fight and find out, the Pequots answered defiantly, "We are Pequots and have killed Englishmen, and can kill them as mosquitoes."[104]

They made good on this threat by killing nine settlers in April 1637. Connecticut and Massachusetts then vied to escalate the war and be first to take the Pequot land by right of conquest.[105] Connecticut's force was the nimbler and more ruthless. Its leader, John Mason, decided to massacre a sleeping town instead of engaging in battle. Some of Mason's officers baulked at this unchivalrous plan—as did his Narrangansett allies, who held back. But after a night of prayer during which the Lord was deemed to give His blessing, the officers went along.[106] "Sometimes the Scripture declareth women and children must perish," one said when criticized afterwards. "We had sufficient light from the Word of God for our proceedings."[107]

The proceedings began on a May morning in 1637, and the chosen place was a stockaded town called Mystic. It would be the most terrible slaughter since Soto burned Mobile a century before. Unlike Soto, Mason did not face many fighting men. Mystic was a soft target, and he knew it: most of the warriors were away, getting ready to defend their capital on the Pequot River to the west.[108]

The English attacked at first light, breaking in the gate and cutting down the occupants while many were still asleep. They soon tired of dragging townsfolk from their beds. "We must burn them," Mason shouted; he then "brought out a Fire Brand, and . . . set the Wigwams on Fire."

> And thus in little more than one Hour's space was their impregnable Fort with themselves utterly Destroyed, to the Number of Six or Seven Hundred. . . . Thus was God seen in the Mount, Crushing his proud Enemies and the Enemies of his People [the English], burning them up in the Fire of his Wrath, and dunging the ground with their flesh. It was the Lord's Doings, and it is marvellous in our Eyes![109]

Cotton Mather later added approvingly, "No less than 600 Pequot souls were brought down to hell that day."[110] The main native force hastened to the scene but got there too late, finding only some Narragansetts stunned by the methods of their Christian allies: "It is too furious, and slays too many," they protested.[111]

The Plymouth colony did not take part, but its chronicler gave details he must have heard from witnesses: "It was a fearful sight to see [the Pequots] thus frying in the fyer, and the streams of blood quenching the same, and horrible was the stincke and sente thereof, but the victory seemed a sweet sacrifice."[112]

The word *genocide* is sometimes bandied about loosely nowadays, but Mason's action against the Pequots fits a strict definition.[113] Puritan authorities later killed male prisoners in cold blood at Boston, selling the women and children into slavery. The English followed up with ethnocide, banning the very word *Pequot* and erasing native place names.[114] So it was that the Pequots became extinct as the ancient Medes; their river was renamed the Thames, and their old capital became New London. Mystic itself escaped the naming purge, perhaps because it was mistaken for an English word.[115]

⋯⋯

Unhappily for the Puritans' hopes of doing as they pleased in the New World, the might of the English Crown followed them across the sea soon after the restoration of the Stuart dynasty. In the mid-1660s, London conquered the Dutch colonies along the Hudson River. Renamed New York, these lands became the personal fiefdom of Charles II's brother, the future James II. The Saints were outflanked and potentially contained.[116]

The answer, the Puritans decided, was to start another war, conquer what was left of native sovereignty around their colonies and let the Indians take the blame. So forty years after their extermination of the Pequots, they provoked and crushed the Wampanoags, the very people who had been helping them for more than half a century. At the same time, the whites turned on their other local allies, the Narragansetts.[117] Known as King Philip's War (from an English name for the Wampanoag leader Metacom), the bloody campaign put an end to native power in much of New England.[118]

But it also spelled the end of the Puritans' own autonomy, which in their dreams had grown from mere isolation to a Puritan theocracy spreading west from Massachusetts and Connecticut to the Pacific. When British officials descended on Boston in 1676 to investigate the settlers' reckless conquest, they were appalled at the destruction on both sides. The war, they reported to London, had cost six hundred white lives, twelve hundred houses, eight thousand head of cattle, a vast sum of money and "upward of three thousand Indians, men, women and children destroyed, which if well managed would have been very serviceable to the English."[119]

The American Revolution was still a hundred years away, but one of its most potent seeds was planted with those words. The settlers wanted the land without the Indians. Britain, taking the wider view of a world power, hoped to enlist indigenous peoples as allies for its empire, especially against the French at Quebec and Montreal. With its line of former Dutch outposts on the Hudson, the Crown now blocked the Saints' path across the continent. The Puritans' divorce from London had suddenly become less distant and more acrimonious, contributing not only to the Revolution but to modern Americans' mistrust of their own central government.

Puritan influence would indeed go on to pervade North America, but it would do so from within the settler culture, spread not by any formal theocracy but by New Englanders migrating westward to the frontier lands. There, where men "hunger after religion," the heirs of the Saints would plant their visions and destinies like apple seed wherever they went. Faith and profit, "jumping together," would become the American way.

5.

WHITE SAVAGES

Savages we call them, because their Manners differ from
ours, which we think the Perfection of Civility; they think
the same of theirs.   —Benjamin Franklin, 1784[1]

No state can achieve proper culture, civilization, and
progress . . . as long as Indians are permitted to remain.
                                    —Martin Van Buren, 1837[2]

In the game of cultural change the winners usually discount
or deny the wisdom they have stolen from the losers.
                            —William Appleman Williams, 1980[3]

A NYONE GLANCING AT A MAP of the Thirteen Colonies
that became the United States will be struck by how small
the white presence still was in the mid-eighteenth
century, a generation before their independence.[4] Halfway in time
between the arrival of Christopher Columbus and the departure
of George W. Bush, British America was merely a seaboard strip
about a thousand miles long and one or two hundred miles deep.
Its claims were much grander—but the area under effective control was not much bigger than the British Isles.

With the Dutch conquered and the Puritans tamed in the mid-1670s, Britain's only European rivals in America were the French immediately to the north and the Spaniards to the south. Spain was too weak to be much of a headache, but France—England's perennial foe—had the garrison towns of Montreal and Quebec plus a loose string of trading forts along the Great Lakes and down the Ohio and Mississippi rivers. The European powers' jockeying for advantage (exacerbated by their endless wars in Europe) relied on alliances with the indigenous American peoples of the interior, especially those whose territories adjoined the settler fringe. As the action slowly shifted westward, a sporadic three-way conflict—known as the French and Indian War—burned up and down the Appalachian foothills from the Great Lakes to Georgia for a century. The ultimate winner would be a new nation—the United States—leaving France expelled, the Indians shattered, and Britain with the consolation prize of Canada.

The heart of this struggle was what is now upstate New York, where the "famous Confederation of the Iroquois," as Tocqueville wrote, "held the balance of power between the two greatest European nations."[5] Like their cousins visited by Jacques Cartier in the 1530s, the Iroquois, often called the League of Five Nations, were farming people with large fortified towns. One pre-Columbian building unearthed near their ancient capital at Onondaga was more than 300 feet long, and there were many such longhouses in each important settlement.[6] Metaphorically, the League was itself a great Longhouse stretching from the Hudson to Lake Erie, with five families under one roof: the Mohawk Nation at the "eastern door" near Albany, the Seneca at the "western door" near Niagara and the Onondaga in the middle, with the small Oneida and Cayuga nations in between.[7] Internally, the League was a democracy governed by a federal council with fifty seats. Externally, it behaved like a small empire, manipulating allies and vassals from Quebec to Kentucky and from New England to Ohio.[8]

The Iroquois could not halt the settler invasion forever, but they slowed it down in their part of America for a hundred years. The outcome could have been foretold from numbers alone. The white population of the Thirteen Colonies grew, by birth and inflow, from a quarter million in 1700 to more than 5 million in 1800, a twentyfold rise in one century.[9] The indigenous population east of the Mississippi plummeted from perhaps half a million in 1760 to nearly nothing in one lifetime—from disease, warfare, some assimilation, and finally the ethnic cleansing known as the Indian Removal of the 1830s.[10] The "winning" of America took place on this one-way demographic seesaw.

Before Old World pandemics reached the Great Lakes in the sixteenth century, the Iroquois alone may have numbered several hundred thousand.[11] They had fallen below seventy-five thousand by the 1630s, when smallpox struck again. "The Indians," wrote a Dutch lawyer who settled near Albany in 1641, "affirm that before the arrival of the Christians . . . they were ten times as numerous as they now are."[12] The Iroquois Confederacy tried to keep its numbers up by assimilating both friend and foe. In the 1640s it conquered its Huron cousins and brought most of them into the Longhouse.[13] Some eighty years later, the Tuscarora joined voluntarily, making the Five Nations into Six. And quite a few Europeans, whether captives, traders or refugees, were also adopted into Iroquois families. Such whites were apt to go native; as Benjamin Franklin remarked, "in a short time they become disgusted with our manner of life, and . . . there is no reclaiming them."[14]

Throughout the eighteenth century, the old and new Americans profoundly influenced each other at all social levels. In his groundbreaking historical essay of 1893, the young Frederick Jackson Turner argued: "The true point of view in the history of this nation is not the Atlantic coast, it is the Great West." By the West, Turner meant the frontier, burning slowly across the continent from the Appalachians in the eighteenth century to the Rockies in the next. In this "crucible," he wrote, "the immigrants were Americanized, liberated, and fused into a mixed race, English in neither nationality nor characteristics."[15]

Much of that liberation came by example. Anyone who had dealings with native people could see their political and social liberties in action: open debate, the rule of consensus and even—when agreement could not be reached on a serious matter—the right to secede, though many of these American freedoms had grown up, like the woods, after the scythe of smallpox.[16]

The Five (later Six) Nations Confederacy may well have been the oldest and most structured democracy in North America. Certainly, this polity was better understood by white Americans than any other, and its influence on their development was considerable. In later years its workings would make a deep impression on Marx, Engels and Victorian feminists.[17]

At an important conference held at Lancaster, Pennsylvania, between several colonies and native nations in 1744, the Iroquois statesman Canasatego—a tall, brawny man of sixty with a winning smile and crafty wit, a veteran of wrangles with the Quaker State—came face to face with Benjamin Franklin, then thirty-eight, later to become famous as an inventor and founding statesman of the American republic.[18] Like many Bostonians of drive and ability, Franklin had fled the Puritan backwater for Philadelphia, at that time the biggest city in North America. There he became a newspaperman and government printer, work that took him to treaty meetings, where "linguisters" translated the imposing Indian speeches on the spot. It was Franklin's job to make and publish the official transcriptions.[19]

Speaking for the Five Nations, Canasatego became exasperated by the bickering among the various colonies. He suggested, a little condescendingly, that the English might do well to emulate his people:

> We heartily recommend Union and a good agreement between you. . . . Our wise forefathers established union and amity between the Five Nations; this has made us formidable; this has given us great weight and authority with our neighbouring nations. We are a powerful Confederacy; and, by your observing the same methods our wise forefathers have taken, you will acquire fresh strength and power.[20]

Franklin took Canasatego's remarks to heart and began studying native political culture. Eventually he promoted the Iroquois model at the Albany Congress of 1754, when the French and Indian War was coming to a head. "It would be a very strange thing," he wrote, "if Six Nations of ignorant savages should be capable of forming a scheme for such a union, and be able to execute it in such a manner as that it has subsisted ages . . . and yet that a like union should be impracticable for ten or a dozen English colonies."[21]

Although the Albany delegates agreed to form a union, the scheme was thrown out by their assemblies and the British government. Federation would not take root until late in Franklin's life, when he helped draw up both the Declaration of Independence and the U.S. Constitution. By the time the latter was written in 1787, the Six Nations had been broken and over-run. Their influence was never formally acknowledged, and the new Americans did not follow the Iroquois model as closely as Franklin had wished.[22]

Yet one memorial to the Iroquois can be seen wherever the United States does business under its Great Seal. The symbol of the Five Nations' combined strength was an eagle clasping five arrows in its talons. The United States raised the number of arrows to thirteen and put Latin in the bird's mouth: E PLURIBUS UNUM. Along with these Roman words and a Masonic pyramid stamped on each dollar bill, the filched eagle became a fitting emblem for the settlers' hybrid empire.[23]

⊷≡◉⊃≋⊷

The Albany Congress went awry in several ways, and the war with the French fared no better. As commander-in-chief, London sent out General Braddock, a military man of a familiar kind: arrogant, none too bright, impervious to good advice. George Washington, for one, tried to impress on him the importance of native troops, worth more "than twice their number of white men."[24]

Braddock took no notice. His contempt for both Indians and colonials cost him his life within a year, when the French routed him at Fort Duquesne (now Pittsburgh). The Iroquois were blunt about the cause of the defeat: "It was the pride and ignorance of that great general that came from England. . . . He looked upon us as dogs and would never hear anything that was said to him."[25]

For a while, the British took heed, setting up a commission of Indian Affairs to liaise with the two centres of native power: the Six Nations in the North and the Cherokee Nation in the South. The northern commissioner was Sir William Johnson, who had lived in the Mohawk Valley near Albany since arriving from Ireland as a young trader in the 1730s. Johnson was a chameleon, a Catholic turned Protestant, a cultured man who paid bounty for French scalps. He soon learned Mohawk, mastered indigenous protocol—which took some doing among the ceremonious Iroquois—and found time for "Pleasures with the brown Ladies," which made for good politics among the matrilineal Iroquois. Johnson owed much of his success to his Mohawk wife, Molly Brant.[26]

After their unhappy experience with General Braddock, most of the Six Nations did their best to stay neutral. But the Great Longhouse was starting to show structural cracks, especially at the Mohawk end, where British influence was strongest. Leading families such as the Brants lived in English-style houses, attended church and sent their children to boarding school. Molly's young brother Joseph, who would fight the American rebels and later take half the Confederacy to Canada, spent his quieter hours translating the Bible into Mohawk from the Greek.[27] With Molly's connections, Johnson managed to draw the Mohawks and some Senecas back into England's war against the French. Helped by these Iroquois at Niagara and on the St. Lawrence, British forces took Quebec City in 1759. With the capitulation of Montreal in 1760, New France came to an end.

With only one foreign power left standing in America, the native nations' leverage as buffer-states was also at an end. They began to fear that the English would now turn on them, to make room for settlers. Unease turned to alarm when Braddock's successor, Lord Jeffrey Amherst, broke every commitment that had been made to Indian allies during the recent war. On Amherst's orders—and to Johnson's dismay—debts were not paid, supplies were not delivered, and squatters were not controlled.

Many Indians had lost farms and homes in the fighting. Starving, desperate and angry, they became susceptible to an apocalyptic message. A Delaware prophet called Neolin, the Enlightened, received warnings from the Master of Life: the Creator had made America for the Indians, but they would soon lose it unless they returned to traditional ways and beliefs. They had to give up European goods, especially alcohol, stop killing animals for foreign exchange, and unite against the invader:

> The land on which you are, I have made for you, not for others. . . . Do not sell to [the whites] that which I have placed on the earth as food. . . . Put off entirely from yourselves the customs which you have adopted since the white people came among us; you are to return to that former happy state, in which we lived in peace and plenty, before these strangers came.[28]

This message was a classic crisis-cult, a call for holy war in desperate times—an American equivalent of the Jewish uprisings against Rome, the Puritan revolt in England or today's jihads against the west. The Ottawa chief Pontiac and others, including some Iroquois, held talks on a united stand to reconquer North America—a feat that still seemed possible. Those who had been to Europe on diplomatic missions knew better: the number of whites in England, some Cherokees reported, "far exceeded what we thought possibly could be."[29] These cooler heads might have prevailed if the full extent of British betrayal hadn't come to light in the spring of 1763, when London signed a peace treaty with Paris in which native interests were ignored.

Pontiac's War began in May—and the native forces initially prevailed. By summer's end, four hundred white soldiers and two thousand settlers were dead. Nine forts fell, leaving only Pitt and Detroit in British hands.[30]

The Indians' "treachery" soon cleared away white scruples about conquest and extermination. In language echoing Samuel Purchas, Colonel Henry Bouquet wrote to Amherst that he planned to "extirpate that Vermine from a Country they have forfeited, and with it all claim to the Rights of Humanity." He suggested infecting the Indians with smallpox. Amherst liked the idea, immediately ordering Bouquet to "innoculate [infect] the Indians by means of blankets, as well as to try Every other method that can serve to Extirpate this Execrable Race."

Indian leaders besieging Fort Pitt were invited to talk beneath a flag of truce and there bestowed with a deadly gift—bedding taken from smallpox victims. Biological warfare was not new— diseased corpses had been lobbed over castle walls throughout the Middle Ages. But by the 1760s, the epidemiology of smallpox was well understood: Jeffrey Amherst and Henry Bouquet must take the blame for the first modern use of germs in war. There can be no doubt that Amherst's objective was genocide. He followed up with a letter to Sir William Johnson, threatening the "Whole Race of Indians" with a "Stop to their very Being."[31]

The disease did its usual work, undermining the native war effort. It also helped Johnson, with his wife Molly's help, to talk most of the Six Nations into staying neutral. In return, he engineered the removal of Amherst and persuaded George III to address native concerns in the Royal Proclamation of October 7, 1763. This key document set a borderline between white and Indian America along the crest of the Appalachian chain.[32] From that day forth, King George decreed, there would be no more squatter invasions and no land cessions, except at the international level between native leaders and the Crown.

The Royal Proclamation would eventually become the legal basis for most of the treaties, reservations and indigenous rights in the United States and Canada. Its immediate effect, however, was to heighten settler unrest. In several of the original charters, written when Europeans had no notion of North America's great breadth, the Crown had granted colonies the right to grow westward to the Pacific. The Proclamation now withdrew this right and confined white America within bounds that only the Crown and the Indians could change. This time it was white Americans who felt the sting of British betrayal.

Just three months after the Proclamation was issued, a white vigilante mob known as the Paxton Boys vented their rage by burning and scalping twenty Conestoga Indians—the entire population of a peaceful mission village near Lancaster, Pennsylvania. Some died in a dawn firebombing on December 14; others were sheltered in the local workhouse by friendly whites, mainly Quakers. Two days after Christmas, the Paxton Boys broke in and killed them, including children. The mob then went on to Philadelphia, intent on ridding the city of Indians. Franklin himself helped calm the riot; later, in a courageous essay, he denounced the killers as "Christian White Savages."[33]

New land was America's safety valve, the last great hope for those outflanked by quicker, luckier and wealthier citizens.[34] Today America's poor are consoled—some say deluded—by the notion that the economic pie, however unfairly sliced, is always growing, that one day it will be their turn to win the lottery, that they are not an exploited proletariat but, as John Steinbeck put it, "temporarily embarrassed millionaires."[35]

Many a frontier family lived in a state of fitful but perpetual motion, homesteading for only a few years before pulling up their shallow roots and moving on, choosing Indians over lawmen, and leaving creditors behind. "Settlers" is hardly the right word for them: rather, they were the true nomads, foot soldiers of the conquest machine first let loose at Jamestown.[36] "Marching before the immense European family of whom he forms as it were the advance guard," Tocqueville noted, "the pioneer . . . builds his rustic hut and waits till the first chance of war opens his way to new wilds."[37]

It was not only the backwoodsmen who stood to lose by an end to "free" land. Big survey and holding companies were usually ahead of the small fry. One of the richest prizes on the frontier was the Ohio Country to the west of Pennsylvania and Virginia, the site of many ancient temple mounds.[38] As far back as 1747, the Washington family and other wealthy Virginians had formed the Ohio Land Company to penetrate the region, deal in furs and speculate in any Indian property they could alienate.[39] The young George Washington, who had trained as a surveyor, joined this and other ventures beyond the Blue Ridge Mountains—land unceded by its native owners and all on the wrong side of what became the Royal Proclamation line. To complicate matters, there were also overlapping claims among the Indian nations: both the Six Nations and the Cherokees claimed sway over most of Kentucky.

Shortly before the American Revolution, Washington confided to a colleague: "I can never look upon that proclamation in any other light (but I say this between ourselves) than as a temporary expedient to quiet the minds of the Indians."[40] Indeed, once the Revolutionary War had ended, the hardest currency available to pension off veterans and pay the rebels' debt was Indian land.

⊹⇒◎⇐⊹

The Revolution claimed not only the land of America and some of its native political ideas but also the very word *American*. Around this time, *American* ceased to mean the indigenous people of the continent (like *Asian* or *African*) and was taken up self-consciously by the invaders. English settlers became Americans in the same way that Dutch Boers in South Africa became Afrikaners.

In his well-known essay "What Is an American?" a self-styled but not entirely honest "American Farmer" spread the new meaning:

> What then is the American, this new man? He is either an European, or the descendant of an European . . . who, leaving behind him all his ancient prejudices and manners, receives new ones from the new mode of life he has embraced. . . . Americans are the western pilgrims, who are carrying along with them that great mass of arts, sciences, vigour, and industry which began long since in the east. . . . The American is a new man, who acts upon new principles. . . . Here the rewards of his industry follow with equal steps the progress of his labour; his labour is founded on the basis of nature, *self-interest*.[41]

Here are the key ingredients of the American Dream: love of the new and dismissal of the old; invaders presented as "pilgrims"; hard work both rewarded and required; and selfishness as natural law—social Darwinism *avant la lettre*.[42]

The author, who went by the alias Hector Saint John, told his readers that he was a man of little education born to English pioneers in Pennsylvania, a simple tiller of the earth. He had no regrets, he claimed, for never setting eyes on Europe, for he was more than satisfied with America, where "everything is modern, peaceful, and benign."[43] In truth, he was a French aristocrat from Normandy, like his later compatriot Alexis de Tocqueville. Hector Saint John was really Michel-Guillaume Saint-Jean de Crèvecoeur, and he had moved from New France to New York in shadowy circumstances after the French and Indian War.[44] Ten years later he married well and bought a farm in lower New York state. It was not Pennsylvania nor a clearing in the wilds, but a going concern. One also wonders how much personal sweat flowed from a man who, while railing against Southern slavery, let slip: "My negroes are tolerably faithful and healthy."[45]

Crèvecoeur was no worse in this hypocrisy than the writers of the Declaration of Independence, many of whom owned Africans. America's wealth and freedom would be built on the slaughter of one race and the enslavement of another. It isn't hard to see how Crèvecoeur could insulate his soul from the chilly underdraught of moral inconsistencies when writing such a banner page in the settler mythology. But his American dream was written a year *before* the American Revolution. How could he have been so unaware—as he later claimed—of the unrest in the society he idealized?

History would later regard the 1776 Revolution as a bold uprising against tyranny, but to many at the time—including

Crèvecoeur in his afterthoughts—it seemed a bloody and squalid civil war.[46] As in America's next civil war (then eighty-five years in the future), brothers ran to rival flags and made each other traitors; farms and towns were set ablaze; white men scalped one another.[47]

Like George H. Bush ("I don't care what the facts are"), Crèvecoeur had a gift for self-deception. But soon he could no longer find perfection, peace or even safety among his fellow whites. In his last essay, "Distresses of a Frontier Man," he transfers his vision of an earthly paradise from the new Americans to the old, switching horses at full gallop from the noble settler to the Noble Savage. He will take his wife and young ones to a quiet Indian town far from "the accursed neighbourhood of Europeans," where the original Americans "live with more ease, decency, and peace, than you imagine."[48]

What Crèvecoeur actually did was leave his wife and children on the farm and flee to Manhattan, where he was flung in jail by British authorities certain that the odd fish they had caught must be a spy. After a few months behind bars, he managed to make his way to London, where he sold his essays to a publisher. From there he went home to France, kept his head down (and on) during the Terror, and later became an admirer of Napoleon.

Crèvecoeur was no Tocqueville. Yet from a hodge-podge of anecdote, wishful thinking and outright boosterism, he made a kind of mythic truth: not what America really was, but what America wanted and still wants to be—"the most perfect society in the world."[49]

While some white Americans of the day saw independence as the making of an ideal republic, the more pragmatic knew it was the takeover of British imperialism in North America by local management, unshackled from London's restraints: in George Washington's words, "a rising empire."[50]

Most Indians saw the faraway Crown as their main hope against the unruly settlers. The Iroquois Confederacy tried to stay neutral, but its government was crippled when smallpox struck its capital at Onondaga.[51] Thereafter, four of the Six Nations sided with the British, two with the new Americans.

In the 1783 Treaty of Paris, which ended the Revolutionary War, Britain yet again abandoned her native allies. "We are . . . as it were between two Hells," wrote Joseph Brant, who had led the Mohawks and others on the losing side. His only recourse was to take his followers to Canada, where their descendants live to this day.[52]

The Iroquois who took the rebel side fared no better. At the Treaty of Fort Stanwix in 1784, the Americans (from here on I will use the word in its modern sense) refused to observe native protocol, avoiding the terms *brother*, *nation* or "any other form which would revive or seem to confirm their former ideas of independence."[53] The United States took the view that it had conquered all Indians, allies or not, and that native title in America was void. Moreover, like the Pequot in the past and the Apache in the future, the Indian was cast as the bestial aggressor: "The savage," George Washington wrote, was like the wolf, "both being animals of prey though they differ in shape."[54]

The settlers took most of the lands of the Great Longhouse. The former owners were left on a small archipelago of grim reservations, where poverty, hopelessness, alcoholism and suicide became endemic. By the 1790s the once-mighty

Confederacy had fallen to a tenth of its strength only a century before.[55]

❖⸺◉⸺❖

With the Iroquois down (though not quite out), the burden of defence fell on the peoples of the Old Northwest—the Ohio Country—who, a generation earlier, had been the backbone of Pontiac's army. These united and challenged the white republic's claim to have conquered America. In 1791 they destroyed two-thirds of the United States' regular army; more than six hundred American troops died, while the Indians lost only twenty-one.[56]

Even before this disaster, Washington's secretary of war, Henry Knox, a clever man experienced in Indian matters, had realized that native military power could not be crushed without a huge expenditure of lives and treasure.[57] He accepted that the nations on the frontier and beyond were still sovereign, and he understood that the main cause of warfare was encroachment by white settlers. He also believed that the United States had a moral duty not to exterminate its indigenous neighbours, if only to protect its own good name: "If our modes of population and War destroy the tribes . . . mankind and posterity will be apt to class the effects of our Conduct [with] that of the Spaniards in Mexico and Peru."[58]

Knox did *not* mean that the United States should cease to expand. Rather, the federal government should press the Indians to cede land by peaceful means, offering them "civilization" and assimilation in return. This approach was in the Enlightenment school of Jefferson, who had written optimistically in 1786, "Not a foot of land will ever be taken from the Indians without their own consent."[59] It also reflected a *realpolitik* that today seems astonishing: a handful of small native polities between the Proclamation line and the Mississippi had been able to check the military expansion of several million whites.[60]

The checkmate would not stand for many years, but it was enough to force a change in national policy.[61] In the early 1790s, Congress passed the *Indian Trade and Intercourse Acts*—its own version of the Royal Proclamation, recognizing the sovereignty of Indian nations and ruling that land could be acquired only by treaties with the federal government. At the same time, Jefferson's idea of civilizing the Indians became official policy. The goal was now "expansion with honor."[62]

Civilization meant acculturation on the Euro-American model, with private property, single-family houses, commercial agriculture, the English language and, not least, the Christian religion. Native Americans had little objection to adopting some of these things. Their cultures were far from static or isolated: they had long been expert with firearms and steel; they had supplemented their own agriculture with orchards and hogs; they were also skilled in trade.[63] Some whites lived amicably with the Indians; some Indians lived and worked in white cities. Native leaders were far from rustic: many had visited New York, Montreal, Philadelphia, London and Paris on diplomatic business.[64] Others, like Squanto long before, had made less pleasant but no less instructive journeys as prisoners and slaves.[65] In short, the old Americans were well informed on the new Americans' way of life and open to cultural change on their own terms.

Key discussions took place at Philadelphia in 1792, where the Iroquois were addressed by the new nation's president, George Washington himself, now chastened enough to follow native protocol. Presenting a white wampum belt, symbolic of peace, the president began:

> Sachems and Warriors of the Five [*sic*] Nations: I
> assure you that I am desirous that a firm peace should
> exist, not only between the United States and the Five
> Nations, but also between the United States and all
> the nations of this land—and that this peace should
> be founded upon the principles of justice and human-
> ity . . . [and] that you may partake of all the comforts of
> this earth, which can be derived from civilized life,
> enriched by the possession of industry, virtue and
> knowledge.[66]

Washington was answered by the Seneca traditionalist Red
Jacket (Sagoyewatha), a stern, thin-lipped man renowned in
his day as "a statesman of sagacity, and an orator of even sur-
passing eloquence."[67] He began by underscoring Washington's
renewed recognition of native sovereignty, then gave a wary
welcome to the civilizing scheme:

> The president, in effect, observed to us that we of the
> Five Nations were our own proprietors—were freemen,
> and might speak with freedom. This has gladdened our
> hearts. . . .
> The president further observed to us that by our
> continuing to walk in the path of peace, and hearkening
> to his counsel, we might share with you the blessings of
> civilized life. . . . To you, therefore, we look to make
> provision that the same may be enjoyed by our chil-
> dren. This wish comes from our heart, but we add that
> our happiness cannot be great if in the introduction of
> your ways we are put under too much constraint.[68]

Red Jacket did not object to ploughs and oxen, but he was unimpressed by white beliefs. When, some years later, a preacher from the Massachusetts Evangelical Missionary Society told the Senecas that he had come to "enlighten their minds" about the one true religion, Red Jacket gave a withering reply: "If there is but one religion, why do you white people differ so much about it?"[69]

⋆⇒◉⇐⋆

The best welcome for the civilizing program came from five ancient peoples at the southern end of the Appalachian chain— the Creeks, Seminoles, Chickasaws, Choctaws and above all the Cherokees. Known to history as the Five Civilized Tribes, these are not to be confused with the Iroquois Five Nations (though the Cherokees were distantly related to them). The Philadelphian naturalist William Bartram, who travelled extensively among the Creeks and Cherokees in the 1770s, was ahead of his time in recognizing that they already had "the refinements of true civilization, which cannot, in the least degree, be attributed to the good examples of the white people."[70] He also noted the Indians' genial character, orderly towns, lack of domestic violence and strict laws against alcohol.[71]

The leap to civilization was therefore not nearly as fundamental a change as most whites imagined: it was more like adding a new storey in European style to an existing structure.[72] As early as 1806, Thomas Jefferson (who was then president) had told an English diplomat that he thought "the Cherokees would in a very short time be civilized enough to be allowed a representative in Congress."[73]

Despite many misfortunes since Hernando de Soto had made his unwelcome visit to their forebears, these Southern peoples occupied broadly the same territories as they had in the 1540s—often building their town halls atop ancestral mounds.[74] They still spoke the same languages, built the same houses, played the same sports and kept many of the same ethnic and place names. Soto's *Chalaque* were the Cherokee, his *Chicaza* the Chickasaw and so forth.[75] Although the kingdom of Cofitachiqui with its Lady and pearls had disappeared, the Creek Nation may have been a direct descendant.

The economic and political pattern that had worked, more or less, for most of the eighteenth century was beginning to unravel. Like the Iroquois, the Southern nations had lost land and numbers in the endless wars, especially the Revolution. Most of their leaders therefore resolved to take the United States at its word: to win peace, security and survival by adopting the civilization of the newcomers.

President Jefferson held out a seductive vision of a mestizo North America: "The day will soon come," he told a gathering of Indians in 1808, "when you will unite yourselves with us, join in our great councils, and form a people with us, and we shall all be Americans; you will mix with us by marriage; your blood will run in our veins and will spread with us over this great continent."[76] Some may have regarded this invitation as patronizing (Why *should* they stir themselves into the invaders' melting pot to "spread across" a continent that had always been theirs?), but at least it wasn't racist, exclusionary or genocidal except by absorption. Indeed, a mixed society was already burgeoning on the frontier. Some Indian families had white blood; some backwoodsmen had native wives.[77] In material culture, the two peoples were becoming much alike, even in dress—young ladies were said to be distracted by the sight of sinewy white lads wearing buckskin breechclouts and little else to church.[78] Both races lived in "the log cabin of the Cherokee and Iroquois," ate American foods and hunted and fought in the same way, including the lightweight form of headhunting known as scalping.[79]

These were violent times, not only in America. Enraged Indians sometimes took terrible revenge on innocents; white Americans did so too. The difference, as always, was that the Europeans were the invaders and most often the instigators. The Duc de La Rochefoucauld, a French social reformer who toured the Southern frontier in the 1790s, concluded that the whites "are in the wrong four times out of five."[80]

Where the two cultures differed sharply was in ideology. Whites were Christians; most Indians were not. The settlers held, or claimed to hold, their land as private property; the Indians owned all land in common, though buildings and other improvements belonged to those who made them. And while Indians had deep spiritual and ethnic ties to the land, whites were always alive to greener grass and the main chance.

Notwithstanding his talk of an inclusive and just nation, President Jefferson (who, for all his enlightenment, was a slaveholder and often argued both sides of a case with equal eloquence) privately admitted to less lofty motives behind the civilizing scheme. Once Indians had become livestock owners on private plots, he wrote in 1803, they wouldn't need their hunting grounds and could be ensnared in the tender trap of debt:

> To promote this disposition to exchange lands which they have to spare and we want . . . we shall push our trading houses, and be glad to see the good and influential individuals among them run in debt, because we

observe that when these debts get beyond what the
individuals can pay, they become willing to lop them
off by a cession of lands.[81]

When debt alone was insufficient, bribery and corruption
often did the job. Failing that, individual ownership would
eventually be imposed by federal law in 1887, when the
nations driven to the Indian Territory (now Oklahoma) were,
in violation of all the Removal treaties, dismantled into private holdings by the *Dawes Allotment Act*—frankly described by
Theodore Roosevelt as "a mighty pulverising engine to break
up the tribal mass."[82]

Jefferson's words of two hundred years ago also help
explain modern America's deep hostility to all forms of ownership and law that try to withstand the alkahest of commerce.
When the conflict arose *inside* western civilization—with
labour's challenge to capital—no nation would show a greater
dread of socialism than the United States. Today, some on the
American right still denounce mainstream social democracies,
including those of Canada and Europe, as "communistic"—a
laughable charge beyond the overheated air of neoconservative
think tanks. Collectivity was savagery: like the red man himself, it was the red menace of its day. The Indians, wrote
Senator Dawes of his *Allotment Act*, lacked "selfishness, which
is at the bottom of civilization."[83]

⋆⇒◉⇐⋆

Just as the two World Wars between 1914 and 1945 can be seen
as a single great war with a long intermission, so the American
Revolution had its second and decisive act a generation later.[84]
Often seen as a fight between Britain and the United States, the

War of 1812 was also the final showdown between militant Eastern Indians, led by Tecumseh, and white Americans for mastery of the continent's future. The progressive Indians—those who had opted to take the United States at its word—regarded Tecumseh as a dangerous agitator who would bring ruin upon all. The militants, mainly traditionalists and young men eager to fight encroachment, saw him as a deliverer.

But it wasn't only the Indian nations who had split into factions. American militants—mainly Southerners and backwoods Westerners known as War Hawks—were fighting government efforts to restrain settler invasions of native land. There was even talk among them of exterminating the Indians and setting up a second white republic beyond the reach of the federal government with its irksome humanitarian concerns.[85] The United States was splitting into the two cultures that still contend within it: educated, establishment Easterners and illiterate, isolated, hard men of the hinterland, many of whom fit Franklin's epithet, White Savages. The Hawks also wanted to finish the job of evicting their former overlord from North America. "On to Canada!" became their war cry.[86]

Ever since President Jefferson had bought Louisiana (much larger than the modern state) from a cash-strapped Napoleon in 1803, the stakes had begun to rise. By extinguishing French claims to the unconquered Mississippi watershed, the Louisiana Purchase aroused appetites for expansion—especially the westward spread of slavery.[87] It was also a potential dumping ground to which all Indians who rejected integration could be "removed." This last idea had been one of Jefferson's own reasons for the purchase. He may have been sincere in proposing it only as a voluntary option; others were not.

By 1813, when Tecumseh was killed near the Canadian border, the South had already become the main theatre of the war. The Creek Nation, which held most of what is now the state of Alabama, had split in two.[88] Militant Creeks had allied themselves with Tecumseh and opened a Southern front against the Americans. In August 1813, near Mobile, where their ancestors had fought Soto long before, they burned Fort Mims and slaughtered several hundred whites.[89]

Reckoning that the United States would win against Britain once more, and fearing their own militants, the Creek establishment, their neighbours the Cherokees and the other Southern nations sent regiments to support the United States. Their leaders were commissioned as officers under the command of Andrew Jackson, "a tall, lank, uncouth-looking personage . . . [an] impetuous, self-willed Scotch-Irish leader of men." At the time Jackson was barely fit to travel—let alone make war—because he was nursing a gunshot wound from one of his habitual duels, this with his own brother Jesse in a Nashville tavern.[90]

The decisive battle came at Horseshoe Bend in March 1814.[91] It would be the last great engagement between Indians and the United States east of the Mississippi.[92] With an overwhelming force, including Sam Houston and Davy Crockett (both to become famous in Texas years later), Jackson took the Creeks' stronghold and paid them back for Fort Mims at double rate.[93] Nine hundred Indians died, including women and children.[94] Jackson took an accurate count by having his men snip the noses off the dead, many of whom were also skinned by the whites to make trophy belts and bridles.

At a vindictive peace treaty, Jackson forced the whole Creek Nation, including his allies, to cede 23 million acres—half the future state of Alabama.[95] For good measure he took 2 million acres from his other allies, the Cherokees.[96]

The Creek War and his defeat of the British at New Orleans would launch Andrew Jackson's political career. In 1829 he became the first Westerner in the White House, elected on a platform to remove all Indians from the United States. A land speculator, lawyer, cotton planter, slave owner and fighter, Jackson had spent most of his life in the state of Tennessee, itself wrested from the Cherokee Nation only a dozen years before he settled there.[97]

Jackson's defenders see him as a rugged democrat—a champion of the small man, especially the frontiersman, against the Eastern establishment. For his detractors, not least Tocqueville, who toured America during his term in office, Jackson was a shallow and unscrupulous demagogue—the first of a presidential line that leads to Richard Nixon, Ronald Reagan and George W. Bush. Jackson's legacy includes the "spoils" system—the giving of top government posts to unelected cronies, known in his day as the "Kitchen Cabinet." As a Bostonian wryly told Tocqueville in 1831, "It took long and patient work to put it into the head of the public that General Jackson was a great man."[98]

After the war, both the whites and the Five Civilized Tribes had carried on building their nations. People of goodwill on both sides still hoped that the old and new Americans could find a way to coexist. There still seemed room and time. In the two centuries that had passed since Jamestown, the Europeans had moved inland only a few hundred miles. Had they continued to move west at the same rate for the *next* two

centuries, the United States might barely occupy the Mississippi Valley today.

But everything was about to change. The precious metals
and crops of the Americas had been transforming the world.
They were about to yield the biggest payoff in history: industrialization, steam-powered imperialism and a population boom
almost everywhere except among indigenous Americans.
During the half-century before 1830, the Cherokee Nation
managed to rebuild its numbers from ten thousand to sixteen
thousand people. In just twenty years before 1830, however,
the settler population of Mississippi and Alabama rose from
forty thousand to more than four hundred thousand. During
the 1820s nearly three hundred steamboats were launched on
the Mississippi and its tributaries. Meanwhile, the Americans
were digging great canals to make an inland waterway from the
Hudson to the Gulf of Mexico.[99]

The progressives in the Five Civilized Tribes saw progress
itself as their only chance of survival. Yet even though some
were of mixed blood, they did not intend to disappear by
assimilation. The leaders wanted to modernize in a way that
would keep their nations intact—as small sovereign countries,
as self-governing protectorates (like those within Europe and
the British Empire) or as native states within the American
union. I shall focus on the case of the Cherokees, the last of the
five peoples to be uprooted and driven west in a death march
that became known as the Trail of Tears.

By the early 1800s, the Cherokees in particular were beginning to beat the Americans at their own game. Chief Vann,
their wealthiest citizen, owned a foundry, several river ferries,
1,100 peach trees, more than 50 black slaves, 6 barns and one
of the best brick houses in what is now Georgia.[100] He never

became a Christian, and the land he farmed belonged to the Cherokee Nation, but his life in other respects resembled that of a thriving Southern planter.[101]

Vann and his like led the transition from traditional societies to nationhood on a Euro-American model, with legislatures, police forces, schools and, in the Cherokee case, a bilingual newspaper. By 1810 the Cherokees had their first written constitution and a Light Horse Guard to settle disputes and evict white squatters. By the mid-1820s they had built a modern capital, New Echota, with an assembly, a supreme court and a printing press.[102] They had codified their laws, adopted a constitution and invented a script for their language. In wealth, education and good order, they had surpassed the frontier society around them. The rate of adult literacy was higher in the Cherokee Nation than in the United States.[103]

On an Eastern speaking tour in 1826, Elias Boudinot (Kuhleganah Watie), a fastidious, brilliant and devout young man who ran the Cherokee newspaper, outlined his people's success: "At this time [we have] 22,000 cattle; 7,600 horses; 46,000 swine; 2,500 sheep; 2,488 spinning wheels; 172 waggons; 2,943 ploughs [and] 18 schools." Yes, he concluded hopefully, "I can view my native country . . . taking her seat with the nations of the earth."[104]

⊷═◉═⊷

The Enlightenment era, personified in America by Franklin and Jefferson, had regarded all men as created equal, at least in theory.[105] In 1785 Jefferson had written, "I believe the Indian to be in body and mind equal to the white man."[106] Francisco de Miranda, a Venzuelan who travelled the seaboard in the 1780s, wrote of Indians and blacks that they "were as apt for anything as anyone else . . . the rational being is the same in whatever form."[107] Sam Houston, who had been adopted by the Cherokees in his youth, said: "These Indians are not inferior to white men. John Ridge [Boudinot's cousin] was not inferior in point of genius to John Randolph."[108]

Such views were falling out of fashion in the early nineteenth century, as the logic of slavery and imperialism wrought a change in white attitudes to other races.[109] Under attack from abolitionists, slaveholders justified their "peculiar institution" on the grounds that black people were not fully human. From there it was a short step to conclude that anyone with a dark skin was genetically inferior. Many Americans came to believe that their Promised Land was "a white man's country," that both Indians and Africans should be expelled.[110] When Boudinot married a white woman in Connecticut, the townsfolk called her a "squaw" and burned the couple in effigy.

The pressure on the Civilized Tribes became openly racist. In a congressional debate on Jackson's 1830 Removal Bill, Senator Forsyth of Georgia argued that Indians could be "treated somewhat like human beings, but not admitted to be freemen."[111] A Vermont lawyer—echoing the victors at Mystic, whether he knew it or not—wrote that "Indians' bones must enrich the soil before the plough of civilized man can open it."[112] President Jackson told Congress that Indians "have neither the intelligence . . . the moral habits, nor the desire of improvement."[113]

To justify its policy of ethnic cleansing, America had to deny the fact of Indian achievement and even destroy the evidence. As if to prove that Indians were "not made for civilization," the Georgia Guard wrecked the Cherokee printing press.[114] The real problem, of course, was that the more the Civilized Tribes progressed on white terms, the more they competed with the white republic."⁵ And as the Indians filled their territory with thriving farms and good houses, they aroused ever more white greed. Why conquer a wilderness when one could take over a ready-made estate? While the politicians schemed, Georgians began to sing:

> *All I want in this Creation*
> *Is a pretty little wife and a big plantation*
> *Way up north in the Cherokee Nation.*"⁶

The U.S. Constitution had made Indian affairs an exclusively federal jurisdiction. The central government also adopted a policy of adding new states to the Union as white settlement moved west, rather than letting old states grow westward indefinitely, as some founding charters from the British Crown had implied. To get Georgia to give up her "right" of endless growth, the Union had paid the state more than a million dollars in 1802."⁷ The federal government had also pledged that it would acquire Indian lands within the state's new boundaries when and if this could be done "peaceably [and] on reasonable terms."¹¹⁸ In 1802 there had seemed plenty of time to fulfill this promise, to achieve "expansion with honour."

Because the United States recognized Indian nations as independent jurisdictions, state boundaries were imaginary lines where they crossed native territory. The Cherokee Nation was not, and never had been, Georgia, but Georgia refused to see it that way. Emboldened by the outcome of the Creek War and aroused by the agricultural boom that followed the invention of the cotton gin, the state grew impatient of the federal government's "failure" to oust the Cherokees and part of the neighbouring Creek Nation."⁹

Indian expulsion became one of the bitterest disputes between centre and periphery, the Union and the South. Others were the future of slavery and "nullification," the supposed right of a state to opt out of any federal law or tax with which it didn't agree. Was the Union a single nation with indivisible sovereignty or was it merely a loose alliance of sovereign states? These questions would be settled a generation later on the battlefields of the Civil War.

Historians have debated who was the more to blame for what happened to the Five Civilized Tribes: Jackson or the Southern states? James Mooney, the great ethnographer who studied the question when events were still in living memory, described Andrew Jackson as "an Indian hater" and thought "there is good ground for believing that the action at once taken by Georgia [after his election] was at his own suggestion."[120]

Jackson himself called the final expulsion of Indians "the leading measure" of his administration.[121] Within months of his taking office in January 1829, the Southern states unleashed an avalanche of anti-Indian legislation. None of it had a sound basis in American law, but it was an effective harassment technique, enabling the states to arrest native leaders and sympathetic whites at will.[122] In 1829 Alabama subjected the Creek Nation to its laws; in 1830 Mississippi banned any Indian from even calling himself a chief. At the same time, Georgia enacted laws to dissolve the Cherokee Nation, prevent its parliament from meeting and bar Indians from testifying in state courts, even in their own defence.[123] "Tyrannical measures," Tocqueville wrote, "have been adopted by the legislatures of the Southern States. . . . it is intended to force [the Indians] to recede by reducing them to despair."[124]

The hunger of poor whites for land was only a part of the pressure. Perhaps more important were speculation (in which Jackson himself had been a player for years) and the concentration of ownership into big plantations, which ensured there was never enough for all. One opponent of Removal pointed out that the Cherokees had long before ceded their best land and that Georgia, which had only "six or seven souls to a square mile," could easily support a hundred.[125] There were also the heavy demands of "king cotton," a crop that exhausted the earth as it ate its way across the South, leaving sandy wastes in which little would grow except peanuts.

The Cherokees knew they were hopelessly outnumbered and outgunned. Any resistance by force was exactly what their enemies were waiting for. So they did what they could: they set about strengthening their small nation-state; they appealed to the American public; and they got ready to fight in Washington before Congress and the Supreme Court. The first article in the Cherokee Constitution defined their nation's boundaries, stating that they "shall forever hereafter remain unalterably the same." It also confirmed the ancient law that all land was "the common property of the Nation."[126]

⋯≈◉≈⋯

Jackson's sympathies were with states' rights, but once in the White House he drank heavily of presidential power.[127] He decided to have it both ways: if need be, he would use federal force to quell South Carolina's bid for nullification; but to satisfy other Southern demands and fulfill his own agenda, he would sacrifice the Cherokee Nation on Georgia's behalf—even if that meant violating the Constitution. In effect, the Indians of the South became the first casualties in America's looming Civil War.

In May 1830 Congress narrowly passed the *Indian Removal Act*, despite fierce opposition from federalists, some church groups, and defectors from Jackson's own party—notably another Tennessee frontiersman, Davy Crockett, who denounced it as "a wicked, unjust measure."[128] Those who write about past atrocities are sometimes accused of "presentism"—projecting current values onto history. But Davy Crockett was by no means the only leading American of the day to denounce Jackson's policy on moral grounds. William Wirt, who represented the Cherokees at the Supreme Court, had this to say: "We may gather laurels on the field of battle, and trophies upon the ocean, but they will never hide this foul blot on our escutcheon. *Remember the Cherokee Nation* will be answer enough to the proudest boasts that we can ever make."[129] Writers, missionary groups and women's organizations also took up the Indians' cause.[130] Frances Trollope (mother of the Victorian novelist), who was living on the Ohio frontier at the time, called the Removal "a base, cruel, and most oppressive act."[131] When Jackson died and the nation went into mourning, Horace Greeley, editor of the New York *Tribune*, denounced the late president as "a jobber in human flesh."[132]

Jackson's State of the Union address for 1830 is worth quoting at some length. Particularly interesting is the way in which the Indians' agricultural way of life is ignored—they are yet again called "wandering savages"—and how greed is dressed as philanthropy. It is also notable that Jackson uses evidence of ancient civilization in North America as a weapon against its heirs, suggesting that the Indians were themselves exterminators. Such arguments are still being made in the United States today.[133] What they reveal is a moral insecurity about the basis of white tenure—"*qui s'excuse s'accuse*"—as with

South African claims in the apartheid era that the Bantu were themselves immigrants and therefore fair game for displacement by the Dutch.

It gives me great pleasure to announce to Congress that the benevolent policy of the Government [for] the removal of the Indians beyond the white settlements is approaching to a happy consummation . . .

True philanthropy reconciles the mind to these vicissitudes as it does to the extinction of one generation to make room for another. In the monuments and fortresses of an unknown people, spread over the extensive regions of the West, we behold the memorials of a once powerful race, which was exterminated or has disappeared to make room for the existing savage tribes . . .

Philanthropy could not wish to see this continent restored to the condition in which it was found by our forefathers. What good man would prefer a country covered with forests and ranged by a few thousand savages to our extensive Republic, studded with cities, towns, and prosperous farms . . . occupied by more than 12,000,000 happy people, and filled with all the blessings of liberty, civilization, and religion? . . .

Is it supposed that the wandering savage has a stronger attachment to his home than the settled, civilized Christian? . . . Rightly considered, the policy of the General [Federal] Government toward the red man is not only liberal, but generous. He is unwilling to submit to the laws of the states and mingle with their population. To save him from this alternative, or

perhaps utter annihilation, the Government kindly
offers him a new home.[134]

In private, Jackson was more forthright. "Build a fire
under them," he told some Georgia politicians. "When it gets
hot enough, they'll move."[135] The president did his part by cutting off the Cherokees' annuity for earlier land cessions,
money the Nation relied on for funding its schools and newspaper.[136] Georgia's governor, George Gilmer, had already dismissed any need for legality or good faith where Indian
treaties were concerned: "Treaties were expedients by which
ignorant, intractable, and savage people were induced . . . to
yield up what civilized people had a right to possess by virtue
of that command of the Creator—be fruitful, multiply, and
replenish the earth, and subdue it."[137]

Armed with this Puritan theology, the state continued its barrage of legislation. One law, aimed at Indian-loving missionaries,
forbade whites from working in the Cherokee Nation without
Georgia's consent.[138] Another banned Cherokees from digging
their own minerals, while the Georgia Guard went in to protect
white prospectors ransacking the nation for gold. The state also
set off a real-estate stampede by surveying the Cherokee Nation
into parcels of land and offering them by lottery.

The Cherokees went to the Supreme Court. In two related
cases—*Cherokee Nation v. Georgia* (1831) and *Worcester v. Georgia*
(1832)—Chief Justice John Marshall set precedents that have
become basic to the political standing of American Indians in
the United States today. In the first case, Marshall defined
Indian nations as "domestic dependent nations," an ambigous
phrase that implied protectorate status.[139] In the second,
having reviewed international law concerning treaties and

protectorates, Marshall explicitly recognized Indian "title to self-government":

> The Cherokee Nation, then, is a distinct community, occupying its own territory, with boundaries accurately described, in which the laws of Georgia can have no force, and which the citizens of Georgia can have no right to enter. . . . The acts of Georgia are repugnant to the Constitution, laws, and treaties of the United States.[140]

"It is glorious news!" Elias Boudinot, the Cherokee news-paperman, wrote home to his brother from Washington. Jackson was heard to say, "Marshall has rendered his decision; now let him enforce it."[141] It became clear that nothing would stop the president—that he would ignore the Supreme Court and the Constitution.

Whether or not Jackson's Removal policy was genocidal by intent—as some scholars believe—it certainly was in execution.[142] About one-fourth of the Cherokee Nation would die when the Removal was carried out by United States and Georgian forces in 1838.[143] By that time, a similar number of Choctaws, Creeks and others had already died when removed, so Jackson and his supporters well knew the true effects of their final solution. During the Creeks' Removal in 1836, the sky above their death march had been filled with vultures.[144]

Once the other Civilized Tribes had gone, the Cherokees found themselves surrounded by whites. In the words of their principal chief, John Ross (Kooweskoowee), the nation was like "a solitary tree in an open space, where all the forest trees around have been prostrated by a furious tornado."[145] After Jackson won a second term, in 1832, the Cherokee leadership split, one faction believing that further resistance was hope-less. Chief Ross stood firm, though, and the overwhelming majority of Cherokees backed him.

In December 1835, while Ross and other Cherokee leaders were being harassed and jailed by Georgia, Jackson's agents drew up a fraudulent treaty with the pessimists, a small group that now included a bitterly disillusioned Elias Boudinot.[146] In May 1836 this Treaty of New Echota passed in the U.S. Senate by a margin of one vote. John Quincy Adams (the pres-ident before Jackson) denounced it as an "eternal disgrace upon the country."

The Cherokees were given two years to get out—years dur-ing which they were invaded more than ever by those hungry for the carcass of the nation they had built. General John Wool, sent to enforce the exodus, reported: "The whole scene . . . has been nothing but a heartrending one. . . . The white men . . . like vultures, are watching, ready to pounce upon their prey and strip them of everything they have." Wool also found that the Indians were "almost universally opposed to the treaty" and would not accept rations or clothing from the United States "lest they might compromise themselves."[147]

Major Ridge, the Cherokee officer who had signed the treaty and served under Jackson in the Creek War, wrote to his old commander: "We are not safe in our houses—our people are assailed by day and night by the rabble. . . . This barbarous treatment is not confined to men, but the women are stripped also and whipped without law or mercy. . . . We shall carry off nothing but the scars of the lash."[148]

During the hardest fighting at Horseshoe Bend in 1814, Andrew Jackson's life had been saved by a Cherokee chief named Junaluska.[149] This man now went to Washington and made a personal appeal. Jackson barely listened, answering, "Sir your audience is ended, there is nothing I can do for you."[150]

⊷══◉═⊷

In the spring of 1837, Andrew Jackson left the White House. But if the Cherokees were hoping for a reprieve from his successor, Martin Van Buren, they were soon disillusioned. The new president affirmed his backing of the other's pogrom: "No State can achieve proper culture, civilization, and progress," he said, "as long as Indians are permitted to remain."[151]

A few months later, the young poet and essayist Ralph Waldo Emerson wrote to Van Buren from Harvard in an open letter, expressing the outrage felt by many:

> A crime is projected that confounds our understand-
> ings by its magnitude, a crime that really deprives *us*
> as well as the Cherokees of a country, for how could
> we call the conspiracy that should crush these poor
> Indians our government, or . . . our country any
> more? . . . The name of this nation, hitherto the sweet
> omen of religion and liberty, will stink to the world.[152]

In June 1838 the U.S. Army began rounding up the Cherokees and confining them in what may fairly be described as concentration camps.[153] The stockades were not designed for extermination, but they might as well have been. Hundreds, perhaps thousands, died within from hunger, overcrowding and disease. Thousands more died that winter on the Trail of Tears to what is now Oklahoma—among them Chief Ross's wife.

Years later the Confederate colonel Z.A. Zele recalled his service with the Georgia Volunteers in 1838: "I fought through the Civil War and have seen men shot to pieces and slaughtered by thousands, but the Cherokee removal was the cruelest work I ever knew."[154]

⋄⭲⭱⭰⋄

In all, some hundred thousand Eastern Indians were expelled in the 1830s—about one in four removed from life in the process, the rest driven beyond the Mississippi.[155] Only a handful of the first Americans managed to stay behind on their old lands: refugees in hills and swamps, and other remnants too small to be a threat.[156] Black Hoof, an elderly Shawnee who had seen a century of frontier fighting for himself, foresaw that the process would never stop: "Wherever we may go, your people, the American Farmers, will follow; and we will be forced to be removed again and again and finally arrive at the Pacific ocean and then be compelled to jump off."[157]

As Emerson and many others understood, the Indian Removal was a test of their new country's character. With the betrayal of the Cherokee Nation, the United States betrayed itself. Sinister elements present in British America since the earliest colonies had surfaced in the republic and taken charge.

6.

MANIFEST DESTINY

The people of this country . . . covet and are ready to grasp
at all that lies upon their borders, and are ambitious of
extending their empire from sea to sea.

—William Sturgis, 1845[1]

The relation now existing in the slave-holding States . . . is,
instead of an evil, a good—a positive good.

—Senator John C. Calhoun, 1847[2]

Man is a money-making animal, which propensity too
often interferes with his benevolence.

—Herman Melville, 1851[3]

ONCE THE INDIANS WERE GONE, the land between the
Appalachians and the Mississippi became an empty
mansion with squatters camping in its silent rooms.
Chicago, one traveller wrote, was "a dull uninteresting place. . . .
in 1832 there were only two houses."[4] Tocqueville called Detroit
an "American village," beyond which "the road goes into the
forest and never comes out of it."[5] St. Louis was dwarfed by the
great earthen ruin of Cahokia, a pyramid covering sixteen acres

and rearing ten storeys high on the opposite bank of the Mississippi. In the 1830s, the big river was about as far as the white empire had advanced.[6]

Tocqueville remarked that America had yet to produce any outstanding writers—a fair comment when he made it—and he was right about the reason: "The majority lives in the perpetual practice of self-applause, and there are certain truths which the Americans can only learn from strangers or from experience. . . . there can be no literary genius without freedom of opinion, and freedom of opinion does not exist."[7]

America could not bear to take a hard look at itself, especially the inconvenient truths of slavery, dispossession and genocide. Religion and profit, "jumping together," had little time for introspection. The slaveholder, the frontiersman and the fundamentalist all hated the historian—and anti-intellectualism has been a strong force ever since.[8] Yet in the generation between the Indian Removal and the Civil War, the intelligentsia tore off the blinkers of the chapel and the counting-house and looked at their surroundings as if for the first time, seeing not some hand-me-down Holy Land shipped across the Atlantic but a mysterious hemisphere with its own life, demanding their engagement. Americans began to think more deeply about their relationship to the peoples who had gone before them, leaving ancient ruins from Ohio to Peru.

The 1840s and 1850s became a golden age in literature and scholarship—in fiction, poetry, history, travel and anthropology—as white America explored its world.[9] The young archaeologist Ephraim Squier made the first scientific studies of pre-Columbian monuments in the United States, deducing that American Indians, not some "unknown race," had built them.[10] John Stephens, a New Jersey antiquarian, travel writer and businessman, went on a long muleback journey through Central America, looking for lost cities "said to exist in the dense forests of those tropical regions." The results were spectacular; on the first trek alone, he found eight major Maya ruins.[11] The mysterious buildings aroused a nascent pan-American pride—and Stephens's commercial instincts. The richly inscribed monoliths of Quiriguá, he mused, "might be transported bodily and set up in New York."[12]

Stephens had already visited Egypt, Greece and the Holy Land, so he was not misled by popular theories claiming that the New World's ancient wonders were the work of Egyptians or other overseas visitors.[13] In the ornate stonework and hieroglyphic writing of the Maya he knew he was seeing a civilization previously unknown to science: "A people skilled in architecture, sculpture . . . having a distinct, separate, independent existence; like the plants and fruits of the soil, indigenous."[14]

While Stephens was chopping his way through Guatemalan jungles, his friend the historian William Prescott was unearthing America's past from forgotten books and archives. Prescott had been studying for the law until he was half-blinded by a crust thrown in a Harvard bunfight—a mishap that steered him into the calmer life of scholarship. His *History of the Conquest of Mexico* and *Conquest of Peru* were sensations when they appeared in the 1840s and are still the classics in their field.[15] Unable to see for himself the land where the great conflicts had taken place, Prescott urged both Stephens and Squier to do the travelling for him, to find what remained of the old American empires overthrown by Spain.

Stephens died before he could go on to South America, his health shattered by the tropics, but Squier did get there in the 1860s, writing his lively *Peru: Incidents of Travel and Exploration in the Land of the Incas.* He found the Andes tough going, with transport, food and lodging hard to come by—while all around him Inca roads, granaries and post-houses lay in ruins. "The influence of Spain in Peru," Squier wrote testily, "has been in every way deleterious: the civilization of the country was far higher before the Conquest than now."[16]

⋅⊷⊐◉⊏⊶⋅

Shortly before President Andrew Jackson left office in 1837, he had abolished the Bank of the United States and handed the funds to private banks that became known as his "pets." As with Ronald Reagan's Savings and Loan scandal of the 1980s, the result was fraud, speculation and collapse, followed by a slump that lasted nearly a decade. Among those ruined was Herman Melville's family: without Jackson's looting of the national treasury, *Moby Dick* might never have been written.

A younger son of old money and Revolutionary fame—one grandfather had been at the Boston Tea Party and the other at Fort Stanwix—Melville found himself unable to earn a living or even finish his studies. In 1840, at the age of twenty-one, he shipped aboard a "world-wandering whale ship" named the *Acushnet.* "If, at my death," he wrote, "my executors, or more properly my creditors, find any precious MSS in my desk, then here I prospectively prescribe all the honor and the glory to whaling; for a whale-ship was my Yale College and my Harvard."[17]

Melville was one of those unlucky authors who lose readers with each title. During his lifetime, his first book, *Typee: A Peep at Polynesian Life,* based on his desertion from the *Acushnet* in the Marquesas, outsold everything else he wrote.[18] The young writer became famous as "the man who lived among cannibals."[19] *Typee* and its sequels turned out to be merely the gateway to *Moby Dick, or The Whale,* but few readers followed Melville there. He had sailed too far beyond the shallows of Romanticism, where Washington Irving and James Fenimore Cooper splashed about in the wake of Sir Walter Scott.[20] Not until the twentieth century, when James Joyce and other modernists rediscovered the waters charted by Melville, would many agree with D.H. Lawrence that *Moby Dick* is "one of the strangest and most wonderful books in the world."[21] If there has to be one Great American Novel, *The Whale* is it.

Melville meant what he said about a whaleship being his education. Owned by New Englanders and manned by men of all races, whalers went everywhere and stayed at sea for years. In its origins, whaling was American as maize: "Where else but from Nantucket," asks Ishmael, "did those aboriginal whalemen, the Red-Men, first sally out in canoes to give chase to the Leviathan?" By the time of the American Revolution, whaleships were sailing from Sag Harbor to Brazil, their crews "in large part Indians, who are the most capable harpoonists and are generally named boat officers."[22] By the 1840s, whaling had become the first worldwide industry dominated by Americans, the forerunner of Big Oil.[23]

Like petroleum in our day, the oil of the sea was soon drained by reckless exploitation. "The moot point," Ishmael asks himself, "is whether Leviathan . . . must not at last be exterminated [like] the humped herds of buffalo, which, not forty years ago, overspread by tens of thousands the prairies of Illinois and Missouri . . . where now the polite broker sells you land at a dollar an inch."[24]

Each age gets the *Moby Dick* it deserves. One can dig forever into the book's rich lodes of allegory. Melville knew the real history of America and trembled for his country's future.[25] By naming the ship after the Pequots exterminated by the early colonists at Mystic, he struck a blow in what Milan Kundera has called the fight of memory against forgetting. The *Pequod* becomes a microcosm of the United States, tricked out with the "chased bones of her enemies," recalling those who thought that Indian bones should sweeten the land for the white man's plough.[26] Captain Ahab is the wrathful Puritan—"a crucifixion in his face"—unhinged by hatred for the sea monster that took his leg, walking "on life and death" with one limb of flesh and the other of whale ivory. Ahab is also the modern American, his faith archaic, yet his means those of the machine: "The path to my fixed purpose is laid with iron rails. . . . Over unsounded gorges, through the rifled hearts of mountains, under torrents' beds, unerringly I rush! Naught's an obstacle, naught's an angle to the iron way!"[27]

Some critics have seen the white whale as the symbol of an evil or hostile Nature, but I disagree. Moby Dick *is* Nature, neither good nor bad but simply itself, abused by human beings at their peril.[28] Ahab-America is doomed by hubris. The great whale rams the ship and swims away, horribly wounded, garrotting Ahab with a harpoon line. The *Pequod*'s mastheads sink into the deep "together with long streaming yards of the flag." It is an end of history.[29]

Moby Dick marked the maturing of an authentic American sensibility: original, bold, self-aware and hence self-critical. The same was true of Melville's later *Confidence Man*. This satirical work has its doldrums and is best known today for the chapter on Indian hating. But anyone who reads it can't fail to be struck by the oddness and freshness of the opening sentence: "At sunrise on a first of April, there appeared, suddenly as Manco Capac at the lake of Titicaca, a man in cream-colors, at the water-side in the city of St. Louis."

At that time, literary allusions were expected to be classical or biblical. Only those who had read Prescott were likely to know that Manco Capac was a legendary Inca king—an American Christ and Caesar sent down to Earth by his father, the Sun, to rule and civilize mankind.[30] By likening one of his riverboat swindlers to this Peruvian hero, Melville insists on a New World frame of reference. He also draws an ironic contrast between the ancient utopia evoked so powerfully by Prescott and the new American empire of Indian haters, hucksters, preachers and confidence men embarking that April First on a ship of fools.[31]

◦═◦◦═◦

While American high culture was starting to digest the historical realities of its presence in the New World, those who set faith above fact had been brewing up spiritual moonshine. In the summer of 1801, a crowd of twenty-five thousand had gathered near Bourbon, Kentucky, in a kind of Pentecostal Woodstock, "jerking, rolling, running, dancing and barking."[32] With such events began the religious wildfires of the Second Great Awakening (the First being the spread of Presbyterianism, Baptism and Methodism in the colonies before the Revolution).

Some sects, notably the Unitarians and Shakers (an offshoot of the Quakers), believed in peace, tolerance and the right to seek God in one's own way without denying that right to others. Unitarianism "took a great weight from the soul of New England" and led to the movement known as Transcendentalism.[33] At its best—in the hands of such thinkers and writers as Ralph Waldo Emerson and Henry David Thoreau—

Transcendentalism was morally courageous, respectful of Nature and skeptical of worldly progress; at its worst it became windy and self-centred, a forerunner of the Me Generation.[34]

The better of these radical movements were sympathetic to the plight of Indians, blacks, women and the poor. Some embraced forms of communitarianism, supporting themselves by cottage industries—Shaker furniture and Oneida silverware. The Oneida Community's free love and the Shakers' no love both caused trouble. The celibate Shakers died out, leaving behind only the vigorous simplicity of their style. The Oneidas went the other way, forsaking social engineering for mainstream manufacturing.

The seeds of these sects had been carried westward by the Puritan diaspora. Far from the deep waters of their own civilization, and able to absorb only superficial elements of the native civilization they displaced, the frontier folk became cultural castaways. Religion decayed into superstition, liberty into anarchy, education (when there was any) into Bible study and little else. "Complex society," Frederick Jackson Turner wrote in 1893, shrinks "into a kind of primitive organization based on the family. The tendency is anti-social. It produces antipathy to control."[35] This culture, in a perpetual state of insecurity and adolescence, exerted a "founder effect" on those who settled in its wake, especially after crossing the Appalachians—a psychological as well as a physical separation from the seaboard.

To modern America the frontier bequeathed positive attributes of boldness, equality and self-reliance; and negative ones of self-absorption, xenophobia, extremism and intolerance. As the historian Bil Gilbert puts it, the legacy of the frontier wars is the delusion "that only a feral man can be genuinely free."[36] Such men bedevil the United States today in the shape of gun-crazy survivalists, Dominionists, and vigilantes patrolling the southern border against a feared "invasion" from Mexico.[37]

⋅➤⫥◯⫥⟨⋅

By 1830, upstate New York—the former Longhouse of the Iroquois—had become so notorious for the frequency and heat of its religious fires that it was called the Burned-Over District, smoking with delusion and quackery. There was a sect of feral men who neither washed nor shaved, and dressed only in bearskins. There were diviners, dowsers and necromancers. There were assorted millennialists, daily expecting the return of Jesus Christ—a strain of Christian belief that has survived two thousand years of disappointment.[38]

One of the Burned-Over District's strangest fires—and ultimately the most successful—was the Church of Jesus Christ of Latter-Day Saints, better known as the Mormons. The sect was founded near Rochester in 1830 by a farm boy named Joseph Smith, a tall, handsome youth with shining blue eyes shaded by unusually long lashes, giving him an otherworldly gaze that enhanced the magnetism of his personality. His creed absorbed almost every element of frontier metaphysics, along with social and sexual unorthodoxy.

The cultural critic Harold Bloom argues that Mormonism and other "post-Christian" sects amount to a form of Gnosticism, an idiosyncratic approach to faith that has become *the* American religion—pervading all denominations, even Catholic and Episcopalian.[39] Certainly, the American way of belief emphasizes a personal relationship with God transcending history and society: a lifelong conversation like that of the lonely child with an imaginary friend. Although radical in their beginnings—posing a moral, political and military threat—most Latter-Day Saints have since become conservative, drawing closer to other Christian fundamentalisms. Americans were not much alarmed when a Mormon, Mitt Romney, ran (briefly) for the U.S. presidency in 2008; it was a different matter when Joseph Smith himself did so in 1844.

Even as they tried to escape the American empire, the Mormons became an important force in its westward march, and their early history opens a revealing window on the frontier soul. Like the Puritans (the original "latter-day Saints"), Smith intended nothing less than to build the City of God on Earth. But he trod where Puritans had feared to go. His peculiar genius was to Americanize Holy Writ by adding the "Bible of the Western Continent," or *Book of Mormon,* claiming to unveil the New World's ancient history.[40] While men such as Stephens and Prescott were making this inquiry through scholarship, Smith (who was at best half-literate) did so by divine revelation. America's two cultures—high and low—were responding to the same need in their distinctive ways.

Since childhood, Joseph Smith had been having visions, possibly linked to seizures. Inspired by his father's looting of ancient mounds, which sometimes held silver and copper artifacts for which collectors would pay well, he became curious about the remote past. At that time the Egyptians and the Lost Tribes of Israel were high on the list of Old World peoples thought to have built the New World's monuments.[41] A fascination with Egypt had been filtering into Euro-American culture since the previous century, not least via Masonic lodges. Early in the 1820s, Jean-François Champollion had made his great breakthrough in deciphering Egyptian hieroglyphics by means of the Rosetta Stone—an achievement widely covered in American newspapers.[42] So Joseph Smith's claim that he had unearthed an ancient book of gold sheets covered with "reformed Egyptian" writing from a New York hill would not have seemed as unlikely as it does today.[43] Even so, his tale of being guided to the find by an angel named Moroni was widely mocked, especially as only a few witnesses were willing to swear they had seen the golden book before the angel came back and collected it.

By then, with the help of magical eyeglasses—also supplied and retrieved by Moroni—Joseph had deciphered the writing and dictated his translation from behind a bedsheet. The resulting *Book of Mormon* makes up for the Bible's awkward silence on the Western Hemisphere. It turns out that a tribe of Israelites had sailed to America in 590 B.C. Before long they split into two clans, the Nephites and the Lamanites, the first righteous by inclination, the other "an idle people, full of mischief [who] seek in the wilderness for beasts of prey."[44]

Originally they had all been European in appearance, but God cursed the Lamanites by darkening their skins. Nevertheless, these two scions of Israel were persuaded to reconcile when Jesus Christ himself visited America soon after the Resurrection. Both clans then became Christian. All went well until the Lamanites slid back into wickedness and unbelief. Things came to a head at a great battle in 384, when the evildoers slew their righteous brethren on the very hill in upstate New York where Joseph Smith would later unearth the golden book.

Only a handful of Nephites escaped the killing, among them their patriarch Mormon and his son Moroni. Soon Moroni was the only Nephite left alive, a paleface Last of the Mohicans. Before leaving Earth for his future as an angel,

Moroni buried the sad story of his people's extermination. From that day until 1492, the New World lay in the bloody hands of the "red sons of Israel"—the American Indians.

This saga has not, I need hardly say, been borne out by scientific research. (Besides all the archaeological problems, American Indians and Semites have no genetic link except as fellow members of the human race.) There are also blunders in Joseph Smith's text that were known anachronisms in his day: pre-Columbian horses, Israelite ships with compasses, and more. Mormons are understandably touchy about factual challenges to their beliefs. Yet, as Jon Krakauer points out in his 2003 book *Under the Banner of Heaven,* their mythology is hardly less credible than that of most other religions, Christianity included.[45] It was Mormonism's bad luck to arise in the glare of newspapers and scholarship instead of the forgiving mists of time.

⌖

There is a startling resemblance in thrust (though not style) between the *Book of Mormon* and President Jackson's State of the Union address on the Indian Removal, quoted in the previous chapter. Both *Mormon* and Jackson appeared in 1830; both claimed that America once belonged to a civilized race wiped out by the existing "savage tribes"; both imply that the extermination of Indians is therefore historically and morally justified.

Of course, I am not suggesting that Jackson perused a copy of *Mormon* before drafting his speech; rather, that both documents reveal the *Zeitgeist.* It isn't hard to see the appeal of Smith's creed on the frontier. His race of fair-skinned Christian Jews become spiritual ancestors for the white invaders, while the real victims of genocide—the Indians—are made the perpetrators of it. And the redskins' evil triumph happens right inside the Iroquois Longhouse, which had been taken over by incomers like the Smiths only a generation before Joseph began talking to Moroni.[46]

Nor was this all. In 1831 Smith revealed that the Garden of Eden hadn't been in the Holy Land but in Missouri, thus making the frontier the centre, not the periphery, of sacred space.[47] He also restored the age of miracles to the here and now, bringing back the days when the Lord spoke out of the whirlwind to prophets and patriarchs. Smith is named Prophet in the *Book of Mormon,* and the head of the church has held that title to this day. Mormons believe their Prophet is in regular touch with the Almighty, receiving orders on policy matters, great and small.[48] New "revelations" often contradict earlier ones. But that doesn't matter, because history doesn't matter: as in all fundamentalisms, faith trumps fact and reason.

The most notorious of Joseph Smith's instructions from God nearly destroyed his sect in the 1840s and has been a thorn in its side ever since. The Prophet told trusted friends that the Lord had given the nod to bringing back the ancient practice of polygyny, or "plural marriage," even though the *Book of Mormon* inconveniently (and ungrammatically) states that a man may have only "one wife . . . for I the Lord God delighteth in the chastity of women."[49] The Lord's change of mind was not made public until some years after Smith's death in 1844, but shocking tales had leaked out long before that. Like many a cult leader, Smith was a ladies' man. "Whenever I see a pretty woman," he admitted, "I have to pray for grace."[50] It seems that grace had not been enough to stop Joseph— already married to Emma—from bedding a fifteen-year-old while the Smiths were lodging with the girl's family in 1832.

For this the Prophet was nearly castrated by a mob. Had his assailants carried out their surgical vengeance, the history of Mormonism might have been quite different. In all, Joseph is thought to have "married" more than forty women, several in their early teens. To a man who had already rewritten the Bible, revising the sexual code of Christendom was no big thing: Smith the Puritan accommodated Smith the seducer by redefining sin.

Their leader's libido, the audacity of their beliefs and the financial clout of their cooperative endeavours did not endear the Mormons to their neighbours. The sect kept wearing out its welcome with local "Gentiles" (non-Mormons), who came to regard Smith as a whoremonger and heretic. Before the golden book had been in print one year, Smith led his flock from New York to Ohio. Less than a year later, they moved on to Missouri, intent on buying up Eden.

But the serpent of slavery had reached the garden first, and the abolitionist sympathies of some Mormons were unwelcome. Local mobs and state militia were soon giving the Saints the kind of treatment the Cherokees were getting from Georgia at the same time. In October 1838 Joseph Smith made a fiery speech, reminding his followers—who then numbered about ten thousand—how they had been driven from one place to another by "unscrupulous mobs eager to seize the land we have cleared and improved." He then veered into megalomania, invoking not Christianity but the founding conquests of Islam: "If they come on to molest us, we will establish our religion by the sword. We will trample down our enemies and make it one gore of blood from the Rocky Mountains to the Atlantic Ocean. I will be to this generation a second Mohammed. . . . Joseph Smith or the Sword!"[51]

In this spirit of jihad, the Mormons attacked their Gentile neighbours, burning down fifty houses. The governor of Missouri responded by ordering his militia to treat the white tribe as enemies and either "exterminate" them or drive them from the state. Thus began the first, and worst, of the three Mormon Wars (of 1838, 1845 and 1857). At Hawn's Mill, eighteen Saints were gunned down inside a log building, including a ten-year-old boy shot in cold blood on the excuse that "nits will make lice."[52]

The Mormons trekked 150 miles east to the Mississippi and crossed into Illinois, where news of their harsh treatment had aroused some pity. The sudden arrival of so many new voters gave them influence in what was then a thinly peopled state, recently emptied of Indians by the Black Hawk War.[53] With energy and speed, the Mormons settled on good land not far from where Black Hawk himself had farmed eight hundred acres and began building a town called Nauvoo (a Hebrew word for beautiful). The Illinois legislature granted Smith a charter with enough powers for him to forge a semi-autonomous city-state.[54] Before long, he was styling himself "King, Priest, and Ruler over Israel on Earth." He was also the commander-in-chief of the Nauvoo Legion—well armed and five thousand strong. Finally, in the electoral campaign of 1844, Smith ran for the presidency of the United States.[55]

Once again the Saints had made too many enemies, and the open secret of polygyny had caused a serious rift within the sect. Smith's heavy crackdown on dissidents fed Gentile fears of theocratic tyranny—fears already aroused by the Prophet's bid for the White House.[56] That summer, militia and vigilante groups gathered for an attack, and Smith was arrested by Illinois on a charge of treason. In June a mob rushed the jail and murdered him. The Mormon faith was barely fourteen years old, and its Prophet dead at thirty-eight.

After a power struggle between monogamists and polygynists, the leadership went to Brigham Young, a short, stout, unprepossessing but gifted man with several wives.[57] No seer or dreamer, Young knew how to get things done.[58] His first accomplishment was to reach terms for ending the Second Mormon War. If the Gentiles would leave them alone for the winter, the Saints would pack up in the spring of 1846 and leave the United States forever. The Mormons prepared to trek west into the Great American Desert, to unconquered Indian territory which, on paper, belonged to Mexico.

And so, only a decade after the Indian removals, a strange white tribe was also driven beyond the writ of the American empire. The Saints were alien enough to be treated like Indians by the settler society from which they sprang—even to the point of expulsion, murder and threats of extermination—an ironic fate for a sect whose beliefs de-nativized the real Indians. In short, the Mormons were both products of the frontier culture and victims of its intolerance. As in conservative America today, talking about freedom was one thing, doing it quite another.

The Mormon wagons rolled west for thirteen hundred miles beyond the Mississippi, wintering on the way. The hardships of the trek cemented the Saints' neo-biblical identity: now they had their Exodus, their Moses and at last their Promised Land. In July 1847 they crested the Wasatch Mountains and looked down on the Great Salt Lake of Utah. The Prophet arose from his sickbed and pronounced, "This is the Place!"[59]

~·—≡○←≡—·~

The western edge of the American empire was still a fretwork of free and semi-independent states, some white, some native and some belonging to Mexico. With its independence in 1821, Mexico had inherited Spanish claims to all territory west of the Louisiana Purchase and south of British America.[60] Some parts, such as Texas, California and New Mexico, had a thin scattering of missions, ranches and outposts. Before the 1849 goldrush, California had only twelve thousand non-Indian residents, of whom perhaps one thousand were Americans involved in whaling, sea-otter peltry and the cowhide trade.[61] In the rest of the territory, indigenous peoples were still free. The ancient Pueblos of Arizona and New Mexico—whose cliff-top towns of stone and adobe may be the oldest continuously occupied buildings in the Americas—had driven out the Spaniards in 1680 and, despite reprisals, had managed to keep a high degree of autonomy ever since.[62]

Texas had so few non-Indian residents (only four thousand Mexicans in 1821) that Mexico had invited Americans to settle there, hoping they would adopt the Catholic faith, become Mexican citizens and form a buffer against the rising Anglo-Saxon empire. The invitation was taken up mainly by slave-owning cotton growers, and Mexico soon saw it had made a big mistake.[63] By 1830 there were three white Americans for every Mexican in Texas. At first these Anglo-Texans tried to work out a *modus vivendi,* but those hopes were quashed by the vainglorious Mexican dictator General Santa Anna, who massacred American settlers at the Alamo and Goliad in 1836, and was then beaten (but spared) by Sam Houston at San Jacinto.

For nearly ten years, the Lone Star became an independent white republic with its own dreams of expanding to the Pacific. Texan desires to join the United States were blocked by Eastern abolitionists fearful of adding another slave state to the Union. Westerners and Southerners took the opposite view; some even toyed with the idea of leaving the Union and joining with Texas to form an empire of their own. In a cynical phrase with recent echoes, ex-president Andrew Jackson argued that the admission of slave-holding Texas to the United States would be "extending the area of freedom."[64] This view eventually prevailed. When the annexation went through in 1845, the London *Times* commented that the Americans had won their new province "as the cuckoo steals a nest."[65]

The subsequent provocation and conquest of Mexico was America's first great foreign adventure and one of its least justifiable. President James Polk (a Jackson protegé) started the war by sending a small force into disputed territory; when this was repelled, as he hoped it would be, he told Congress that Mexico had shed American blood on American soil—a statement Abraham Lincoln later called "the sheerest deception."[66] The eighty-year-old statesman John Quincy Adams charged Polk with "unscrupulous suppression" of facts and said that Congress's control of the right to declare war was "utterly insufficient . . . as a check upon the will of the President."[67] Adams would be proven right: Congress's last declaration of war was immediately after Pearl Harbor; all America's wars since 1945 have been fought without one.

Henry David Thoreau, then dwelling on Walden Pond, denounced the Mexican war, withheld his taxes and spent a night in jail. (The story goes that when Emerson came in the morning to get him out, saying, "Henry, why are you in here?"

Thoreau answered, "Waldo, why are you *not* in here?") The incident sparked Thoreau's famous essay "Civil Disobedience," which would inspire opposition to other wars, above all Vietnam. But not all the intelligentsia could resist the drumbeat. The young poet Walt Whitman, drunk with patriotism, cheered Polk on: "Yes, Mexico must be thoroughly chastized. . . . Let our arms now be carried with a spirit which shall teach the world that . . . America knows how to crush, as well as how to expand!"[68] And then there were those—as there always are—who found a way to dress greed as altruism: "The universal Yankee nation," cried the *New York Herald* in 1847, "can regenerate and disenthrall the people of Mexico in a few years; and we believe it is a part of our destiny to civilize that beautiful country."[69]

Besides locking its hold on Texas, the United States wanted California and the great natural harbour of San Francisco. Of course, everything in between would have to come too. Instead of simply occupying the desired territory, the Americans struck at the Mexican heartland. After bombarding Veracruz, where Cortés had landed in 1519, they marched through the mountains to the high Valley of Mexico, where the ancient capital of the Aztecs lay within its ring of smouldering volcanoes.

In September 1847 the Americans took the castle of Chapultepec outside Mexico City and at last reached the National Palace—the "Halls of Montezuma."[70] Peace was signed in 1848. Some of Polk's backers wanted to annex all of Mexico, but that had never been his objective—a nation of 7 million was too much for white America to swallow. Polk's strategy was to conquer the whole but keep only the northern half. The rest could be left independent, sovereign in name yet subservient to American interests and investment: the same kind of relationship the Aztecs had once forced on their unhappy neighbours. Mexico became the first client-state under American hegemony.[71]

The mood of the day—after this victory and just before Commodore Matthew Perry's "opening" of Japan—was well expressed in a colourful outburst by the Southern journalist and cotton trader James De Bow.

> We have a destiny to perform, a "manifest destiny" over all Mexico, over South America, over the West Indies and Canada. . . . The gates of the Chinese empire must be thrown down by the men from the Sacramento and the Oregon, and the haughty Japanese tramplers upon the cross be enlightened in the doctrines of republicanism and the ballot box. The eagle of the republic shall poise itself over the field of Waterloo, after tracing its flight among the gorges of the Himalaya or the Ural mountains, and a successor of Washington ascend the chair of universal empire.[72]

Not even Joseph Smith at his most Mohammedan had soared quite so high on his own updraught. "Manifest destiny" was on every patriotic tongue—a reissue, in broader currency, of the old Puritan (and new Mormon) belief in Americans as the Chosen People.[73] Like other self-serving notions of what Providence had in mind, the phrase shone a beam of divine approval on anything America might seize or do in the Aladdin's cave of the New World. In his 1935 book *Manifest Destiny*, the distinguished historian Albert Weinberg called it a monstrous alchemy turning "democratic nationalism into a doctrine of imperialism."[74]

-⊷≡◉⊜≡⊶-

While their former countrymen were conquering Mexico, the Latter-Day Saints had been busy building their desert holy land. Under Brigham Young's able leadership, they had laid out the grid of Salt Lake City and begun ditching water to their fields from the "Jordan" and other streams feeding the lake.

These irrigation works are often said to be the first in North America, but the Mormons were following indigenous practice, whether they knew it or not. (They probably did: not far south of Utah, ancient Americans had been building irrigation systems since the time of Julius Caesar. The elaborate Hohokam canals of Arizona were so well built that white settlers put them back to work in the 1860s. Phoenix was named in recognition of this rebirth.) The new Israel did a lively trade, provisioning overland trekkers to the California goldfields. The colony began to prosper and to draw new members, some from as far away as the slums of England. Brigham Young became bold enough to tell the world about the Lord's endorsement of polygyny, "one of the best doctrines ever proclaimed."

So it may have seemed in Utah; most outsiders were appalled. "It is a scarlet whore," thundered one congressman: "It is a reproach to Christian civilization, and deserves to be blotted out."[75] Under the treaty that ended the Mexican War, Utah had become part of the United States: the Mormons had escaped the American empire for only one year. Polygamy was against federal law, and that—plus Brigham Young's harassment of American officials—gave the new President James Buchanan reason to deny Utah statehood and send an army to enforce the writ of Washington in 1857.

But that was far from the whole story. Only months before, the Supreme Court had handed down the infamous Dred Scott decision, ruling that slaves were property, not persons, and thus unprotected by the freedoms of the Constitution even in free states.[76] A Northerner with Southern sympathies, Buchanan decided to take a leaf out of Jackson's book and sacrifice a marginal group on the altar of national unity, hoping to eclipse "Negro-Mania with the . . . excitements of an Anti-Mormon Crusade."[77]

The Third Mormon War (or Utah War) never came to a straight fight. The worst violence happened at a desert watering hole called Mountain Meadows, where a California-bound wagon train was butchered by "Indians," most of whom were Mormons in disguise.[78] Brigham Young was deposed as territorial governor but not deported. The federal appointee who took his seat was no match for his machinations: the Prophet still ran Utah.

Among the celebrity visitors who trekked to Utah to see the new American religion was the eccentric English Orientalist Sir Richard Francis Burton. Disguised as a "dervish," Burton had recently penetrated Islam's forbidden cities of Mecca and Medina—a journey for which unbelievers were likely to pay with their lives. The perils of Mormondom were nothing to such a man; the worst, in his view, being Salt Lake City's sanctimonious gloom and the lack of a bar at his hotel. Burton, who favoured polygamy for his own reasons, regarded Mormons as underdogs and liked the Islamic echoes in their "faith of the poor." He ignored, or did not see, the Saints' less saintly side: their plundering of Indians and Gentiles, their endorsement of slavery (despite earlier abolitionist leanings) and their ban on blacks in the priesthood (which stayed in effect until 1978).

"The Prophet," Burton wrote admiringly, had "stood up to fight with the sword of the Lord . . . against the mighty power of the United States."[79]

That power soon had to pull back to fight the Civil War. The Saints hailed the conflict as fulfilling prophecy that the Gentiles would destroy themselves and Christ would come back to Earth. Though the war did give the Mormons time to consolidate, the decisive "coming" in Utah was that of the railroad in 1869. Little by little, the City of God reached terms with earthly powers: in 1890 the Lord again changed his mind about polygyny; plural marriage went underground, and, in 1896, Utah became a state at last. Some Mormons continued to practise "plural marriage" quietly, and a few still do—in remote "fundamentalist" Mormon strongholds such as Bountiful, British Columbia. There are now about 12 million Mormons worldwide, and the faith still grows.

⋅⋙◉⋘⋅

Thirty years before the Civil War, in one of his most prophetic insights, Alexis de Tocqueville foresaw that the moral contradictions and headlong drive of white America might lead to self-destruction:

> The future of the New World belongs [to] a restless, calculating, adventurous race which sets coldly about deeds that can only be explained by the fire of passion, and which trades in everything, not excluding even morality and religion. A nation of conquerors that submits to living the life of a savage without ever letting itself be carried away by its charms, that only cherishes those parts of civilisation and enlightenment

which are useful . . . and presses forward to the acquisition of riches, the single end of its labours . . .

It is a wandering people whom rivers and lakes
cannot hold back, before whom forests fall and
prairies are covered in shade; and who, when they have
reached the Pacific Ocean, will come back on its tracks
to trouble and destroy the societies which it will have
formed behind.[80]

As the empire grew, so did the pressure on its contradictions. One by one the Indian Removal, the conquest of
Mexico, the taking of California and the westward march
of Mormons, Texans, goldminers and other colonists wrenched
open the suture between North and South. Texas was a slave
state, Utah became a slave territory and the former home-
lands of the Civilized Tribes had become not so much
republics as forced-labour plantations. By 1860, of the
South's 12 million people, 4 million—one-third of the total—
were slaves.[81]

Europeans had not practised servitude on such a scale
since the days of pagan Rome.[82] Its revival—which would not
have happened without the Columbian bonanza of loot, labour
and land—belied western civilization's ideal of moral progress. Tocqueville's outrage was well aimed (if not wholly accurate) when he wrote, "I reserve my execration for those who,
after a thousand years of freedom, brought back slavery into
the world once more."[83] Though thralldom had never died out
and has existed in many societies, the forms it took in the New
World after 1492 were among the worst in history.

The first American slaves were indigenous Americans, but
they died away too soon to be a significant labour pool except in

Mexico and Peru.[84] Four-fifths of the Africans taken to the New World were shipped after 1700. Between then and about 1810, by which time the trade (though not slavery itself) had been banned by the British Empire and the United States, at least 6 million slaves crossed the Atlantic.[85] As many as one in three may have died on the way.[86] Another 2 million were taken *after* 1810, mainly to Brazil and some unlawfully to the American South.

Quite apart from its moral stink, slavery was inefficient. During his travels, Tocqueville had been struck by the contrast in wealth and development on opposite sides of the Ohio River. "The only reason," a local explained to him, "is that slavery reigns in Kentucky, but not in Ohio. There work is a disgrace, here it is honourable."[87] A Louisville merchant agreed, identifying the weakness that would doom the Southern system: "Slavery is even more prejudicial to the masters than to the slaves. . . . If the South is not as industrialized as the North, that is not because slaves cannot work in factories, it is because slavery deprives the masters of . . . energy and spirit."[88]

By the time of the Civil War, the South had become an archaic, rural and exposed society. The slaveholding states had only 8 million free citizens to the North's 19 million. The North had embraced the Industrial Revolution. Understanding this disparity, President Abraham Lincoln expected a quick victory before antiwar feeling tied his hands. But the South put up a much tougher fight for its way of life than the North had expected. One reason was patriotism: the South was well on its way to becoming a separate nationality. Another was fear: the South dreaded a black uprising, a great settling of scores for what everyone knew, deep down, was wrong.

The Civil War needs no retelling here, except as it influenced American expansion and the emerging world order.[89]

It haunts America just as the Great War haunts Europe, and for similar reasons: it was not a fight against an outlandish foe who could be demonized and dropped in the oubliette of history; rather, it was between kin, sometimes literally. And its impact on society was immense. More than six hundred thousand soldiers died: ten times the number who fell in Vietnam and *seventy* times more when adjusted for population.[90]

Despite *Gone with the Wind* kitsch and "Lost Cause" nostalgia, the Civil War is the one aspect of America's past that America takes seriously: "our only *felt* history," in Robert Penn Warren's memorable words, a "history lived in the national imagination."[91]

⋈

In his 1996 book, *Exterminate All the Brutes,* the Swedish writer Sven Lindqvist draws a link between nineteenth-century colonial atrocities and the horrors of the two World Wars. In the twentieth century, he argues, Europeans reaped on their own turf a harvest of racial hubris and mechanical slaughter which they had sown years before overseas. Their easy victories over tribesmen—for example, at Omdurman in 1898, where a Sudanese army was mown down by Gatling guns before it could get within musket shot of the British—fostered an illusion that technology had made war simple and one-sided and that the deaths at the far end of the gunsight did not matter. "This kind of war was full of fascinating thrills," recalled Winston Churchill, who had been at Omdurman. "It was not like the Great War. Nobody expected to be killed."[92] Nobody white, that is.

A similar link can be drawn between America's "easy" victories over Indians and its slide into the Civil War, which, like the World Wars, Vietnam and Iraq, was wrongly foretold to be simple and quick. The age of the machine gun had not quite dawned by 1861, but the gunboat, the railway and the percussion-cap rifle had all been at work for some time. Like European imperialists in Africa, Americans had grown used to enemies with obsolete weapons, little ammunition and no artillery. The leaders of both North and South shared this colonial conceit. Indeed, the Union president, Abraham Lincoln, and the Confederate president, Jefferson Davis, had served together during the Black Hawk War of the 1830s.[93] (As for racial hubris, the governor of Iowa kept Black Hawk's skeleton hanging up in his office.[94])

The breakaway South formed the Confederate States of America with its capital at Richmond, Virginia—the very place where, two and a half centuries before, King Powhatan had ruled a smaller confederacy from his Tower. The city on the James certainly had historic prestige and fine buildings, but the location was unwise. Only a hundred miles separated President Davis in Richmond from President Lincoln in Washington City.

According to the secessionist theory of the Constitution, the South—or any state—had the right to leave the Union. And many Northerners were ready to let the South go. Could white America have divorced calmly and left it at that? The answer must be no; sooner or later the diverging nations would have fought it out. For one thing, the Confederacy had dreams of building a slave empire, incorporating Cuba and other Caribbean islands. The North would not have brooked such a rival. So Lincoln made his Faustian bargain, employing "one evil, empire, to destroy another evil, slavery."[95]

The Confederates had early successes, won by brilliance and daring against the odds, but after the losses of Gettysburg and Vicksburg, the South was doomed. Throughout 1864 the North fought an "anaconda campaign" of attrition, bringing ever more men, ships and weapons to bear on a shrinking front. Finally, in April 1865, General Ulysses S. Grant—a kindly man, a heavy drinker and sometime store clerk who disliked war but was surprisingly good at it—accepted the sword of his adversary, the more sober and equally gifted commander, Robert E. Lee, at Appomattox.

By the end, the Confederacy was in a state like that of Germany in 1945: its fields burnt, its slaves freed, its railways torn up, its cities in ruins.

⋯⟾◉⟽⋯

Late in 1863, when it was becoming clear that the North would win, the great orator and antislavery activist Frederick Douglass, who was himself a former slave, said that the work of the "abolition war" would never be done "until the black men of the South, and the black men of the North, shall have been admitted, fully and completely, into the body politic of America."[96] For the dozen years of postwar Reconstruction, the North came down hard on the South, and Douglass's dream— later Martin Luther King's and Barack Obama's—seemed almost within reach. But the work of rebuilding America was hindered by the corruption of carpetbaggers and war profiteers who bedevilled Lincoln's successors.[97]

Meanwhile, a terrorist insurgency threatened to break out in the conquered states. Death squads with ominous names and bizarre rituals arose to restore white supremacy: the Pale Faces, the White Brotherhood, the Knights of the White Camelia and the Ku Klux Klan. By the late 1870s, it was clear that the price for national reconciliation would be paid by African

Americans. Washington turned a blind eye as segregation and Jim Crow laws overturned the new racial order, keeping the South a white man's country for another hundred years.[98]

Little by little, the subdued if unrepentant states were readmitted to national life, a process that subtly changed the language. When Walt Whitman had written "The United States *themselves* are essentially the greatest poem" in 1855, he reflected the usage of the time. After the war, the country's name shifted from a plural to a singular noun: the United States became *itself.*[99]

⋆⟾⟾⟾⋆

The Civil War did not affect only white Americans and former slaves.[100] Native Americans played a greater role than is generally known, and on both sides. Sandwiched between Texas and Missouri, the Civilized Tribes—by then re-established as semi-sovereign nations in the Indian Territory—were inevitably drawn into the invaders' war, splitting into pro-Union and pro-Confederate factions. The last Southern commander to surrender his sword was Brigadier General Stand Watie, a brother of the Cherokee newspaperman known in English as Elias Boudinot.[101] On the winning side, the terms of surrender signed by Robert E. Lee at Appomattox were written by Colonel Ely Parker, General Grant's right-hand man and a Seneca chief of the Iroquois League.[102] As a young man, Parker had worked with Lewis Henry Morgan on the ground-breaking ethnography *League of the Iroquois,* which brought the ideas of the ancient Longhouse to the attention of Marx, Engels and other Victorian thinkers.

When Ulysses Grant became president in 1869, he made Parker head of Indian Affairs—the first Indian to hold the post, and the last for a century. But neither Grant nor Parker could stop the spiral of violence in the West, and their best intentions were undermined by corrupt Washington contractors, who, like their counterparts today, padded accounts and siphoned off public funds.

With its easy money and lack of oversight, the four-year emergency had corrupted all levels of American government. It had also produced an industrial surge, especially in weapons, shipbuilding and railways. And like all great wars, it had bequeathed problems of debt and demobilization.[103] The Union alone had a million men under arms; they couldn't all retire at once. Americans also realized that if they were to avoid fighting each other again in future, they would need an outside enemy against whom their divided nation could unite. So Washington turned its war machine on the unconquered peoples of the West. By 1868 General Philip Sheridan of the Army of the Potomac was out in Oklahoma, uttering his notorious words, "The only good Indians I ever saw were dead."[104]

We are now speaking of the West in the modern sense of the word—the Great Plains where the horse Indians hunted the buffalo.[105] In the American myth that Hollywood has sold to the world, these are the only *real* Indians: wild, nomadic, noble and unchanging.[106] Forget all that. The horse Indians were never typical of America, and their life was built on change. Many of them—including the Cheyenne, the Sioux and the Arapaho— were refugees from the invaded East, obliged to take up buffalo hunting when their farmland had been overrun by whites. Their culture was a brief and brilliant response to a shifting world, a hybrid flower that bloomed and died within a hundred years.

Of course, a few people had been living on the Plains ever since the end of the last Ice Age. But they hunted on foot and had only dogs to drag everything—tipis, lodge poles, food, the elderly—on small travois across the ocean of grass. When the first horse appeared in the eighteenth century, they named it "holy dog."[107] The horse shrank distance, carried goods, and turned footsloggers into knights. The Plains Indians quickly became as skilled on horseback as Mongolians, growing rich on the great herds of buffalo, trading meat for corn and guns.

The white expansion onto the Plains was also driven by a combination of new needs, opportunities and means. Just weeks after the American conquest of Mexico, a gold strike at Sutter's Mill in California had set off the wildest goldrush since the old Spanish conquests of Mexico and Peru. Prospectors and adventurers rolled west in tens of thousands, heedless of the "permanent" Indian frontier, spreading the usual plagues of disease, alcohol and violence. By the end of the Civil War, it was clear that the Western mountains held enormous wealth—not only the traditional gold and silver but other minerals newly in demand as the world industrialized. The whites also saw that the land was not as barren as they had thought; some parts were indeed desert, but much of the West was a savannah of deep, black earth kept treeless by the buffalo.

Anyone who drives across the Great Plains today can't fail to be staggered by their extent—some million square miles, more than the entire area occupied and claimed by the United States before the Louisiana Purchase. It seems impossible that nineteenth-century armies could find, let alone subdue, the Western nomads in a single generation. Yet the Indians weren't the only moving target; so, in a different way, was the civilization that attacked them.

White numbers and technology were taking off as the Columbian Age began to bear its greatest fruits. Having grown at compound interest in the Old World for two centuries, the stolen wealth of Mexico and Peru had now returned to the New—to feed, finance, equip and populate the new American empire. In 1830 the United States had 13 million people; in 1860, 31 million; and by 1900, 76 million—more than any European country.[108] Just thirty years after the Indian Removal, the railway joined the coasts and split the buffalo, which shied at the gleaming rails. The first motorcar crossed America thirty-four years after the first train.[109]

In the eighteenth century, both whites and Indians had used the same weapons: smooth-bore muskets with powder and ball. But as the Industrial Revolution accelerated, the arms race became ever more one-sided. While the Indians were still using muskets, the whites had repeating rifles; by the time the Indians acquired rifles, the whites had machine guns.[110] The Sharp rifle, the Gatling gun and the steam train were the brightest stars in a constellation of inventions that enabled white America to take the West.[111]

The decisive weapon, however, was nothing more glamorous than a new tanning process, perfected in 1871. Buffalo leather suddenly became part of the world economy, prized for machinery belts and army boots. The United States government realized it could subdue the Plains tribes by letting freelance hunters (many of whom were Civil War veterans) kill off their food supply. "It would be a great step forward in the civilization of the Indians," said Senator James Throckmorton, "if there was not a buffalo in existence."[112] He got his wish. Whites with repeating rifles wiped out the great herds—perhaps 30 million animals—in just ten years, taking the hides and leaving the flesh to rot."[13] By 1890 only a few hundred buffalo were left. The Indians had a Hobson's choice: starvation or surrender. Often it was both, on reservations little better than death camps.

The definitive general history of this period is Dee Brown's 1970 bestseller, *Bury My Heart at Wounded Knee,* which quotes extensively from eyewitnesses on both sides.[14] The race war followed much the same pattern as the one that began at Mystic, complete with Puritan bloodlust. One of the worst massacres was led by a Methodist preacher named John Chivington, who fell on a sleeping village of friendly Cheyennes at Sand Creek, Colorado, with these words: "I have come to kill Indians, and believe it is right and honorable to use any means under God's heaven to kill Indians."[15] What followed was the My Lai massacre of its time. Coming early in the Western wars, Sand Creek quashed whatever hopes of peace the tribes still held. It set the stage for the short-lived Indian victory over General Custer at the Little Bighorn, the Ghost Dance crisis cult, and the final squalid murder of Sioux prisoners at Wounded Knee.

The year of Wounded Knee, 1890, was chosen by the United States Census to mark the closing of the frontier. With the final defeat of the Western Indians, three hundred years of warfare for "free land" came to an end. At the same time, the Creeks, Cherokees and other Southern nations who had been driven to the Indian Territory ("theirs forever . . . under the most solemn guarantee of the United States") were broken up by the *Dawes Allotment Act,* and the "surplus" opened to a white stampede.[16] Since the Removal, the Five Civilized Tribes had made good progress establishing themselves in what is now Oklahoma, building schools, hospitals and towns, with national legislatures of stone and brick in high Victorian style. They had also freed their former slaves and rebuilt after the destruction of the Civil War. Their level of education was superior to the American norm, and their communal land ownership acted as a social safety net, keeping them free from the poverty of many frontier whites. But as Senator Dawes noted, they lacked "selfishness"—that essential ingredient of Anglo-American civilization. When the Cherokee and Choctaw nations fought the *Dawes Act* in court, Congress dissolved their national governments. When all Five Tribes then applied to join the United States as an Indian state, their request was denied. The Removal treaties had promised that the Indian Territory would never "be included within . . . limits or jurisdiction of any [white] State." Yet in 1907, once whites safely outnumbered Indians in the territory, Theodore Roosevelt proclaimed it the state of Oklahoma. Despite all these attacks, the Five Civilized Tribes are still a significant portion of Oklahoma's population today, and they have revived their national governments as much as possible. Their lands, however, remain fragmented.

By one reckoning, the United States made 370 treaties with Indians and broke them all.[117] Three centuries after Roanoke and Jamestown, the conquest of North America was done. Much the same had happened in Canada, the most violent episode being the war against the Métis leader Louis Riel and his Indian allies in Manitoba and Saskatchewan. There was less fighting north of the forty-ninth parallel, but the extermination of the buffalo, the building of a railway from coast to coast, and the settlement and treaty process were all quite similar.

It was only in this last period that white America's oldest and biggest lie had any truth: in the Far West, the settlers really did face a "wilderness" inhabited by nomads. Until then, Europeans had made their way across the continent by taking over fields and houses emptied by disease, warfare or—where those failed—by state-enforced ethnic cleansing. From Jamestown and Plymouth to the edge of the Plains, the takeover was parasitic: America's true pioneers were Indians. Indeed, the Civilized Tribes sent west and robbed again fifty years later became the first wave of "settlement."

The Far West had been left to hunters because neither Indians nor whites could farm a grassland mown by buffalo and wildfire. For the first time, the white man could not purloin "the fruits of others' labours."[118] Luckily for him, industrial technology did the job instead. After the slaughter of the buffalo, cattle briefly offered a tame substitute. But the open range was soon diced into farmland by the invention of barbed wire.[119] The steel rope came west on steel rails. It also took steel and steam to flay the earth itself—to slice through ten thousand years of matted sod and turn the Prairie into wheat fields. The same Mr. Gatling whose gun reaped Sioux and Sudanese also made farm machinery and the first steam plough.[120] And so the Great Plains became a chessboard, its pawns set out by industries and banks.

In 1987 a settler named Leroy Judson Daniels published his memoirs when he was more than a hundred years old. Born in 1882, breaking wild horses in Montana at fifteen, he saw the Great Plains turn into monoculture: "What a sight in the spring! Grass as far as the eye could see, wild flowers of all kinds, wild strawberries . . . millions of prairie chickens and quail, wolves and squirrels, foxes. . . . Of course, now we can see what we did to that wonderful world . . . took it away, destroyed what God and nature gave man to support his life. Then there wasn't a fence anywhere."[121]

The winning of the West was immediately laundered into
entertainment, first by Buffalo Bill Cody's Wild West Show and
ever since by dime-store novels and films. The last word on the
"conquest machine" must go to the great Sioux leader Sitting
Bull, who fought Custer at the Little Bighorn, toured Europe
with Cody in the 1880s, and died during a botched arrest two
weeks before Wounded Knee:

> The love of possession is a disease with them [the
> whites]. They take tithes from the poor and weak to
> support the rich who rule. They claim this mother of
> ours, the earth, for their own and fence their neighbors
> away; they deface her with their buildings and their
> refuse. That nation is like a spring freshet that overruns
> its banks and destroys all who are in its path.[122]

A Sort of Empire

The Eagle is the chief of the feathered race . . . fierce, rapacious, and holding a sort of empire over the whole.

—Noah Webster, 1812[1]

The real truth of the matter is, as you and I know, that a
financial element in the larger centers has owned the
Government ever since the days of Andrew Jackson.

—Franklin D. Roosevelt, 1933[2]

The Americans may have preserved a cult of Liberty but
they do not feel the need to liberate themselves from the
servitude which their capitalism has created.

— Hubert Beuve-Méry, 1944[3]

THREE YEARS AFTER SITTING BULL'S DEATH, Chicago
hosted the 1893 World's Fair—marking the four hun-
dredth anniversary of Columbus's first voyage (albeit a
year late). This was America's coming-out party, its answer to
the Great Exhibition of 1851, when the might and splendour of
the British Empire had been displayed to 6 million visitors at
London's Crystal Palace. By the 1890s the United States had

outstripped the mother country in population and was fast overtaking the old workshop of the world in industrial output and technical progress. Only a tenth of American production was being sold abroad, but that was already enough to make the United States second only to Britain in world trade.[4]

It was also at the Chicago Fair that the young historian Frederick Jackson Turner presented his famous paper on the frontier as America's "crucible," in which the higher elements of European and native civilization had been vaporized, leaving a coarse yet resilient alloy. In later essays, Turner took a rosier view of the frontier culture, emphasizing the opportunities of "free land," rather than the three-century legacy of warfare. But he got it right the first time.

Perhaps the most troubling aspect of that legacy was the creation of a social system dependent on endless expansion. "To stop the march of empire would doubtless have proved too much for any philosophical principle," wrote Albert Weinberg in *Manifest Destiny,* "for each advance of the frontier solved one set of problems only to create another, satisfied one desire only to stimulate a new one."[5] Until industrialization, North America had seemed so vast that the day of reckoning would never come. But in the thirty years after 1870, white Americans took and settled more land than they had in the previous three hundred.[6]

On the eve of the twentieth century, the United States ran out of *Lebensraum:* the frontier safety valve was shutting down. Back in America's East, pressure was building up as railways, mines and other industries owned by "robber barons" formed monopolies, driving down wages by using immigrant and child workers in the midst of an inflationary boom. In 1893 the bubble burst—in bank failures, strikes and riots—followed by a five-year slump.

The best cure for home unrest, as King Henry IV on his deathbed advises Prince Hal, is foreign quarrels.[7] Instead of weaning itself from a diet of territorial expansion, America spilled into the Pacific.[8]

⊷⩴◉⊜⊶

By the 1890s most of the Polynesian islands had been snapped up by European empires, leaving one great prize unclaimed: the Kingdom of Hawaii. American whalers, missionaries and planters were already well established there, but the islands were still ruled by a native dynasty founded by King Kamehameha I in 1795. Recognizing the threat of the white strangers who had suddenly appeared on their shores, he and his heirs had responded much like the Civilized Tribes. For a hundred years, the Hawaiian nobility adopted foreign ways in a bid to build a modern nation strong enough to resist the outlanders.

But, as in the Americas, the indigenous population was struck hard by imported disease, worsened by alcohol, prostitution and cultural breakdown.[9] In the 1820s the old religion was suppressed; in the 1850s, on the advice of American missionaries, the land was severed into private plots. Many commoners lost their farms to sugar and cotton estates. Many nobles were seduced by the life of Victorian aristocrats.[10] Hawaii became "globalized," a pawn in what was then called the World Market. "In the midst of these evidences of prosperity and advancement," wrote David Kalakaua, the last king, "the natives are steadily decreasing in numbers and gradually losing their hold upon the fair land of their fathers. Within a century they have dwindled from four hundred thousand . . . to a little more than a tenth of that number of landless, hopeless victims to the greed and vices of civilization."[11]

King Kalakaua himself sickened and died in 1891, leaving the throne to his sister, Queen Liliuokalani.

The white settlers—most of them Americans—had long dreamed of getting the islands annexed by the United States, France or Britain, or simply seizing Hawaii for themselves. These aims were sometimes encouraged and sometimes rebuffed by foreign powers, depending on political winds at home. In 1881 James Blaine, the U.S. secretary of state, called Hawaii the "key to the dominion of the American Pacific."[12] Six years later America secured Pearl Harbor for a naval base. By 1893 the settlers were strong enough to over-throw the queen in a coup d'état, saying that her efforts to strengthen Hawaiian rule were undemocratic.[13] While Washington dithered over backing their revolt, the rebels set up a "Gospel Republic" led by Sanford Dole, a missionary's son with a wiry patriarchal beard. Dole held the islands until Republicans—most of whom favoured imperialism, then as now—came to power in the United States in 1897. The new regime quickly annexed Hawaii without qualms and made Dole the first governor.[14]

Like Texas, Hawaii was taken "as the cuckoo steals a nest." It was the last place that could be overwhelmed by settlers and remade—in American eyes—from an imperial possession into a piece of home.[15]

⋄⟞◉⟝⋄

At the end of the nineteenth century the machine guns were rattling everywhere—in Sudan, French Indochina, the Congo—and they had been as genocidal on Argentina's pampas as on America's Great Plains. The European powers had built empires around the world and were getting ready to carve up

China. Why shouldn't the United States join in too, before all the pickings were gone?

With the Republicans carrying both White House and Congress, imperialism was firmly in the saddle. When President William McKinley took office in 1897, he chose a red-blooded expansionist and militarist, Theodore Roosevelt, to be his assistant secretary of the navy and, later, his vice-president. "I should welcome almost any war," Roosevelt wrote to a friend at the time, "for I think this country needs one."[16]

But other leading Americans were uneasy about overseas ambition and keenly aware of the moral danger for a nation that deemed itself the apostle of freedom. Such unlikely bedfellows as the distinguished philosopher William James (brother of the novelist Henry James), the industrialist Andrew Carnegie and a variety of socialists, church groups and pacifists came together to form the American Anti-Imperialist League.

After Hawaii the imperialists' next target was the forgotten remnants of the Spanish Empire: Cuba, the Philippines, Guam, Wake and a few other islands in the Pacific and Caribbean. Local uprisings provided an excuse for American "concern." In February 1898 the U.S. battleship *Maine,* showing the flag at Havana, mysteriously blew up and sank with all hands. Hawkish newspapers immediately blamed Spain, though the explosion may well have been an accident. Within days of the sinking, Roosevelt sent a squadron to the Philippines to make a surprise attack on a Spanish fleet half a world away—giving the order more than two months before the war itself began anywhere.[17] The deed is doubly suspicious in light of a letter Roosevelt had written to Henry Cabot Lodge the previous September: "Our Asiatic squadron should blockade, and if possible, take Manila."[18] President McKinley had ample time to recall the squadron, but he did not do so. Roosevelt's order must have had White House support. Clearly, the United States had been planning the Spanish war long before a good *casus belli* could be found—a policy similar, in several ways, to the hunting of Iraq a century later.

Spain's Caribbean islands went down like old horses at a bullfight. Few Americans died, and Roosevelt's Rough Riders covered themselves with glory. The secretary of state called it a "splendid little war." Under peace terms denounced by the Anti-Imperialists as "colonial vassalage," the United States made Cuba a protectorate and took the naval base of Guantánamo Bay as its commission.[19] Things would not go so smoothly in the Philippines, America's "first Vietnam."[20]

◦⊷≡◉⊜⊶◦

Looking back on these events from the far side of the twentieth century, one can see the seeds of future war being planted as if by a malevolent Fate: Pearl Harbor, Guam, Wake, the Philippines, Cuba, Guantánamo. All are famous names today, not for the events of the 1890s but for those of the 1940s, 1960s and 2001. The death of the old world empire built by the conquistadors became the birth of a new world empire that would claim the coming century as its own.

In the Philippines, America would learn the limits and costs of imperial reach, as Spain had long before. It was one thing to conquer indigenous Americans and Polynesians who could be counted on to "melt away" from introduced diseases; quite another to acquire a large subject population that was biologically a part of Asia. The Filipinos then numbered about 8 million—five times more than the Cubans, thirty times more than the surviving American Indians and two hundred times more than the Hawaiians.[21]

By his own account, President McKinley had cold feet, which spent many a wakeful night pacing the White House floors. In 1897 he had spoken out against annexing Cuba because, "by our code of morality [it] would be criminal aggression."[22] But now he wanted the Philippines. How could he justify the inconsistency? Like a Mormon prophet, McKinley entered into long conversations with God about this moral dilemma. Obligingly and unsurprisingly, the Lord told the president it was nothing less than America's duty to "educate the Filipinos, and uplift and civilize and Christianize them."[23]

So the United States turned against the local rebels it had initially backed. McKinley claimed that Filipinos had started the fighting, but evidence later came out that U.S. officers had been ordered to provoke it. The Philippine leader, Emilio Aguinaldo, offered McKinley a deal: he would settle for a protectorate. All he needed were "some tangible concessions from the United States" that he could present to his people. It is still unclear why McKinley didn't take his offer. After all, the United States was driving that very bargain with the Cubans.[24]

The reason for Washington's hard line seems to have been a mix of racism, national pride and rivalry with other powers. Senator Albert Beveridge, the barking dog of the imperialists, told the president that God had been preparing Anglo-Saxons and other Germanic folk "for a thousand years . . . as the master organizers of the world . . . And of all our race He has marked the American people as His chosen nation." Such rhetoric came down from the Puritans, but, as Weinberg noted prophetically in 1935, it was also a foretaste of Hitlerism.[25]

Greed had to be dressed up as a sacred duty to bring the "savage" into civilization.

"The Philippines are ours forever," Senator Beveridge told Congress (in a speech he entitled "In Support of an American Empire"). "And just beyond the Philippines are China's illimitable markets. We will not retreat from either. . . . We will not renounce our part in the mission of our race, trustee, under God, of the civilization of the world."[26] Rudyard Kipling weighed in, penning his "White Man's Burden" on the Philippine affair, a poem best remembered for its title. (Roosevelt wrote to Senator Lodge that it was "poor poetry, but good sense from the expansionist standpoint."[27]) One senator declared that letting the Filipinos keep their freedom would be "the highest cruelty."[28] Another said America need not shrink from imperialism, because hers would be "the imperialism of liberty."[29]

Whatever his reasons, McKinley wanted the Philippines just as George W. Bush wanted Iraq. Words written by historian Tyler Dennett in 1922 could easily apply to either war: "The policy [was] adopted in great ignorance of the actual facts . . . and in a blissful and exalted assumption that any race ought to regard conquest by the American people as a superlative blessing."[30]

It took sixty thousand U.S. troops two years to confer that blessing and capture Aguinaldo. From the scanty reports that leaked out between 1899 and 1901, it is clear that, in cruelty and injustice, the Philippine War reprised the Indian wars and foretokened Korea, Vietnam and Iraq. William James said that "McKinley's cant . . . has reached perfect expertness in the art of killing silently."[31] The Anti-Imperialist League did what it could to break that silence by publishing soldiers' letters. One officer wrote home about the town of Caloocan, the My Lai or Mystic of the war: "Caloocan was supposed to contain 17,000

inhabitants. The Twentieth Kansan swept through it, and now
Caloocan contains not one living native." A private confessed
that he had, with his own hand, "set fire to over fifty houses
of Filipinos."[32]

When journalists at last got to the war zone, they confirmed
the worst, including use of a torture that is again in the news
today as "waterboarding"—a near-drowning technique that the
Americans had condemned the Spaniards for practising, but
then adopted themselves in the Philippines and have again been
using in the so-called war on terror.[33] "Our men," reported the
Philadelphia *Ledger*, "have killed to exterminate men, women,
children, prisoners, and captives, active insurgents and sus-
pected people from lads of ten up, the idea prevailing that the
Filipino was little better than a dog. . . . Our soldiers have
pumped salt water into men to make them talk."[34]

Meanwhile in Washington, Elihu Root, the secretary of war,
was answering the critics with sang-froid: "The war in the
Philippines has been conducted by the American army with
scrupulous regard for the rules of civilized warfare . . . with
self-restraint and with humanity never surpassed."[35] In 2003
Root's modern successor, Donald Rumsfeld, would use the very
same word—"humanity"—to describe his bombing of Iraq.[36]

⟶⟡⟵

In 1901 President McKinley was assassinated—not by an
aggrieved Filipino but by an American-born anarchist shout-
ing that the president was an enemy of the workers. When
Tocqueville had travelled through the United States seventy
years before, he had been struck by the equality and opportunity he saw: almost everyone was middle class; concentration
of ownership was discouraged by law; competition seemed to

be working as Adam Smith had said it would. John Quincy Adams told him, "Many more generations will yet pass before we feel that we are overcrowded," and Tocqueville wondered, if that were so, why Americans were in such a hurry: "They rush upon their fortune as if but a moment remained for them to make it their own."[37]

The canny homesteaders knew something the French nobleman did not: *good times don't last; get yours while you can.* In the 1860s it had been said that the frontier would "postpone for centuries" and perhaps forever "all serious conflict between capital and labor."[38] The decades after the Civil War saw the United States' fastest territorial growth—yet also a massive upward shift of wealth as industrialization made a handful of Americans into plutocrats. By the turn of the century, the self-sufficient yeomanry admired by Tocqueville had all but disappeared. Big land and railway companies had bagged the winnings of the West. The farmer was in thrall to banks and faraway markets; the city dweller was ground down into a proletariat. Manhattan had more than 3 million people, many of them in slums.

This was no longer government "of the people, by the people, and for the people," said the veteran statesman John Hay, who served under both Lincoln and McKinley, but "government of corporations, by corporations, and for corporations."[39] The huddled masses alighting at New York found that an American factory of 1900 was much the same as a British, French or German factory of 1900—or, for that matter, a Third World factory of today. A sixty- or seventy-hour week was typical; work was hard, unsafe and unhealthy.[40] Nearly a third of a million American children under fifteen were working in mines, mills and factories. The plight of women and girls in

New York sweatshops was exposed by the Triangle Shirtwaist fire of 1911, when 146 died in a locked building. In 1904 alone, about half a million people were injured at work in the United States and twenty-seven thousand killed.

Despite America's social safety valve—all the "free land" taken from the Indians at such cost and with such hopes—exploitation of the weak by the strong had crossed the Atlantic and taken charge in the new Eden. Industrial imperialism was not simply mowing down tribesmen far from the public eye; it was devouring the very society from which it sprang.[41] As free enterprise congealed into monopolies and trusts, radical workers responded by forming "one big union"—the Industrial Workers of the World (IWW), nicknamed the Wobblies. There was something messianic about the Wobblies, a dream of bringing down the whole edifice of capitalism and building a socialist millennium in its stead. Their strikes were met with violence, even murder, from police, militia and vigilante squads. Society was polarizing along class lines.[42]

It dawned on the more thoughtful industrialists and politicians that a way to expand the market for American goods and take the heat out of social unrest would be to raise the buying power of the working class. Though an imperialist and a Republican, Theodore Roosevelt understood this equation—and he had the political guts to tackle big business. He broke up some of the monopolies, sought arbitration for labour disputes, slowed the raping of natural resources and imposed federal standards on food and drugs. He was also a supporter of the Hague Tribunal, the first stirrings of an international order.[43]

Ironically, these farsighted policies have since been undone or demonized by more recent Republican politicians—a measure of the drift in American politics from a pragmatic middle ground typical of modern democracy to a neo-Victorian extremism bent on unlearning the lessons of the twentieth century.

Those lessons—learned at a cost of 80 million lives—are that injustice, inequality and mass poverty lead to terrorism, war and revolution. The shooting of President McKinley was only one of many attacks during the long summer of imperial greed before the palm-court orchestras were silenced by the guns of 1914.[44] In Joseph Conrad's novel of the times, *The Secret Agent,* a suicide bomber prowls London wearing an explosive jacket, detonator in hand. That was published in 1906.[45] In 1920 a truck bomb blew up on Wall Street outside the headquarters of J.P. Morgan.[46] Now we are being told that terrorism is new, that nineteen fanatics have changed the world, that such people are so powerful and pervasive that the "war" against them must trump democratic freedoms that survived two World Wars and the threat of nuclear annihilation.

The first gun of 1914 was the pistol with which a nineteen-year-old extremist shot the Archduke Franz Ferdinand, heir to the Austro-Hungarian throne, and his wife at Sarajevo.[47] The attack was provoked by ethnic injustice in the Balkans, but that was neither new nor enough, in itself, to make a continent commit mass suicide. The first lesson of 1914 is the risk of overreacting to terrorism.

Historians still debate how Austria's revenge for that murder touched off a bloodbath that would blight all subsequent history. Perhaps the western world had forgotten the disasters of war. Perhaps the Great Powers had grown bored with the endless jousting of the Edwardian afternoon. The wealth of the long peace had been distilled into an arms race. In one generation, battleships had changed from things of wood, sail and cannon into turbine-powered castles of steel.[48] The leaders were seduced by the beauty of their weapons: modern war, they said, would be easy and quick. You'll be "back before the leaves fall," they told the troops that August. But as today's foremost historian of war, John Keegan, writes, "It would be four years and five autumns before the survivors returned, leaving on the battlefields some 10 million dead. The vast crop of fit and strong young men which formed the fruit of nineteenth-century Europe's economic miracle had been consumed by the force which gave them life and health."[49]

In the 1912 American elections, Theodore Roosevelt's Progressives had split the Republican Party, handing victory to the Democrat Woodrow Wilson—a lean, scholarly Virginian with a record of fighting for the underdog.[50] In his idealism, Wilson was the Jimmy Carter of his times, though he lacked Carter's humility. He also had a weakness for self-deception, which led him into some ill-advised meddling in Latin America; but against that must be set his reforms in the Philippines, including a promise of independence that was eventually followed up by Franklin Delano Roosevelt.[51] America re-elected Wilson in 1916 on a platform of keeping America out of the Great War except as a supplier and lender to the Allies.[52] Soon, however, German outrages threw American opinion behind Wilson's reluctant decision to take part. The last straw was the exposure of a German plot to help Mexico get back the territory she had lost in 1848 if she would make war on the United States.[53]

As the American Civil War had already shown, modern conflicts are won in factories as much as on battlefields. The Western Front—that long wound of mud, blood and wire across the body of Europe—was a stalemate. The winner would be the side that could exhaust the other's economy and starve its population: the medieval siege at an international scale.[54] While America's belated involvement had a relatively small military impact, it was probably decisive for these economic reasons.[55]

Not all Americans sent to Europe had as good a war as Dick Savage of the "grenadine guards" in John Dos Passos's *Nineteen Nineteen*, but many shared his moral vertigo at the abyss he found there: "I swear I'm ashamed of being a man. . . . God, we're a lousy cruel vicious dumb type of tailless ape."[56]

⋯⟹⟸⋯

Weeks after the guns were stilled by the Armistice, Woodrow Wilson steamed to the Paris Peace Conference aboard the *George Washington*.[57] In their tail coats and black silk hats, the peacemakers who gathered at Versailles in 1919 looked like an undertakers' convention. And so they were. They had to bury the bodies, clean up the mess and find meaning in pointless slaughter.

It was an overwhelming brief: to settle terms and borders, to sterilize the seeds of future war, to foment liberal democracy, to find a balance between capital and labour. Every European government east of France had fallen, mostly to Marxist revolution.[58] Of Wilson's Fourteen Points for peace, the sixth, in particular, makes ironic reading today. The new Communist Russia, he wrote, should be given "an unhampered and unembarrassed opportunity for the independent determination of her own political development [and] a sincere welcome into the society of free nations under institutions of her own choosing."[59]

The task, Wilson argued, would demand not merely a peace treaty but "a new world order" enshrined in an international body, which he called the League of Nations. The idea itself wasn't new—at the dawn of the Victorian Age, the poet Alfred Tennyson had called for the "Parliament of man, the Federation of the world"—but never before had such need and opportunity come together.[60] Europe was morally and financially bankrupt; wars and empires were discredited; America's idealism really did seem to be the world's best hope.

The battlefields were slowly ploughed over or left to armies of the dead: acres of crosses and headstones in perfect array. Above them reared silent temples of white stone to the "Great War for Civilization"—as if civilization had won. In truth, civilization had died with the mustard-gas and the maggots, with the torpedoed passenger liners, with the aerial bombing of civilians in their beds.[61] The fond belief of the Enlightenment—that technological and moral progress go hand in hand—was dead. The civilized had learned what many "savages" already knew: that civilization behaves no better than savagery and does its worst on a far greater scale.

The spectacle of the "master organizers of the world" butchering one another had not been lost on the "lesser breeds" they ruled. The pretensions of imperialism were undone. Independence movements sprang up in the tottering empires, especially India. It became a matter of when—not if—the white man would unload his burden.

❖⟩═◑═⟨❖

If the great epic of western progress was a lie, writers and artists asked themselves, what was true? What beautiful? Although inklings of modernism had appeared before the Great War, the aesthetic canon was overthrown wholesale in its wake. To the uninitiated, stories became riddles, paintings became nightmares, music became noise, buildings became boxes and machines. The public turned to popular culture—to film, jazz, comics and romances.

The only modern style with wide appeal—art deco—was in fact the least modern and most American. When Frank Lloyd Wright and other young designers were casting around for new ideas at the Chicago World's Fair of 1893, they saw a spectacular outdoor exhibit of Maya buildings from Yucatán: full-size casts of doorways, façades and an entire triumphal arch. The steel-frame skyscraper was being developed at just that time. While American architects were trying various styles for the high-rise form, New York City passed a setback bylaw, requiring tall buildings to step inward as they rose, to let sunlight reach the streets. The law encouraged pyramids.[62] Indeed, a steep Maya temple at Tikal in Guatemala (to which the New Yorker building bears a strong resemblance) had been the tallest structure in the New World for more than eleven hundred years.[63] Ancient American forms and motifs—unfamiliar enough to seem new and "modern"—came to dominate art deco design, appearing on everything from skyscrapers to radio sets.

✦≡◐⊂≡✦

Perhaps only an American of Woodrow Wilson's background and wide learning could have dreamt that a League of Nations might put an end to war. Wilson—a Southerner who admired Lincoln—took history seriously. Like Benjamin Franklin nearly two centuries before, his thinking was influenced by the ancient Iroquois League, which had been formed for the same reason: to stop warfare among closely related nations.[64] The Europeans, more cynical but also broke, had little choice but to go along with Wilson's dream. While the old empires had been sending their treasure up in smoke, the American empire had enjoyed a boom. The United States was now the world's banker, owed 10 billion dollars by the Allies.

Wilson got his League, but his own nation never joined it. Congress would not ratify the treaty—for reasons that foreshadow the American right's dislike of international agreements to this day.[65] The League of Nations, the Law of the Sea, the Mine Ban Treaty, the Kyoto Accord on climate change and the International Criminal Court have all been rejected by the United States (after initial involvement) because a vote in Congress or a change of regime gave spoiling power to a vested, parochial, even paranoid interest. Tocqueville had a point when he noted that American democracy "is able to control the internal affairs of society. But I cannot persuade myself that it is in a state to manage foreign affairs."[66]

As Margaret MacMillan writes in her fine book on the Peace Conference, *Paris 1919*, the League "underlined the idea that there were certain things that all humanity had in common and that there could be international standards beyond those of merely national interest."[67] Wilson failed to make America the heart of this endeavour—his efforts wrecked his health and failed to forestall an even greater war—but the League of Nations set a precedent that would eventually bear fruit in the United Nations and the European Union.

⋯⊙⊂⋯

Many historians have blamed the Second War on the First, "in so far as one event causes another."[68] From this distance in time, the two World Wars look like a single tragedy with a long intermission. Before the mortar was even dry between the stones of the great memorials, the "vicious dumb apes" began jostling for the second act. Although it is hardly fair to blame the 1919 peacemakers for being unable to see the future, it is true that the Nazi Party thrived on mass unemployment and hyperinflation caused by the reparations extracted from Germany in the early 1920s: millions of young men were looking for scapegoats and a saviour.[69] It is also true that the high-handed carve-up of the Middle East would lead to the Iraq War of today—via the Suez Crisis of 1956, various Arab-Israeli wars and the Gulf War of 1991. Furthermore, the Great War's sociopolitical lessons—the need for capitalism to be tamed, for workers to be protected, for unemployment to be checked—were soon forgotten. In America the Republicans not only rejected Wilson's League but undid many of his (and Theodore Roosevelt's) progressive business laws, leaving the stock market to roar until it choked in October 1929.

A return to madness might still have been avoided had there not been a fatal concurrence of financial, moral, political—and natural—turmoil. As the cliché has it, the Dirty Thirties were a perfect storm. Human affairs were not being played out like medieval politics in a static world. The population boom was speeding up. Modern farm technology was being applied recklessly, if with the best intentions. By the early 1920s it was becoming evident that those who had thought the Great Plains too dry for farming had not been altogether wrong. The notion that "rain follows the plough" was wishful thinking.[70] The bumper years after breaking the land had been a coincidence: a wet period in a natural cycle coupled with a one-time issue of fertility from ten thousand years of turf. Just as the nutrients of a rainforest are in the trees, not the ground, so the life of the prairie had been in the matted grasses fed on buffalo manure.

Left in that state, the land could have waited for rain. But with the sod busted, the earth flew into the sky.

The Western droughts went on for a dozen years. Fields became dunes, farms failed, towns died. "The land would wear just so much architecture and society," Jonathan Raban writes in *Bad Land,* "and no more."[71] In Oklahoma the transported Cherokees had turned previously undesirable land into a thriving collective republic, only to have it broken up into lots and taken from them piecemeal in the 1890s. Incoming white settlers, equipped with steam and gasoline tractors, then overdrew Nature's account in one generation. After that the "Okies" too had to make a mass removal—in jalopies down Route 66 to California. A few lines from John Steinbeck's novel *The Grapes of Wrath* amount to a terse history of the West: "Grampa took up the land, and he had to kill the Indians and drive them away. And Pa was born here, and he killed weeds and snakes. Then a bad year came and he had to borrow. . . . The bank owned the land then."[72]

With the Wall Street Crash of 1929, the boom-and-bust cycle of free-market capitalism yet again produced a panic, this time on a giant scale. Yet the Soviet Union, the Marxist alternative, seemed to be immune from the worldwide slump, or Great Depression. While American factories were idle, Joseph Stalin was turning the primitive empire of the czars into an industrial hive. Western visitors came back repeating what Lincoln Steffens had said in 1919: "I have seen the future and it works."[73]

In fact, they had seen only what they were allowed to see. Just as the American empire had been built at the expense of Indians and blacks, Stalin industrialized by looting and dragooning the peasantry. Offstage were dispossessions, famines, executions and forced-labour camps. Stalin and Hitler may have regarded themselves as opposites on the political spectrum, but like all fanatics, they were much alike—right down to their moustaches and phony names.[74] In both tyrannies, the party became the state. (The main difference was that Hitler had a pact with business, while Russia had no private sector.)

Soviet industrial production tripled during the 1930s—and with full employment.[75] The Russian share of world output rose from 5 to 18 percent. Many drew the obvious conclusion: capitalism was failing; communism worked. In the 1932 presidential elections won by Franklin Delano Roosevelt, a million Americans voted hard left.[76] If capitalism did not reform, it risked being overthrown. There was already a model of reform to follow: the government credit and controls that had worked during the Great War. Money had always been found to make war; why not find it to keep the peace?

So Franklin Roosevelt, a cousin of Theodore and a young colleague of Woodrow Wilson at the 1919 Peace Conference, built on his forerunners' best ideas.[77] The New Deal, announced in his 1932 campaign, regulated capital and put people to work building infrastructure: roads, dams, national parks, public housing. With the *Social Security Act* of 1935, America had the makings of a modern welfare state. The *Indian Reorganization Act* righted some old wrongs and restored a degree of native autonomy.[78] Abroad, Roosevelt renounced gunboat diplomacy (his Good Neighbor Policy), took up Wilson's promise of independence to the Philippines, and avoided war over oil with Mexico.[79] Opposition from diehards grew—FDR was called a "traitor to his class"—but the coming of war quelled the backlash.

❖⟿◉⟿❖

As with the First War, the slide to the Second was set off by a terrorist attack: the firebombing of the German Reichstag (Parliament) on February 27, 1933. It is still moot who was to blame, but Hitler immediately exploited the outrage—jailing opponents, suspending civil liberties and tightening his grip on power.[80] Nazism, said Hitler, was "a doctrine of conflict." Germans were told that their nation had no choice but to expand or die. As the novelist Thomas Mann wrote in a letter: "If the idea of war, as an aim in itself, disappeared, the National Socialist [Nazi] system would be . . . utterly senseless."[81]

With its notion that "Aryans" were the Chosen Race, its Führer-worship and its promise of a Thousand-Year Reich, Nazism was not so much a political party as a crisis cult. "The Germans are under a spell," wrote the young lawyer Sebastian Haffner when he fled to England in the late 1930s. "They live a drugged life in a dream world. They are terribly happy, but terribly demeaned. . . . As long as the spell lasts, there is almost no antidote."[82]

Japan's participation is harder to explain. In the First War she had sided with the Allies; in the Second, under the control of militarists, she unwisely challenged the United States for the Pacific. Japan had no need to invent a kitsch ideology like that of the Nazis. Reigning (though not ruling) over the militarists was a divine emperor of the old school, a Son of the Sun whose dynasty had held the throne since long before the Incas and the Caesars. In a way, Pearl Harbor was the belated fruit of Commodore Perry's attack on Japanese seaports eighty-eight years before: the response of an old empire awakened at gun point by a new.[83]

On August 6 and 9, 1945, the first nuclear weapons used in war exploded above Hiroshima and Nagasaki. Days later, Japan surrendered. More people may have died in the conventional firebombing of Tokyo, yet the first Allied journalists to defy orders and reach the atomic-bomb sites knew straight away that something strange and terrible had happened there.[84] "The atomic bomb's peculiar 'disease' . . . is still snatching away lives," George Weller, one of America's most accomplished and tenacious war correspondents, wrote from Nagasaki a month after the blast: "Men, women and children with no outward marks of injury are dying daily." All dispatches from Weller (who had won a Pulitzer Prize in 1943) were suppressed by American censors.[85] The Australian Peter Burchett, who reached Hiroshima at the same time, managed to get a story out to London's *Daily Express:* "People are still dying, mysteriously and horribly . . . from an unknown something which I can only describe as the atomic plague. . . . Hiroshima does not look like a bombed city. It looks as if a monster steamroller has passed over it."[86]

Man's weapons had outgrown him. History had given the first half of the twentieth century a grim sandwich of hard lessons: two thick slices of war, with communist revolution, capitalist exploitation, economic depression, environmental disaster, fascist nightmare and mass genocide in between. If 12 million people died in the First War, at least 50 million died in the Second.[87] Even the hell of the trenches was trumped when the Nazi death camps were exposed. "There is Auschwitz," wrote the survivor Primo Levi, "so there cannot be God."[88]

8.

The Winds of Fear

Leaders like wars because wars remind people they
need leaders.   —Plato, ca. 400 B.C.

The history of the United States is not the story of tri-
umphant anti-imperial heretics. It is the account of the
power of empire as a way of life, as a way of avoiding the
fundamental challenge of creating a humane and equitable
community or culture.

—William Appleman Williams, 1980[1]

What think you of Terrorism, Mr. Jefferson?

—John Adams, 1813[2]

PROBABLY THE BEST MIND at the 1919 Paris Peace
Conference had belonged to "a very clever, rather ugly"
young member of the British team who was no team
player—the economist John Maynard Keynes.[3] He'd foreseen
that the crippling reparations imposed on Germany would lead
to further conflict, and he'd had the courage (or arrogance) to
resign when his warnings went unheeded. Twenty-five years
later, as the Great War's sequel came to an end, Keynes was in

demand. If the world didn't want more Nazis and Bolsheviks, something had to be done to prevent mass unemployment and poverty.

Keynes's ideas for smoothing out the boom-bust ride of free markets had already influenced the New Deal, and his *General Theory of Employment, Interest and Money* (1936) is still widely regarded as the twentieth century's most important work of economic thought. Simply put, Keynesianism argues that governments should tax during the good times and spend during the bad. It doesn't always work and is subject to temptations and abuses, but no one has ever had a better idea. Even Richard Nixon would proclaim himself a Keynesian, though with fingers characteristically crossed behind his back.[4]

In July 1944 Roosevelt invited Keynes to a three-week conference at Bretton Woods, New Hampshire, to plan the postwar economic order.[5] From these meetings—and others among the Allies—emerged the United Nations, the World Bank and the International Monetary Fund. The latter institutions were intended to act like national treasuries at the world level: as counterweights and stabilizers of the market cycle. Three years later the United States and other countries agreed on the Marshall Plan for economic reconstruction, especially in war-torn Germany and Japan. The big mistake of 1919 was not repeated: instead of trying to bleed the vanquished for their sins, the Allies helped them rejoin the world economy.

In financial terms, the "Allies" meant the United States. America had emerged from the war with no damage on its home turf, and an industrial capacity greater than the rest of the world's put together.[6] The war economy had shown that planning worked, that government provision of jobs and basic needs could eliminate the underclass. Keynes had found a balance between capitalism and socialism. Even Britain—bombed, broke and rationed—saw a steady improvement in nutrition and health throughout the war and a narrowing gap between rich and poor.[7] Almost all western democracies used their wartime experience to build modern welfare states along Keynesian lines in the 1940s and 1950s.

This was the high-water mark of American prestige, the moment at which the United States, admired for bravery in war and generosity in peace, eclipsed Britain as world leader.[8] In those few charmed years between the end of the World War and the beginning of the Cold War, America was seen to be pragmatic, sophisticated and engaged. America did business with Russia, allowed the Japanese emperor (shorn of empire and godhood) to keep his throne, and installed a stable German republic on the western side of the line across Europe which Churchill dubbed the Iron Curtain.

The dismantling of Britain's empire soon began, the British consoling themselves with the "special relationship" they thought they enjoyed with their successor.[9] This warm, hazy and one-sided illusion (few Americans have even heard of it) would lead Tony Blair disastrously astray half a century later.

-⋅≡◦⊂≡⋅-

The Bretton Woods world order was both strengthened and undermined by the Cold War. The threat of Soviet and Chinese communism ensured that reconstruction funds for Germany, Italy and Japan did not dry up too soon. And within the western democracies, capitalism was obliged to do what it does best: compete with the rival product. So big business, especially in Europe, learned to get along with big government—with redistributive taxation and "socialist" programs such as national health care, today a cornerstone of life in every advanced country except the United States. The result was a generation of prosperity.

For a while it looked as though the "developing" countries (or Third World) would also benefit. If something like the Marshall Plan had been extended to the poorest regions of the planet—as seemed likely for a while—the world might be a very different place today. But the rivalry between the power blocs soon took the form of an arms race, as the United States and the U.S.S.R. built arsenals of nuclear weapons vastly more powerful than those dropped on Japan.[10] To settle their quarrel over how life should be lived, both sides made it clear that they were willing to destroy all life on Earth. The stand-off (compared to two men knee-deep in gasoline, each with a lighter in his hand) was known as MAD: Mutually Assured Destruction. Yet it doesn't really help to call the cold warriors or even the Nazis "madmen"—for such language suggests that these events were anomalies from which we can learn nothing. The unsavoury truth is that they stem from common human flaws that grew uncommonly dangerous through technology, culture and circumstance.

Other civilizations had feared that angry gods might end their world, but never before had men held the means to do it themselves. The social, political and psychological costs were incalculable: paranoia, nihilism, escapism and mysticism spread like toadstools beneath the overcast. Charlatans, extremists and the weapons trade thrived in the atmosphere of doom. General Douglas MacArthur, whose long career began in the Philippines and ended in Korea, had this to say in 1951: "Our country is now geared to an arms economy which was bred in an artificially induced psychosis of war hysteria and nurtured upon an incessant propaganda of fear."[11]

The most brilliant critique of the atomic age was a dark comedy, Stanley Kubrick's *Dr. Strangelove, or How I Learned to Stop Worrying and Love the Bomb.*[12] Non-Americans who saw the film may have thought the script absurd: Who could credit a rogue U.S. general setting off Armageddon because he believes that adding fluoride to drinking water is an "international Communist conspiracy to sap and impurify all of our precious bodily fluids"?[13] But in truth, many American extremists of the time did believe exactly that, as Richard Hofstadter showed in his 1963 essay "The Paranoid Style in American Politics." Among similar ideas touted by the likes of Senator Joseph McCarthy and the John Birch Society were these: that the Marshall Plan had served "the world policy of the Kremlin"; that the Supreme Court was "one of the most important agencies of Communism"; that President Eisenhower (a Republican and war hero) was "a dedicated, conscious agent of the Communist conspiracy"; and that a gun-control measure proposed after the shooting of President Kennedy was a plot to make the United States "part of one world socialist government."[14]

In most countries, thinking of this sort is confined to a few harmless cranks. The exceptions—places where the cranks are too many to be harmless—tend to be ethnically polarized backwaters, such as Northern Ireland and apartheid South Africa, or nations in trauma such as Germany after the First World War. Yet such thinking is widespread in America, part of a circle of beliefs including anti-Darwinism, anti-intellectualism and the neo-Manichaean view that Americans are God's Chosen beset by satanic enemies—whether heathen Indians in the seventeenth century or an "axis of evil" in the twenty-first.

The United States has been modern history's big winner— the culmination of the five-century Columbian Age—so why do many Americans exhibit a mindset typical of losers? One answer is that the frontier culture descends from the Puritans who lost the English Civil War and from the equally beleaguered "Scots-Irish" Presbyterians who forsook their role as British colonial pawns in Ulster for the American colonies in the eighteenth century. In his amusing yet serious book *Deer Hunting with Jesus,* Joe Bageant (himself a gun owner of Scots-Irish background) argues that "Scots-Irish Calvinist values all but guarantee anger and desire for vengeance against what is perceived as elite authority."[15] Isolated, unschooled, messianic in their thinking, threatened by the Establishment's (sometimes) enlightened policies towards Indians and blacks, the frontier folk came to see themselves as victims. Of all white Americans, they worked the hardest and ran the highest risks, yet the profits flowed to the big cities in the East. Caught between the central power and the outlying "savage," they feared the loss of their precarious gains to the network of governance dogging their heels across the continent.

Barry Goldwater, the 1964 Republican presidential candidate, once said, "This country would be better off if we could just saw off the Eastern Seaboard and let it float out to sea."[16] Such a statement from a major politician in any other country would be unthinkable. It exposes not only the mental desert of the hinterland but the rift between what we might call Backwoods America—descended from the frontier—and Enlightenment America, descended from the likes of Benjamin Franklin and Thomas Jefferson. These two subcultures interpenetrate (as they always have), the friction between them feeding the polarity and starving the middle ground. Backwoods America clings to its fundamentalism and its firearms because they are touchstones of the pioneering myth, of an autonomy that has slipped from the small man's grasp. During the Cold War, many such Americans felt newly empowered by righteous might against the godless Soviet horde. They became, as it were, Afrikaners with atomic weapons—locked in their ethnic bunker, armed with Jehovah's wrath and with his fires.

Consider these two quotations:

> Secret and systematic means have been adopted and pursued, with zeal and activity, by wicked and artful men, in foreign countries, to undermine the foundations of [our religion] and thus to deprive the world of its benign influence on society. . . . These impious conspirators and philosophists have completely effected their purposes in a large part of Europe.

> How can we account for our present situation unless we believe that men . . . are concerting to deliver us to disaster? This must be the product of a great conspiracy, a conspiracy on a scale so immense as to dwarf any previous such venture in the history of man. A conspiracy so black that, when it is finally exposed, its principals shall be forever deserving of the maledictions of all honest men.

One of the above was said by Senator Joseph McCarthy in 1951 as he pursued his communist witchhunt. The other comes from a Massachusetts sermon preached in 1798. Readers may be able to tell which is which by the diction, but not, I think, by the content.[17]

Backwoods America not only fears outsiders but has always needed them to define itself, to make the parochial central, to sustain an archaic worldview rooted in a biblical apocalypse it both dreads and desires. This America also, paradoxically, serves the needs of a centralized secular power, famously called by Eisenhower the "military-industrial complex"—the love match of capital and conquest first brokered during the Civil War.[18] It is no accident that the "wild" Indian of the West is attacked soon after the rebel South is vanquished; that the communist bogeyman appears soon after the last Indian is confined on a reservation; that the Muslim fanatic is inflated to the level of a worldwide conspiracy soon after the Red Menace gives up and starts dining at the Moscow McDonald's. "Evangelicals have substituted Islam for the Soviet Union," a leading evangelical admitted in 2003. "The Muslims have become the modern-day equivalent of the Evil Empire."[19]

The Third World War has been fought in the Third World.[20] The hydrogen bombs haven't killed us yet, but for billions they killed the future. The warmongers were sane enough to stop short of bombing each other (though they came close during the Cuban Missile Crisis), confining themselves to bombing each other's non-white allies by conventional means, including napalm and chemicals.[21] Since 1950 some thirty countries have been bombed and invaded by the United States, the U.S.S.R. or China—in that order of activity, with the United States far ahead.

The military historian John Keegan pointed out (in 1989) that the nations which had fought the Second World War learned "that the costs of war exceeded its rewards" in proportion to their losses. The United States, with fewer than three hundred thousand battle deaths and an untouched mainland, was "the least damaged and most amply rewarded."[22] The

Soviet Union, which lost 7 million troops and as many civilians, bore the brunt. America, Keegan concluded, was the most ready among the Second War's winners to fight new wars; Russia, for all its bluster, was one of the least.[23]

In Korea some fifty-four thousand Americans died, and in Vietnam, nearly sixty thousand.[24] The number of local people killed in those wars cannot be accurately known, but it was certainly many millions; mid-range estimates are 2 and 3 million, respectively. As in the frontier wars, the Philippines, and the Middle East today, non-white life was cheap. The comedian Dick Gregory summed it up: "What we're doing in Vietnam is using the black man to kill the yellow man so the white man can keep the land he took from the red man."[25]

For most of its forty years—if we assume it ended with the Russian withdrawal from Afghanistan in 1989—the Third World War was a stalemate. In Indochina the Americans lost, and in Central Asia so did the Soviets. The hidden toll was the squandering of the world's hope and treasure and the strengthening of the worst elements—warlords, weapon dealers, fanatics, profiteers—in many countries, including the big two. Military budgets spun out of control, absorbing more and more of the wealth of the postwar boom. Funds for developing countries failed to keep up with promises or even with population. The sideshow of the Space Race—intended to persuade the enemy that the missiles really worked and the public that missiles could be fun—added to the cost. In the long run, the capitalist superpower was able to outspend the communist one, and to do so without beggaring too large a sector of its citizenry. But both powers, especially the United States, lived high by exploiting an offshore "underclass" in the Third World.

⋆⇒◯⇐⋆

At the start of this book, I discussed the two main types of empire: centralized and tribute (also called territorial and hegemonic). The ancient New World provides a textbook example of each: the centralized Inca Empire of Peru, and the tribute network of quasi-independent states dominated by the Aztecs of highland Mexico. By the early twentieth century, all the European empires had become the centralized kind, with formal systems of law, education, health, public works and (in some cases) citizenship extended to their colonial subjects.[26]

When the United States took the Philippines from Spain, it acquired this set of imperial obligations. It soon found that unless there is a strong source of colonial revenue or good prospects for white settlement, such an empire can be more trouble than it's worth. This realization, along with the collapse of China's "illimitable" market, influenced America's decision to get out of the overseas empire business in the 1930s.

Much the same calculation lay behind the breakup of the European empires after the Second World War. Some territories were let go reluctantly, but most were freed because liabilities were growing faster than returns. The inherent contradiction between democracy at home and dominion abroad also ensured that the age of formal empires was done: there could be no such thing as an "imperialism of liberty."

Yet both Cold War superpowers needed worldwide economic empires to pay for their military machines and home prosperity. So they opted for the other, cruder type of imperialism, where quasi-independent vassal states are dominated and milked of their surplus through compliant local elites. Both Washington and Moscow reinvented the Aztec Empire.[27] Like the Aztecs (and earlier hegemons such as Sparta and the

Mongols), the superpowers overthrew baulky regimes, installed puppets, exploited labour and resources, yet shouldered no obligations for the welfare of the people indirectly under their control. In most cases the local ruler was a loathsome dictator, propped up on the principle that "he may be a sonofabitch, but he's *our* sonofabitch." One example of the breed was Saddam Hussein, in the days when President Reagan's envoy, Donald Rumsfeld, was shaking his hand.[28]

President John F. Kennedy had dressed this new imperialism in frontier rhetoric, making it sound altruistic, complete with an echo of Kipling: "Our frontiers today are on every continent. . . . Only the United States . . . bears this kind of burden."[29] Inside the active theatres of war, puppet regimes were pressed, as in Vietnam or Afghanistan, to "request" military help; outside, order was kept by coups d'état. Of the coups engineered by America, the most notorious—because they overthrew freely elected governments—were those ousting Mohammad Mussadegh in Iran (1953), Jacobo Arbenz in Guatemala (1954) and Salvador Allende in Chile (1973), condemning those countries to years of state terror, torture and, in Guatemala, one of the vilest civil wars of modern times.[30] In the Soviet sphere, democratic governments never had much chance to get elected in the first place, but reformers such as Imre Nagy in Hungary (1956) and Alexander Dubček in Czechoslovakia (1968) were ruthlessly toppled.

While the United States quashed freedom abroad, it remained (unlike the Soviet Union) a relatively free society at home. However, the American left was no more immune than the right from the old Puritan ague of extremism. By disrupting the 1968 Democratic Convention, by the terrorism of the Weathermen and other outrages, left-wing radicals handed the White House to Richard Nixon in 1968, albeit by less than 1 percent of the popular vote.

⁌⟩═◉═⟨⁌

By the time Richard Nixon resigned in disgrace in 1974, a majority of Americans said they had lost confidence in both business and government. A Harris Poll found that "65% of Americans oppose military aid abroad because they feel it allows dictatorships to maintain control."[31] Many had forsaken the view that the fight against communism justified any means. Nixon's successor, Jimmy Carter, the best-intentioned if not the most effective president of recent times, edged away from the "sonofabitch" policy, allowing a popular revolt to oust Nicaragua's strongman Anastasio Somoza, a villain from the pages of Gabriel García Márquez.[32]

Carter had the bad luck to hold office during the energy crisis and the Iran hostage affair. Conservative ideologues such as Irving Kristol complained that there was far too much talk "about the need for Americans to tighten their belts . . . even resign themselves to an economic philosophy of no growth. It is dangerous and irresponsible."[33] The sweater-clad Carter lost the 1980 election to the B-actor Ronald Reagan, who told folks what they wanted to hear: there was lots of oil and no need to turn down the furnace. It was "still morning in America." (One of Reagan's deeds was to undermine the new Sandinista regime in Nicaragua by fomenting and arming freelance terrorists, based in neighbouring Honduras and funded by the "Iran-Contra Affair.")

The economic problems of the 1970s—"stagflation," falling shares, soaring gold—were caused mainly by the Vietnam War and Middle Eastern politics (just as a similar set of problems has now arisen from the war in Iraq). But the right seized its chance to blame the New Deal and the Keynesian consensus, and to try to undo them. Conservatives wanted a return to laissez-faire capitalism, rebranded as monetarism or "Reaganomics." Their guru was Milton Friedman, a far-right economist at the University of Chicago who revived the ideas of Keynes's old foe Friedrich von Hayek.

Instead of subordinating business to the public good through democratic institutions, as Keynes had argued, Friedman wanted to let the stock market run the world. There was no need to tax and redistribute wealth: so much money would be made that it would "trickle down" to the poor. Greed was good.[34] It was as if the World Wars, the Russian Revolution, the Great Slump and the growing ecological and energy crises had never happened. History didn't matter anymore. What mattered was *belief*: the world had simply to take the preacher's hand and throw away the crutches.

What is remarkable is how easily these shopworn ideas were touted as new. Friedman was not an original thinker but a salesman. His recipe of deregulation, free trade and tax cuts for the wealthy was simply a revival of the late Victorian status quo—the laissez-faire chariot race that had ended in the wreckage of 1914–45. Predictably, the slashing of regulation brought fraud, speculation and crisis. Half a trillion dollars disappeared on Reagan's watch in the Savings and Loan collapse. Equally predictable was a sharp widening of the gap between rich and poor. "Since 1975," says the CIA's *Factbook* on the United States (a source that can hardly be accused of leftist bias), "practically all gains in household income have gone to the top 20% of households." While America's streets filled with beggars, the ratio in salary between a shop-floor worker and a CEO in the top U.S. corporations climbed from thirty-nine to one in 1970 to more than a thousand to one by 1999.[35]

⋯≒◉⊂≒⋯

When the Cold War ended and the Berlin Wall came down, there was talk of a "peace dividend." Many in America and the outside world thought they had seen the last of the *Dr. Strangelove* generals. Military budgets everywhere could be cut back, and the resources they had wasted could be put into improving human lives and tackling the environmental crisis.

In 1989 British prime minister Margaret Thatcher—a good friend of Reagan and Friedman, but no fool—warned the world: "The problem of global climate change is one that affects us all, and action will only be effective if it is taken at the international level. It is no good squabbling over who is responsible or who should pay."[36] Her words are a sad measure of how much time has been lost, how action on the environment has been derailed for twenty years, mainly by Big Oil.

The peace dividend was squandered during the Clinton years, partly because of pressure from Republicans—both in Congress and through the Federal Reserve chairman, Alan Greenspan. Once the communist alternative had given up, the full arrogance of monopoly capitalism returned. With automation and rising population, labour became cheap and easily replaced. Workers could be kept docile—especially on their rights and the environment—if they were always in debt and always worried about losing their jobs.[37] A constant barrage of advertising, new gadgetry and easy credit lured the biddable consumer into peonage. During Bill Clinton's last year as president, banking regulations in place since the 1930s were rashly discarded—clearing the way for the lending boom and mort-gage bubble that burst in 2007–08.[38]

In Jonathan Franzen's 2001 novel, *The Corrections,* a charac-ter who takes a shady job with mobsters in a post-Soviet Baltic republic is "struck by the broad similarities between black-market Lithuania and free-market America. In both countries, wealth was concentrated into the hands of a few; any meaningful distinction between private and public sectors had disappeared; captains of commerce lived in a ceaseless anxiety that drove them to expand their empires ruthlessly; ordinary citizens lived in ceaseless fear of being fired."[39] What made monetarism seem to work in the United States was not so much the "free market" touted by Friedman as de facto protectionism against foreign competitors and, above all, "military Keynesianism"—a steep increase in weapons spending under Reagan and both of the Bushes.[40] Unlike genuine Keynesianism, in which public money, stored up in good times, is spent during bad times on education, health, housing and other labour-intensive proj-ects of lasting worth, *military* Keynesianism pours taxpayers' money down missile silos, feeding only the military-industrial complex.

While the United States, through the International Monetary Fund and the World Bank, has been imposing free markets and "small government" on other nations, it has borne little resemblance to an open market itself. In the form of service-men's benefits and pensions, America runs a generous welfare state. But only for the military. The dearth of such programs in civilian life ensures a steady supply of cannon fodder from city ghettoes and struggling farms. So many American jobs depend on defence spending that the military machine has a ready-made constituency at election time.

Corporations such as General Motors, Chrysler and Boeing do so much military business on easy terms that they are, in effect, state-subsidized industries. Newer military contractors have burgeoned since 2001, supplying U.S. forces with everything from gasoline to mercenaries. Such firms—which include Halliburton (run by Dick Cheney before he became vice-president and in which he retains large holdings) and Blackwater—feed so exclusively on government money that they amount to state-*owned* industries, except that their well-paid executives and investors are entirely unaccountable to the electorate. The citizen bears the cost but has no control; it is the worst of both worlds. Halliburton has even moved its headquarters to the tax haven of Dubai.[41]

Republicans are fond of attacking "tax-and-spend" Democrats. Recent Republican administrations should be called "spend-and-borrow"—because they are taxing the future instead of the rich. George W. Bush has repeated Reagan's policies even more recklessly, pushing for colossal tax cuts in the midst of a war now costing $150 billion a year. "Our Congress has been hijacked by corporate America and its enforcer, the imperial military machine," wrote the acerbic novelist Gore Vidal in 2002.[42] In 2003 the conservative *Financial Times* of London agreed: "On the management of fiscal policy, the lunatics are now in charge of the asylum."[43]

It seems to be the unspoken goal of the neoconservatives to beggar the public purse in order to wreck social spending and leave a mess for Democratic or moderate Republican successors.[44] Certainly, it is a Friedmanite article of faith that the state should spend only on law enforcement and defence. If such policy continues, the United States will become like a Third World dictatorship where the military is the only effective institution. Or not even that—if the nation's right of force is sold off to "contractors" and mercenaries.

⁕⇒�〇⇐⁕

The worldwide spread of free-trade agreements, known as globalization, is the modern version of the nineteenth-century World Market dominated by the British. Yet when Queen Victoria died in 1901, the world economy—a rough index of the human load on natural systems, on earth, air, water, fisheries, forests and minerals—was only one-fiftieth (or 2 percent) of what it is today. Monetarism's great fallacy is to assume that the world is infinite and growth can therefore be endless. It takes no account of human and environmental costs or of long-term limits. Deregulation is just what it says it is: a free-for-all to grab the most in the shortest time. Globalization is a feeding frenzy. Its "efficiency" is measured only in the short term and by criteria that ignore depletion, pollution, waste disposal, social harmony and public health. The supposed "rights" of capital trump those of sovereignty, ecology, labour—and future generations. The economy has become a tyranny. Unless trade agreements include tough environmental and labour standards (as they do to some extent within the European Union), capital will always seek out the dirtiest river and the most exploitable human being.

The quest for easy money is as old as money itself. But it is hardly surprising that the delusion of endless growth and the denial of natural limits have taken their most virulent form in the United States—in the culture forged on the frontier. "The very essence of the frontier experience," writes the naturalist Tim Flannery, "is to exploit [resources] as quickly as possible, then move on."[45] The world is less a home in which to live than a treasury to ransack, and the loot needn't be shared out fairly or even used wisely, because there will always be more somewhere else. Back in the 1830s, an American explained to Tocqueville why Mississippi steamboats were so flimsily built: "There is a general feeling among us about everything which prevents us aiming at permanence. . . . We are always expecting an improvement."[46] Because the United States, alone of nations, was formed by both the Industrial Revolution and an ever-receding frontier, the expectation of growth and throwaway plenty has become a cultural norm.

When John Steinbeck made a midlife road trip across America with his dog Charley more than forty years ago, he was appalled by the middens he saw along his way: "American cities are like badger holes, ringed with trash," he wrote. "In this, if in no other way, we can see the wild and reckless exuberance of our production . . . chemical wastes in the rivers, metal wastes everywhere, and the atomic wastes buried deep in the earth or sunk in the sea."[47] (Then, most evenings, Steinbeck cooked his dinner in a throw-away aluminum frying pan to save himself the bother of washing dishes on the road.)

There was a time when those hoping to live the American dream had to move to America to do so. Now the dream has Americanized the world. As Walter LaFeber wrote of the Open Door Policy of the late nineteenth century: "Capitalism, like Christianity, was a religion that would not keep. It had to be expanded constantly, imposed if necessary."[48] The new form of the old myth of unending plenty is that everyone will be able to *live* like Americans if they *think* like Americans. No matter where they are and how downtrodden they may be, if they convert to the faith of market fundamentalism they will become consumers of goods and enjoyers of democracy. This is the Big

Lie of our times.[49] While its spell lasts, a few will get obscenely rich, others will thrive as middlemen, and the rest will either scrape by or starve. We can already see this happening: after a generation of Friedmanite trade policy, there are a thousand billionaires on Earth, yet 2 billion people—one-third of mankind—live in the deepest poverty.

China has embraced the new economics, yet shows few signs of becoming the free society that, according to Friedman's dogma, free markets will produce. In *The Shock Doctrine,* Naomi Klein persuasively argues that the opposite has more often been the case: monetarism thrives in dictatorships and sweat-shop tyrannies. Despite phenomenal growth, "Communist" China now has no universal health care, and 700 million Chinese (more than half the population) earn less than two dollars a day. Numbers in India, a liberal democracy, are similar. What kind of progress is this? Did America throw off the divine right of kings only to enthrone, worldwide, a divine right of things?

The abject poor now outnumber the whole of mankind when Queen Victoria died. In one century, the world has become a small and crowded place. All frontiers have long been overrun. The climate itself is already buckling under our demand. Even if the current economic myth were to work as advertised and enrich us all, before 6 billion (soon to be 9 billion) human beings could become consumers on anything like an American scale, the Earth would be unable to support them.

⤙⟹⟸⤚

But for Bill Clinton's dishonourable discharge on an intern's dress, the 2000 election might not have been close enough for George W. Bush to steal.[50] The world then watched in disbelief

as the United States failed to carry out a thorough recount—
something that would have been done as a matter of course in
any other democracy.[51]

While many people had been worrying about the planet,
America's war profiteers had been wondering how to keep the
lucrative game of militarism on the go without the Russians.
They needed a new enemy, and for a while they auditioned
China for the role. A Defense Planning Guidance document
written early in 1992, while George H. Bush was president and
Dick Cheney secretary of defence, argued that the United States
should achieve such a lead in weaponry and military capability
that it would be unassailable. This doctrine, known as "full-
spectrum dominance," was a demand for a blank cheque.[52] It
was also life support for Ronald Reagan's (and later George W.
Bush's) unworkable Star Wars fantasy—a "missile shield" that
would allow America to shoot without being shot at, a modern
version of shooting Indians from the train.[53]

In 1997 Dick Cheney, Jeb Bush (George W.'s brother),
William Kristol (son of conservative ideologue Irving) and others who would surface in or near the future Bush regime
founded what they called the Project for a New American
Century. Their opening statement called for "an international
order friendly to our security [and] our prosperity." In January
1998 the group sent a letter to President Clinton, urging him to
"aim, above all, at the removal of Saddam Hussein's regime from
power."[54] The letter's signatories included Donald Rumsfeld,
Paul Wolfowitz and Richard Perle, all of whom became leading
members of Bush's staff. Most had longstanding ties, director-
ships and holdings in the weapons, military supply and oil
businesses—as did Cheney (the former CEO of Halliburton) and
Condoleezza Rice (a former Chevron executive).[55] An oil tanker

called the *Condoleezza Rice* had to be quietly renamed when Rice went on the public payroll.

On September 11, 2001, a new, though not unknown, enemy took three thousand lives on American soil.[56] Of the nineteen hijackers, fifteen were Saudi Arabians and most had been living and training in the United States for years. However, there was little doubt they had links to the Saudi terrorist Osama bin Laden and that his organization, al Qaeda, was training in Afghanistan, a theocratic dictatorship ruled by the Taliban (at one time fostered by the Americans as anti-Soviet "freedom fighters"). The subsequent war on that country was therefore seen by many world leaders as legitimate, or at least tolerable.

The war against Iraq in the spring of 2003 had no such legitimacy. None of the September 11 terrorists was an Iraqi, nor was there any evidence that al Qaeda ever had ties to Saddam Hussein's regime. There was also no evidence that Iraq still held "weapons of mass destruction"—a shorthand cliché for nuclear or chemical weapons in the wrong hands. (Of course, the nations that have by far the most WMD are the United States, its allies and the former Soviet Union.) As recently as February 2001, General Colin Powell had said that the sanctions applied since the Gulf War against Saddam Hussein "have worked. He has not developed any significant capability with respect to weapons of mass destruction."[57]

Two years later, at a televised meeting of the United Nations, Powell (then secretary of state) was obliged to argue exactly the opposite. He did not make his case: the best evidence he presented was weak; the worst was already known to be false.[58] Furthermore, Hans Blix, the United Nations weapons inspector, was already achieving real disarmament by destroying Iraq's Scud missiles.[59]

While Washington would settle for nothing less than conquest in Iraq, it pursued a policy of negotiation with North
Korea, a far more dangerous dictatorship with proven nuclear
technology and long-range missiles, but no oil. The last-
minute argument for war—that Saddam Hussein was a vicious
tyrant—was true enough, but so were several of America's close
friends in the Middle East and elsewhere.

The world was dragooned to war on false pretences. Bush
knew it, Powell knew it, informed opinion around the world
knew it, and so did Bush's most pliant ally, British prime minister Tony Blair.[60] Millions protested in the streets of the
world's great cities, including a large demonstration in New
York, where al Qaeda had struck only eighteen months before.

Some recalled that the first Gulf War, started by the first
President Bush, had also been sold on false pretences: an emo-
tional report to the Human Rights Caucus of Congress by a
fifteen-year-old girl, saying that Iraqi troops had torn hundreds of Kuwaiti babies from incubators. This was later
exposed as a lie concocted by a PR firm; the girl, identified only
as "Nayirah," turned out to be the daughter of the Kuwaiti
ambassador to the United States.[61]

-→-=◉⊂=-→-

Let me be clear that I do not subscribe to claims that the George
W. Bush regime might somehow have known in advance about al
Qaeda's plans for September 11, 2001. (Of course, it was known
that al Qaeda and other groups posed a threat, and there are
documents to that effect, nothing more.) Nor do I belittle the
horror and suffering of that day. But there is plenty of evidence
to suggest that, like Austria-Hungary in 1914 and Germany in
1933, those in Washington seeking to advance a militarist

agenda swiftly took advantage of the terrorist outrage to do so. This exploitation of the September 11 attacks is inexcusable.

The banners in the streets saying "No Blood for Oil" were dismissed as cant by Bush and Blair. We now know better. Alan Greenspan, the head banker of the United States government throughout most of Bush's tenure, recently confirmed what the evidence suggested and what Paul Wolfowitz (Rumsfeld's deputy at the time) also admitted in June 2003: the Iraq War, Greenspan said, was "largely about oil."[62] In short: a cabal of weapons dealers and oil profiteers who came to power in the world's mightiest nation by dubious means took advantage of the September 11 attacks to start an unrelated war they had been wanting to wage for years. And Tony Blair helped them do it.

Blair is the one I find hardest to understand. Britain was the former colonial power in Iraq; there were seasoned experts on hand who understood the special dangers of the country and the region. Why did Blair squander his political capital on backing the most extreme policies of the Bush administration—and all for nothing in return? Bush, whose war made oil prices triple, would not even throw Blair a crumb on the issue of climate change because it might "hurt the American economy."

The kindest assumption one can make is that Tony Blair thought he was talking to the America of Franklin Roosevelt, unaware that the heirs of Joseph McCarthy had taken charge. Perhaps, like many Britons, he harboured the naïve idea that America is not really a foreign country—just a bigger, richer England. Clearly he believed in the "special relationship" which he thought London still enjoyed with Washington, and he himself with George Bush. One theory is that he hoped he could use the American alliance to enhance Britain's power within the European Union. Another is that strong religious feelings played a role both in his friendship with Bush and in the conviction that his actions were, as he so often claimed, "the right thing to do." Both theories reveal how deeply British politics have become Americanized in recent years.

Whatever Tony Blair's motives may have been, they had a side effect in which the American right rejoiced: the Iraq War split the European Union, the world's only credible democratic counterweight to American hegemony. If Europe had stood together against the war, the disaster might have been avoided or at least contained.

As everyone now knows, the experts' warnings were fulfilled: the war was won but the peace lost, the entire region destabilized. The consequences to world peace are still unfolding and may yet become more serious. The suffering has far outweighed the benefit of deposing Saddam Hussein: some four thousand Americans dead, perhaps ten times that number of Iraqi battle deaths, more than 150,000 civilian deaths and over 2 million Iraqi refugees driven into exile—a tenth of the country's population.[63]

The damage to human rights and to the moral standing of the United States has been incalculable. Ancient freedoms such as habeas corpus, a foundation of English-speaking democracy for a thousand years, were lightly brushed aside. Since the initial attack on Afghanistan, the Bush regime has violated Geneva Conventions on the treatment of war prisoners that even Nazi Germany observed.[64] Guantánamo Bay (in eastern Cuba, only one hour's flight from Miami) is merely the most visible Gulag in an archipelago of offshore prisons where men and boys have been held without charge, trial or access to lawyers for years. The full extent of the abuses is still unknown, but they certainly include torture, solitary confinement and degradation of the sort that came to light at Abu Ghraib, the infamous prison outside Baghdad.

The methods countenanced in Bush's "war on terror" have given all repressive regimes of both right and left an excuse for their own atrocities. Vladimir Putin sings the antiterrorist song as he leads Russia back to autocracy. The Castro brothers savour the irony that Washington keeps its prison camp in Cuba to escape the reach of U.S. law.[65] Those who stand to gain most from the war on terror are the terrorists themselves. In this sense, writes the cultural historian Morris Berman in *Dark Ages America*, "Rumsfeld, Perle, Abrams, Bush, Cheney, Wolfowitz, Rice [etc.] are bin Laden's comrades in arms." Propaganda about Iraq and terrorism became a self-fulfilling prophecy: "We took a country that was not a terrorist threat and turned it into one."[66]

9.

THE WORLD'S BEST HOPE

Some honest men fear . . . that this Government, the
world's best hope, may by possibility want energy to
preserve itself. I trust not.   —Thomas Jefferson, 1801[1]

As a result of the war, corporations have been enthroned and
an era of corruption in high places will follow, and the money
power of the country will endeavor to prolong its reign by
working upon the prejudices of the people until all wealth is
aggregated in a few hands and the Republic is destroyed.
                                   —Abraham Lincoln, 1864[2]

The real war always has been to keep alive the light of civil-
isation everywhere. . . . The end of the world begins not
with the barbarians at the gate, but with the barbarians at
the highest levels of state.   —Ben Okri, 2003[3]

T HE SO-CALLED WAR ON TERROR will breed only more
terror and more war. The neglect of the world's poor
will lead to chaos. The rape of the environment will
take our civilization to catastrophe. Our only hope, as great
Americans such as Woodrow Wilson and Franklin Roosevelt

understood, is to build a world order in which everyone has a say and shares the rewards. A full belly and a fair hearing won't stop a fanatic, but they will greatly reduce the number who become fanatics.

George Orwell once likened the British nation to a family with the wrong members in charge. In America the "wrong members"—the Bushes, Reagan, Nixon and others who have betrayed America's founding ideals since the days of Andrew Jackson—seem to get hold of the nation about once every third or fourth presidential term, the time it takes for memory to fade and a crook or an incompetent to mature by the glow of nostalgia into a statesman. As Tocqueville foresaw, the great risk in a democracy is that the voters can choose tyranny. Sometimes the enemy of the people is the people. This risk is probably higher in the age of the sound bite, the televangelist, Fox News and the politics of fear than it was in the 1830s. Tocqueville may also be right that "nothing is more opposed to the well-being and the freedom of man than vast empires."[4] Rome was only slightly and briefly democratic; Spain never so. The only precedent for a world empire run by a democracy is Britain—and Britain opted to keep its democracy and let its empire go.

Since the mid-term elections of 2006, there have been encouraging signs that the great machine of American democracy is still capable of repairing itself. In the caucuses and primaries for the 2008 presidential election, the field of candidates was less predictable than it had been in half a century. Turnout was unusually high, especially among the young. Whatever else George W. Bush may have done, he awakened American voters to the importance of taking part. Republicans could choose from a Vietnam War hero, a Mormon millionaire, a Christian fundamentalist, or a maverick libertarian who agreed with many on the left that the terrorist threat to America has been caused by his own nation's foreign policy. Democrats were ready to make history by nominating either a woman or an African American (literally).[5]

The Republicans settled on Senator John McCain, whose forthrightness, courage and military background made him the candidate most likely to draw swing voters. The Democratic contest (still open at the time of writing) was hampered by its embarrassment of riches. In a normal election year, Hillary Clinton's candidacy alone would be remarkable. But the young outsider, Barack Obama, managed to inspire a broad range of voters with what he called (in a book title) the "audacity of hope." His policies did not differ much from Clinton's, but his eloquence, intelligence and liberal record—notably as one of the few senators to vote consistently against the war in Iraq— aroused a national mood for change. Change and hope were soon on every candidate's lips; even those of McCain, whom George W. Bush publicly endorsed, and whose inner circle includes William Kristol and other neoconservative ideologues close to the Bush White House.[6]

The hope so easily aroused will be far less easy to fulfill. Much will depend, as always, on which party carries Congress. Whether it is Backwoods America or Enlightenment America who takes charge, the new leader will inherit the wreckage of the past eight years: wars that seem both unwinnable and inescapable, a ruinous public debt and a financial crisis that may prove to be the worst since the 1930s. Hope may be a virtue—and it can win elections—but hoping for the best instead of learning from the past has often led America astray.

It remains to be seen whether the count in November will be accurate and fair; whether moderation and thought will prevail over extremism and personality; whether the outgoing regime will resist the temptation of exploiting a crisis such as a "terror alert" (real or not) to throw the election its way.[7] The latter possibility is less far-fetched than it may seem. In mid-2004, when George Bush's re-electoral prospects were looking dim, the White House and the Justice Department actually discussed postponing the general election because of the "terrorist threat." Such a thing has never been done in the history of the United States—not even in world wars.[8]

No matter who wins the keys to the White House in 2008, it would be a mistake to think that the outgoing presidency was an aberration and that its like will not be seen again. Politicians such as George Bush and Dick Cheney—who feed on superstition, fear and the worst kind of patriotism—are "grounded in a widespread cultural pattern."[9] Their power base is one half of a polarized nation. Roughly half the electorate may be expected to agree with Katherine Harris, who presided over Florida's voting fiasco in 2000, tried to disenfranchise as many blacks as possible, and later said that "God is the one who chooses our rulers."[10] This is Backwoods America talking—or being talked to (Harris herself is a wealthy banking, fruit and chemical heiress). Enlightenment America is outraged by such statements, which cater to a fundamentalist mindset not vastly different from that of the Taliban, al Qaeda and other extremists whom the "godly man" in the White House vowed to destroy.

In short, a significant part of the United States still belongs to an archaic, aggressive and colonial culture that has drifted a long way from the mainstream of western civilization. If this judgment seems harsh, consider these departures from the modern norm. The United States is the only major western nation

- where the death penalty is still used—only China and Iran outdo America in executions; George Bush alone, while governor of Texas, issued 152 death warrants;[11]
- where one person in 130 is in jail—the world's highest rate of incarceration (about seven times higher than in Canada or Europe);[12]
- where automatic pistols and assault rifles are readily on sale;[13]
- where five out of ten think the Creation myth in the Bible is literally true;
- where only one citizen in eight holds a passport;
- where there is no universal health care (47 million have no coverage).[14]

America also has the widest gap between wealthy and poor, and the lowest direct taxation. Education is locally funded: poor districts get poor schools—another problem first identified by Tocqueville.[15]

⊷⇒◉⇐⊷

In a 2008 opinion poll taken for the Canadian Broadcasting Corporation, 52 percent of those interviewed chose the United States as "the country that stands out as a negative force in the world." (The second choice, Iran, came in at 21 percent.)[16] It is likely that a similar poll taken in Europe, Australia or Latin America would yield similar results. American prestige has never been lower; yet, whether we like it or not, the United States is such a military and economic power that what it does is everyone's business. All of us, Americans and outsiders, must live with this land of paradox: a democracy hobbled by theocracy and plutocracy; a "peace-loving" country at war almost constantly for four hundred years; a nation both well-meaning and rapacious, welcoming and suspicious, devout and materialistic, friendly and fearful, innocent and corrupt, libertarian and repressive, individualistic and conformist, generous and grasping, imperial and parochial, modern and archaic.

We may still hope for progressive American leadership in the world, but we can no longer afford the old twentieth-century habit of depending on it. Repeatedly seduced by atavistic impulses, America has become an unreliable member of the world community.[17] Despite the sorry record of the past eight years, the 2008 elections could still go either way. Too many voters, like the first President Bush, "don't care what the facts are"; too many opt for the fast food of the national myth instead of the sobering nourishment of history—even history so fresh that its dead are not yet cold.

The tragedy of American diplomacy since 1918 has been that the United States *did* learn the hard lessons of world history in the first half of the twentieth century, and then forgot them in the second. Over the same period—especially the last four decades—mankind has begun to grasp that its problems have grown beyond the purely political. The human boom set off by history's Big Bang in 1492 is reaching Nature's bounds. The crops, metals and "free" land of the New World gave western civilization a new lease on life which has lasted five hundred years, the period I have called the Columbian Age. Now the lease is up for renewal on much steeper terms. We are still enjoying the wealthiest times of *all* times, but we are eating into Nature's capital instead of living on her interest, wrecking the very ecosystems on which we depend.[18] The economic "surplus" is in fact an overdraft—mortgaged against the future of all, squandered by the few on luxury and weapons.

If there is to be order, not chaos, in the twenty-first century, we must build a new world order strong enough to manage the ending of the boom and make the best of what the Earth provides. We must opt for quality over quantity, thrift over opulence, right over might, stability instead of reckless change. These aims will be extremely hard to fulfill: they require a new politics, a new economics and a new demographics, all cutting against the grain of human nature. But there is no other choice. As the great British historian Eric Hobsbawm warned more than a decade ago: "The price of failure, that is to say, the alternative to a changed society, is darkness."[19]

Many Americans, from Rachel Carson to Al Gore, have done their best to awaken us to what we face. In the 1970s the United States led the world in environmental standards and protection. But that momentum has since been lost. Government regulation and conservation have been demonized, international cooperation undermined, and the public good abandoned to the despotisms of the market and the military. For the past eight years in particular, the American empire has become the problem, not the solution, a neo-Aztec pyramid of force and greed.

It is one thing to answer the question "What is America?" with such unflattering words. We must also ask if there are any other candidates for the title of "the world's best hope," any better models for how the future might be run. The former Soviet Union seems to be returning to a corrupt authoritarianism, tossing its short-lived liberal democracy on the same midden as its socialist dreams. The rising powers of India and China, who together make up more than a third of the human race, seem locked in the embrace of globalization, repeating the worst mistakes of the Industrial Revolution: dirty industries, exploited workers, reckless urban sprawl. Chinese communism has mutated into a surreal hybrid of dictatorship, state corporatism and chaotic private enterprise.[20]

There is one big, bumbling, yet remarkably successful attempt to find a new way forward: the European Union. For some sixty years now, Europe has grown away from tribalism, fanaticism and militarism, and towards a new commonwealth built not on the threat of war but on its memory. The Union has gelled little by little, expanding from six members to twenty-seven, with others on the waiting list. More than a trading alliance but not quite a federation, this evolving supranational organism now has more people and a bigger economy than the United States.[21]

The Union's political structure is adaptive, pragmatic and uncertain. There is still no formal constitution or unified foreign policy. Per capita income in the richest member nations is ten times higher than in the poorest—but that is partly because the EU is admitting the ruins of the Warsaw Pact and the Balkans. New members with weak economies and civic standards are being upgraded as they join what began as a rich man's club. The European Union seems able—or at least willing—to refit whole countries, while the United States can barely restore New Orleans.

Europe still has considerable sins: marginalized "guest" workers, exploitive investment in the Third World and unsustainable levels of consumption. That said, energy use per head is half that of the United States and Canada, while the average standard of living is about the same.[22] A better balance has been struck between the interests of capital, labour and the environment than in any other trading bloc. The greatest threat to the European experiment is Americanization: Friedmanite pressure to weaken social and environmental laws in the name of business "efficiency." So far the Union is standing its ground. As Mark Schapiro wrote in *Harper's,* "Europe is now compelling other nations' manufacturers to conform to regulations that are far more protective of people's health than those in the United States. Europe has emerged not only as the world's leading economic power but also as one of its moral leaders. Those roles were once filled by the United States."[23]

Early in 2008, the European Union announced a plan to spend €60 billion (some $90 billion) each year for twelve years to reduce carbon emissions at least 20 percent by 2020.[24] This reduction still may not be enough—especially if diehards such as the United States and Canada fail to join in—but it is leadership. If carried through, the Europeans' financial commitment to fighting climate change will rival what America spends fighting the enemies it has made in Iraq.

Like a rehabilitated criminal, Europe seems to have confronted the grim realities of its own past. The peace within the Union since 1945 offers hope that peoples, like individuals, can learn from their mistakes. Nations who had been killing one another for centuries are now at work on a shared future. If the human race as a whole is to avoid a worldwide catastrophe caused by its own desires, fears and delusions, it will do so along such lines.

The Columbian Age was built on colonial attitudes: on taming the wilderness, civilizing the savage, and the American dream of endless plenty. Now there is nothing left to colonize.[25] Half a millennium of expansion has run out of room. Mankind will either share the Earth or fight over it—a war nobody can win. For civilization to continue, we must civilize ourselves. America, which helped set the Europeans on their new path half a century ago, must now examine its own record—the facts, not the myths—and free itself from the potent yet potentially fatal mix of forces that created its nation, its empire, and the modern world.

Afterword

[America] goes not abroad in search of monsters to
destroy. She is the well-wisher to the freedom and
independence of all.   —John Quincy Adams, July 4, 1821[1]

The hardening of lines, the embrace of fundamentalism
and tribe, dooms us all.   —Barack Obama, 2004[2]

SINCE THIS BOOK WENT TO BED (as printers say) about
a year ago, there have been two remarkable transformations in the political life of America and the world.
First, the thirty-year pyramid of debt, folly and fraud built up
by the worshippers of Milton Friedman has toppled down upon
us—a result that should have surprised nobody with even a
passing knowledge of history and human nature.

Second—and partly because of the first—the United States has
elected Barack Obama, arguably the brightest star to appear in the
world's political sky since Mikhail Gorbachev. Like Gorbachev,
who presided over the fall of the Soviet empire, Obama has
undertaken the colossal task of reforming a corrupt and crippled
system. Unlike Gorbachev, Obama was freely elected after a
gruelling campaign, an outcome which many believe confirms

the health of the American political process and offers hope that lasting change may be achieved without disaster.

Obama's election revived one of the nation's most cherished yet most seldom realized ideals: that by hard work, brilliance and integrity a worthy underdog can reach the very top. Few such underdogs have done so since Abraham Lincoln famously rose from log cabin to White House. As Lincoln himself foretold, the "money power of the country" usually manages "to prolong its reign by working on the prejudices of the people." But Obama went one better than Lincoln, and in a way that crowned Lincoln's own accomplishment. Although Barack Obama's African heritage is Kenyan, his self-definition as a black American—explored frankly and eloquently in his 1995 book *Dreams from My Father*—gave great symbolic force to his electoral triumph.

I do not mean to rain on this parade, but while such symbols are highly important they do not, by themselves, slay the worm of racism; and to dwell too much on the genetic side of Obama's victory is to risk diminishing other aspects of his achievement, not least his political liberalism, environmental awareness and skill at inspiring others across entrenched lines. While for many Americans the mere presence of a black family in the White House may wash away the moral stain of slavery and the bloodstains of the Civil War, for the outside world the colour of Barack Obama's skin is nowhere near as important as the content of his policies. Nor is the United States the only nation to have chosen one of the chronically oppressed for top office: Benjamin Disraeli, who served many years as British prime minister in Victorian times, was of Jewish immigrant heritage; Mexico's most revered president, Benito Juárez, was a native Zapotec; and since 2005 an indigenous Aymara, Evo Morales

Ayma, has led Bolivia—the first native American to do so since the Spanish conquest of the Inca Empire.

As Canadians also know to our shame, it is a very hard thing for a nation built by incomers to acknowledge, let alone rectify, the moral insecurity of its title to the land. That task has scarcely begun anywhere in North America. Even Barack Obama, who in his inaugural address made a point of being inclusive toward immigrant races and cultures, forgot to mention the first Americans—a surprising oversight from one who is not only half black but part Cherokee.

⋯⊸⊜⊷⋯

Millions flocked to the inauguration in Washington; hundreds of millions watched from their homes around the world. Emotion ran high: a blend of hope and relief, inspiration and *schadenfreude*. Hello to President Obama also meant good riddance to President Bush who, while outwardly gracious in departure, had used his last weeks of power before the January handover to pursue his assault on the environment with a flurry of executive decrees. Many in the throng booed loudly whenever the outgoing president was mentioned by name, and the BBC World News showed Dick Cheney (who had hurt his back) scuttling away from the halls of power in a wheelchair like a superannuated Dr. Strangelove, black leather gloves and all.

After some very dark years, American democracy has done exactly what it *had* to do to begin renewing itself at home and redeeming itself abroad. The nation has chosen a president who promises to return the United States to the political centre and to internationalism, and who seems to have the political and intellectual gifts to fulfill this promise, insofar as anyone can under the present circumstances. Yet it's only prudent to keep this outcome in perspective: to bear in mind why change became so urgent, and how, despite that urgency, so many Americans still rallied to the old banners of God, guns and glory during the campaign. Despite the appalling record of the Bush years, the numerous mistakes of the Republican campaign and the deftness of the winning candidate, the popular vote was still alarmingly close: a spread of only 6 percent. And it would have been much closer than *that* without the financial tailspin before election day; close enough, perhaps, for the Republicans to win, or to steal.

Throughout the electoral campaign the cultural rift between Backwoods America—descended from the Puritans and the frontier hinterland—and Enlightenment America—descended from the intellectual tradition of the Founding Fathers—was thrown into sharp relief. While Barack Obama acknowledged the Iraq War as a colossal blunder, John McCain's running mate, Sarah Palin, called it "a task from God." Some Republicans even sank to exploiting Obama's middle name, Hussein, implying he was a closet Muslim or somehow akin to the ousted tyrant of Iraq. Others burrowed even deeper into superstition, saying Obama was the Antichrist.

The constituency of the far right has not gone away, nor is it likely to any time soon. The fundamentalist, anti-intellectual strain in America still sways nearly half the electorate. It was probably the overreach and incompetence of the neo-conservatives, as much as their professed ideology, that sank them, thereby opening up sea-room for a change that might otherwise have been unthinkable. In this sense, it took George Walker Bush to elect Barack Hussein Obama.

⋄⇒◉⇐⋄

A democracy such as the United States, which is so dependent on the qualities of its leader that in some ways it resembles an elective monarchy, is indeed lucky that a president has emerged who seems to have what it will take to tackle the domestic and international crises. Moments of great ruin are also chances for great change, and it is here that progressive forces in America and the outside world have pinned their hopes. In these early months of the new government, it's still too soon to know what can and will be done. One thing we can be fairly sure of is that the needs are so pressing, and the expectations so high, that there are bound to be disappointments. Many will recall similar times of hope for change: notably the euphoria less than twenty years ago when the Berlin Wall came down, the Cold War ended and America elected another charismatic Democrat, Bill Clinton, who, partly for reasons of his own making, did not live up to that historic opportunity.

The Obama administration has got off to a good start, helped by a wide Democratic margin in the House, though a smaller one in the Senate. Obama healed the rift in his own party by appointing Hillary Clinton and other "establishment" Democrats to high office. In his choice of advisors and heads of federal agencies, Obama has restored intellectual excellence and science—especially environmental science—to positions of influence. His controversial decision to keep Robert Gates on as defence secretary may prove wise in winding down the Iraq War and finding a fresh approach to Afghanistan: Robert Gates is no Donald Rumsfeld. Obama has announced a phased withdrawal of combat troops from Iraq by August 2010, leaving "support troops" in place until the end of the following year. On his first day in the White House he announced the closure (within a year) of the Guantánamo Bay prison, and in his first address to Congress he underlined that the United States "does not torture."

On the economic front, Obama has self-consciously assumed the mantle of Franklin Delano Roosevelt, naming the first phase of his financial stimulus plan the "American Recovery and Reinvestment Act"—language evoking the National Industrial Recovery Act of 1933, FDR's launching pad for the New Deal. In the 2009 budget presented to Congress— with expenditures of $3.6 trillion, nearly half of which must be borrowed—Obama fulfilled his election promise by announcing that taxes for the wealthiest Americans (those earning more than $250,000 a year) would rise, while taxes for the other 95 percent of taxpayers would be cut. Large sums have been allotted to public works, health care and education. To help pay for these initiatives, Obama proposed reining in extravagances such as farm subsidies and weapon systems, vowing to cut the federal deficit in half within four years.

Around the world there has been an "Obama Effect" as governments trying to deal with environmental and social crises— especially climate change, poverty and banking reform—now see an America willing to join instead of hinder their efforts. Most of Bush's firmest allies and fellow travellers—Britain's Blair, Spain's Aznar, Australia's Howard—had already been voted out when Obama came to power; those still standing (among them Canada's Harper) became political dinosaurs with little choice but to adapt or go extinct. The neo-conservative project now lies everywhere in ruins. The G20 group of leading nations has announced that deregulated hyper-capitalism (also called "Anglo-Saxon" capitalism, after the Reagan-Thatcher axis) is dead, and must be replaced with something resembling the Keynesian consensus of the mid-twentieth century.

I need hardly point out how much the world has changed since the two world wars. That said, their lesson—that the only way forward for civilization is a middle way combining the better features of both socialism and capitalism—is more cogent than ever. Nobody yet knows how serious the financial collapse will prove to be, nor how long it may last. The opinions of the so-called experts who fostered this mess must be treated with the utmost skepticism. As Adam Smith noted long ago, "money is belief." When that collective illusion is abused, prosperity vanishes almost as quickly as fraudsters flee in their private jets to South America.

Of particular concern is the stability of China, whose authoritarian regime has survived mainly by delivering rapid economic growth. If the promise of modernity evaporates in the world's most populous nation, so may the legitimacy of the Beijing elite. The same is true of smaller and less important countries, some of which are already sliding into anarchy. Only time will tell whether an economic recovery will take root within a year or two, as optimists claim, or whether the capital-ist order is now disintegrating as profoundly as the communist order did twenty years ago.

Unlike twenty years ago (let alone sixty years ago) the health of the natural world, which is the sole root of the economic world, is now frailer than at any time since civilization began. Nothing short of a massive international effort, in which the wealthy nations of the European Union and the United States take the lead, will be equal to the threats we have all ignored for too long. After too many lost decades and lost opportunities, the United States should be congratulated for electing a government that has declared itself ready to take up the avoided yet unavoidable task.

But I shall end by underlining something I said in the last chapter of this book: while those of us in the outside world may hope for progressive American leadership, we cannot afford to rely on it. Internationalism, and anything smacking of socialism, are anathema to about half the American people. It is encouraging that during Obama's first hundred days in office, two in every three Americans approved of their new president. But that was during the honeymoon. If history is any guide, the political right will harden and regroup, especially when problems at home and abroad prove expensive or intractable. Many will be as keen to thwart the policies of Barack Obama as they were to undo the work of FDR.

In his inaugural address, President Obama called upon Americans to "set aside childish things. The time has come . . . to choose our better history. . . . Greatness is never a given. It must be earned." These words acknowledge past failings and future burdens; they propose a new skepticism toward the national myth, a return to the hard facts. It behoves us all not merely to salute but to engage with the return of Enlightenment America, and to help it endure—not least for our own good.

Ronald Wright, 2009

Notes

In the notes below, all sources are cited by their short forms only. For full citations, see the Bibliography immediately following this Notes section.

Author's Foreword

---

1. Crèvecoeur, *Letters from an American Farmer.* In the introduction to his 1782 first edition, Crèvecoeur claims to have written most of his text shortly before "the troubles that now convulse the American colonies."
2. From Kerouac, *On the Road,* part 2, chap. 3.
3. Strachey, *Eminent Victorians,* vii.
4. Quoted in Armstrong, *I Have Spoken,* 145–47.
5. Misreading his observations of the stars as he sailed south toward the coast of Venezuela, Columbus came to believe that the Earth was not round but resembled a woman's breast in this area and that he was sailing up the nipple toward Eden. See Fernández-Armesto, *Pathfinders,* 183.
6. See Fernández-Armesto, *Amerigo.* The name *America* first appeared in 1507 on a map of what is now Brazil and soon spread like a rash over the whole of the New World. (An alternative derivation, suggesting the name was coined from that of Richard Ameryck, who backed John Cabot's voyage to Newfoundland in 1497, is intriguing but has little support.)
7. The book was published in the original French and in a definitive English translation by Henry Reeve in 1835.
8. Edited by J.P. Mayer and translated by George Lawrence in 1959.

9. Tocqueville, *Democracy in America*, 298–99.

10. Ibid., 333, 183.

11. He dismissed Canada as a threat, despite bitter fighting between Canada (and its Indian allies) and the United States in 1812–14. He deserves credit for raising the spectre of Mexico, but he also dismissed it (Tocqueville, *Democracy in America*, 195). The United States would be at war with Mexico fourteen years after his visit and with itself in just twice that time.

12. Tocqueville, *Journey to America*, 158. Michael Mann, in his 2007 book *The Dark Side of Democracy*, singles out the Indian Removal as one of the worst cases of ethnic cleansing by a democracy.

13. One early critic, Charles Sainte-Beuve, said Tocqueville had "begun to think before he had begun to learn" (see Tocqueville, *Democracy in America*, xxx, and *Encyclopaedia Britannica* 1911, vol. 26, 1043).

14. The Puritan historians, writes Peter Conn, depicted "themselves and their New World experiment [as] a latter-day chosen people, enacting in the New World Zion the decisive chapters of human history" (Conn, *American Literature*, 24.–25).

15. The demoralized remnants of indigenous societies that Tocqueville saw aroused his pity but did not shake his received and mistaken idea that Indians were nomadic, unable or unwilling to "civilize" and therefore doomed by progress. "Three or four thousand soldiers," he wrote, "drive the wandering races of the aborigines before them; these are followed by the pioneers, who . . . make ready the triumphal procession of civilization across the waste" (Tocqueville, *Democracy in America*, 337). To be fair, at the end of his first book, Tocqueville does protest the treatment of the Five Civilized Tribes—given up by the federal government "as subjects to the legislative tyranny of the states"—but he fails to explore or appreciate the context.

16. Turner explored this cultural mixing in the first version of his thesis. In later years, his idea became less nuanced and more triumphalist, emphasizing "free land" rather than cultural exchange.

17. Turner, *Significance of the Frontier*, 5.
18. Tocqueville, *Democracy in America*, 410.
19. Lapham, "Terror Alerts," 9–11.

Chapter 1 — The New World Order

1. William Henry Drayton (South Carolina's chief justice), "A Charge on the Rise of the American Empire," 1776, quoted in Van Alstyne, *Rising American Empire*, 1.
2. Jefferson, *Notes on the State of Virginia:* "Indeed I tremble for my country when I reflect that God is just: that his justice cannot sleep for ever." Jefferson, himself a slaveholder, was referring here to slavery.
3. Bush, speaking soon after the *Vincennes* accidentally shot down an Iranian airliner (quoted in *Harper's Magazine*, November 1990, 48). The attack happened on July 3, 1988, while Ronald Reagan was still in office and Bush was campaigning.
4. This exact phrase seems to have originated with Woodrow Wilson at the time of the 1919 Paris Peace Conference and the founding of the League of Nations. Others, among them Cecil Rhodes and H.G. Wells, had said something similar.
5. See my Chapter 7 and relevant notes for more on Wilson and the League; MacMillan, *Paris 1919*, gives an excellent account. Isolationists and hardliners, mainly Republican, feared restraints on their national sovereignty. Al Gore (*Assault on Reason*, 174) writes that G.W. Bush "sabotaged" the International Criminal Court (ICC). Bush said he used his veto to protect torture— including simulated drowning, or "waterboarding"—because the bill took "away one of the most valuable tools in the war on ter- ror." See "Bush Vetoes Interrogation Limits," BBC World News, March 9, 2008.
6. Of course, although Rome controlled about one-quarter of the Earth's population, its influence did not reach far beyond Europe, North Africa and the Middle East. It had no contact whatever with

the New World, which was already developing its own empires by that time.

7. Anne-Marie Slaughter of Princeton University wrote in 2007: "Citizens of over ninety nations lost their lives in the attacks. The United Nations passed a unanimous resolution supporting the United States . . . everyone was with us—until we told them, both in word and deed, that if they weren't with us they were against us. The Bush administration announced that we had no use either for treaties or international institutions" ("Diplomacy," in "Undoing Bush: How to Repair Eight Years of Sabotage, Bungling, and Neglect," *Harper's Magazine,* June 2007, 59).

8. When he died in 1506, Columbus still thought he had been to Asia. The matter was not settled until the 1520s, when the survivors of Portuguese explorer Ferdinand Magellan's fleet returned after sailing around the world. See also Chapter 2.

9. Turner, *Significance of the Frontier,* 17.

10. The historian Leland D. Baldwin wrote in 1981: "The narrow conservatism and religious bigotry of the Bible Belt are the creation of forces that emerged from the decaying corpse of Puritanism" (Baldwin, *American Quest,* 50).

11. George Washington, quoted in Van Alstyne, *Rising American Empire,* 1. Also quoted in Turner, *Significance of the Frontier,* 18.

12. Kennedy, quoted in Williams, *Empire,* 198–99.

13. The fighting in North Africa, which went on for many years, was sparked by tribute and piracy in the waters off what is now Libya, then nominally part of the Ottoman Empire.

14. Thomas Jefferson, in his inaugural address in March 1801.

15. Clendinnen, "History Question," 64.

16. Events cascading, in Hannah Arendt's words, "like a Niagara Falls of history" (see Jerome Kohn's introduction to Arendt, *Responsibility and Judgement,* x). In his study of the twentieth century, *Age of Extremes,* Eric Hobsbawm writes: "The destruction of the past, or rather of the social mechanisms that link one's contemporary experience to that of earlier generations, is one of the

most characteristic and eerie phenomena of the late twentieth
century. Most young men and women at the century's end grow up
in a sort of permanent present lacking any organic relation to the
public past of the times they live in. This makes historians, whose
business it is to remember what others forget, more essential at
the end of the second millennium than ever before"(3).

17. See Chapter 5.
18. Falwell, one of the first television preachers and a founder of the
    Moral Majority, died in May 2007. For a short obituary, see BBC
    World News, May 15, 2007. See also my Chapter 4.
19. Gore, *Assault on Reason*, 1, 271.

Chapter 2 — Loot, Labour and Land

1. Adam Smith, *The Wealth of Nations*, 273, 307.
2. Tocqueville, *Democracy in America*, 27–28.
3. Boorstin, *Genius*, 1.
4. Tocqueville, *Journey to America*, 242. "I have often come across
   fortified works which bear evidence of the existence of a people
   who had reached a fairly high state of civilization," Houston
   said. "Whence did that people come? Whither did it vanish?
   There is a mystery there." Houston was a firm believer in the
   equality of races, telling Tocqueville that both Indians and
   blacks were as intelligent as white people, but even so, he thought
   the ruins were more likely the work of Mexicans than of any
   local people.
5. Tocqueville, *Democracy in America*, 27–28.
6. "Modern industry has established the world market, for which
   the discovery of America paved the way. . . . An indispensable
   condition for the establishment of manufacturing industry was
   the accumulation of capital, facilitated by the discovery of America
   and the importation of its precious metals" (Marx and Engels,
   Manifesto, and *La Misère de la philosophie* [Poverty of Philosophy,
   1847], excerpted in Marx, *Karl Marx*, 137–38).

7. The first accurate modern census did not take place until 1801, in England. Among scholars dealing with the more distant past, there are "high counters" and "low counters," and some estimates are absurdly low or high. I have chosen figures in what is now the mainstream. Estimates for the Inca Empire range from 6 million to 32 million. I think it unlikely to have had more than 25 million or fewer than 10 million. Mesoamerica, though smaller in area, was more densely inhabited, as it is today. The parts under Aztec control may have had as many as 25 million, with another 5 to 10 million in the Maya area and autonomous parts of what is now the Mexican republic. For an excellent summary of research and debate in this area, see Lovell, "'Heavy Shadows and Black Night.'"

   The current population of what was the Inca Empire is about 50 million all told, including 32 million for Peru alone, of whom about half are ethnically indigenous and most of the remainder mestizo. (Mestizo is often more a cultural than a genetic term, denoting degrees of westernization.) The current population of what was the Aztec Empire is close to 100 million, almost 30 million of whom live in greater Mexico City.

8. Lovell, "'Heavy Shadows and Black Night,'" 426.

9. These calculations are based on reckoning the mid-1700s as the start of the Industrial Revolution, though it didn't gather full steam for about another century. I discussed civilization as an "experiment" and assessed its risks in my previous book, *A Short History of Progress*.

10. Civilizations "are large, complex societies based on the domestication of plants, animals, and human beings. [They] vary in their makeup but typically have towns, cities, governments, social classes, and specialized professions" (Wright, *A Short History of Progress*, 32–33).

11. Until a few years ago, archaeologists thought that American civilizations, including the Peruvian, did not get under way until about 2000 B.C. However, dramatic findings at Caral, Huaricanga

and other coastal sites north of Lima have shown that cities with monumental architecture had arisen there by five thousand years ago or even earlier—as in the Middle East. See also note 16, below.

12. There were a few fleeting contacts (by Viking, Polynesian, Peruvian and perhaps Asian seafarers) between the Western Hemisphere's initial peopling and 1492, but it is clear from linguistics, plant biology and epidemiology that these interactions were not significant in the development of civilization there.

13. All experts agree that humans, like other apes, are Old World animals and that our remote ancestors first evolved in Africa. There is growing but uncertain evidence that humans reached the Americas by forty thousand years ago—not long after they reached Australia. In 2004 some archaeologists announced that a series of footprints had been found in volcanic ash in Mexico and securely dated to at least thirty-nine thousand years ago, but the dating has since been widely questioned. The fate of other very early sites, mainly in South America, has been similar. All these finds have their champions, but there is still room for doubt. However, reliably dated remains in Chile and elsewhere have persuaded most scholars that humans must have reached America by at least fifteen thousand years ago.

14. Humans are not the only two-legged hunters: chimpanzees sometimes hunt small game, including monkeys, and rival troupes even make war on each other in the wild. When early modern humans first spread out of Africa, they enjoyed a feast of game in the cold latitudes of Eurasia, where big, hairy beasts roamed the steppes and forests below the icefields. Trouble began when these ancestors of ours became too good at what they did. As their hunting craft grew deadlier, they thrived and multiplied. Eventually they were killing the game faster than it could breed, a problem worsened by natural climate change as the Ice Age began to lose its grip.

15. Today there are two species of wild camelid in South America (the vicuña and the guanaco) and two domesticates, the llama and the

alpaca, which are closely related to, and thought to be descendants of, the guanaco.

16. Research on the earliest Peruvian cities is summarized by Mann,
1491, 174–203. They were growing not only food, but also large
amounts of cotton and gourds for fishing nets and floats. In
February 2008, monumental ruins at Sechín Bajo, including a
round, sunken plaza, were dated by radiocarbon to between 3000
and 3500 B.C.

17. More productive and generally more numerous. See, for example,
National Research Council, *Lost Crops of the Incas,* for a fascinating
survey of "lost" Andean crops with modern potential.

18. Quoted in Viola and Margolis, *Seeds of Change,* 36–37. See also
Pagden, *Hernán Cortés.*

19. Díaz, *Conquest,* 235. In later times, after the era of the conquistadors had passed, such statements would be dismissed as prepos-
terous exaggerations, but modern archaeology has borne them
out. For a whole generation after 1492, European explorers kept
missing the American civilizations, both North and South, by a
whisker—an accident of winds and currents. Mired in Caribbean
islands and mangrove coasts, Columbus and others found simpler
societies that did not match their expectations of what Asia
should be. This "undiscovery" helped establish the image of
America as backward and sparsely peopled. It was the equivalent
of Mexicans crossing the Atlantic but getting stuck for twenty-five
years on the Canary Islands and West African coast.

20. In central Mexico, the immediate forerunners of the Aztecs were
the Toltecs, but the imperial model for both was the ancient city of
Teotihuacan, which flourished between the first and seventh centuries A.D., with a population of perhaps a quarter million—about
the same as that of Aztec Mexico City. More than two thousand
years before the Aztecs, astronomy, mathematics and writing
were invented from scratch and brought to high levels of refine-
ment, especially by the Maya, who lived (as they still do) in the
southeastern half of the Mesoamerican hourglass.

The Inca heartland around Cusco lay near the border between two forerunners: the Wari, who had controlled much of what is now modern Peru from a city of that name near Ayacucho between the sixth and eleventh centuries A.D., and Tiwanaku, a city on the shores of Lake Titicaca, which controlled highland Bolivia and parts of the Peruvian coast between the first and eleventh centuries A.D.

21. The Mexican capital lies at an altitude of more than 7,500 feet in the fertile Valley of Anahuac (or Mexico). It had begun as separate towns, called Tenochtitlan and Tlatelolco, on a pair of small islands in the great shallow lake. As time went by, the islands were artificially extended and the city merged into one. The lakes were mostly drained in Spanish times, though enough remains at Xochimilco to give an idea of Aztec canals and *chinampa,* or "floating garden," cultivation.

22. I make no excuses for the Aztecs, who slaughtered many thousands of war prisoners. However, Europeans, with their own record of mass killings—the Roman circus, the burning of heretics and witches, the Inquisition, and the Nazi death camps—are in a weak position to cast the first stone. At the games of Trajan, for example, five thousand men and eleven thousand animals were slaughtered in the Colosseum.

23. Clendinnen, *Aztecs,* 8.

24. See Luttwak, *Grand Strategy,* for a discussion of imperialism in the context of the Roman Empire; he refers to the two kinds as "hegemonic" and "territorial." Clendinnen (*Aztecs,* 26) felicitously describes the Aztec structure as an "acrobats' pyramid."

25. Perhaps the best example is China, which identified itself with Heaven, assimilated enemies and ethnicities, gave opportunity to merit and drew its borders on the Earth in stone. Despite several periods of disintegration, China has lasted three thousand years.

26. The Quechua name breaks down as *Tawa* (four) with *suyu* (region, direction or division) joined by the suffix—*ntin*—denoting a set. It

can also be translated as the Four Directions, the Four Corners of the World and the like.

27. This empire was the last of three great phases of Andean unification, which archaeologists call "horizons." Beginning before 1000 B.C., the first two had each lasted between five hundred and a thousand years. There's no knowing how long the Inca Empire would have endured if the outside world hadn't overtaken it; my guess is that it might have done about the same.

28. Each ethnic group sought to control a range of ecological zones: seaside fishing grounds, irrigated desert valleys, temperate mountain terraces for maize, cool highland fields for potatoes and, higher still, pastures for llamas and alpacas—animals kept for wool, meat and pack trains.

29. Throughout their domain the Incas had built imperial cities, temples, and garrisons with standard architectural forms, linked by some fifteen thousand miles of paved roads; there were ambitious terracing, irrigation and warehousing projects; a government courier system; and an army of officials and statisticians, who ran the imperial economy, using *quipu* records. Some independent trade was carried on by member peoples, especially by ship along the coast, but the state economy was centrally planned. Kendall, *Everyday Life of the Incas,* 96–139, gives a good summary of Inca imperial practices (for road building, see p. 138). Urton (*Signs of the Inka Khipu*) gives evidence that the *quipu* system was complex enough to be deemed a form of writing, though no surviving *quipu* has yet been fully deciphered.

30. There was no slavery of the Old World type, but some conquered peoples were known as *yanakuna* ("the helpers") and used for royal service and the working of imperial lands. However, *yanakuna* seem to have been well provided for and could rise to become "Incas by privilege" in the administration. The rest of the populace was taxed in the form of labour, providing ten or twenty days' *mit'a* work each year. Women in the "nunneries" wove fine cloth, looked after temples and often became wives of royalty and

high officials. These institutions were based on pan-Andean community practices. After the Spanish conquest, they did indeed become forms of slavery, especially the dreaded *mit'a* in the mines. The workload also became much heavier as the population collapsed.

31. Cieza de León, *Crónica del Perú,* vol. 2, 54–55.
32. Quoted in Clendinnen, *Aztecs,* 38; Pagden, *Hernán Cortés,* 75. When the Spaniards marvelled that there were no beggars in Peru and wrote that the late Inca Huayna Capac had been a "great friend of the poor," they were more or less right: one of his titles was *waqchakuyak,* meaning "he who cares for the poor or befriends those without kin." Central Mexico has since become a mestizo nation of great vitality. But in the Andean republics— Peru, Ecuador and Bolivia—the events of the 1500s have yet to be resolved; the descendants of conquered and conqueror live together uneasily, like partners in a bad forced marriage.

    During the dark centuries of colonial and postcolonial oppression, no major uprising in Mexico proposed a return to Aztec rule, but almost every revolt in Greater Peru, from the sixteenth century to the present, has aimed either to restore the Inca Empire or at least to invoke it as a golden age. For examples, see Millones, "Time of the Inca"; Gott, "Brave New World"; and Gott, *Guerrilla Movements.*
33. Bernal Díaz, who was there, says the Aztecs killed 860 Spaniards, including some deaths at Otumba. Of the sixty-nine horses, forty-six were lost, many killed and an unknown number captured (Díaz, *Conquest,* 305).
34. This point has been made by Borah and Cook, "Conquest and Population," by Jennings (*Invasion of America,* 21) and J. Klor de Alva, cited in Thomas (*Conquest of Mexico,* 593). Thomas underplays both the scale of the Aztec victory in 1520 and the importance of smallpox in the Spanish recovery and eventual victory in 1521.
35. Francisco de Aguilar, ca.1525.

36. A Spanish friar, Toribio Motolinía, quoted in Crosby, *Columbian Exchange*, 52, estimated more than half in most provinces, adding: "They died in heaps like bedbugs." The ruler killed by smallpox was Cuitlahuac, elected after Moctezuma died in Spanish custody. Spanish sources claim that Moctezuma was stoned to death by his people while appealing for calm from a palace rooftop; Aztec sources say he was either strangled or stabbed up the anus with a sword, execution methods the Spaniards favoured when they wished to avoid an obvious wound. See my *Stolen Continents*, 42, for sources.

37. Cook and Borah (*Essays in Population History*, vol. 1, viii, cited in Lovell, "'Heavy Shadows and Black Night,'" 430) calculated a decline in Mexico from 25.2 million in 1518 to 2.7 million by 1568 to 1.1 million by 1605 and even lower by 1620—a total of more than 95 percent. Even if we were skeptically to deduct 10 million from their 1518 estimate, the decline would still be more than 92 percent.

38. Crosby, *Columbian Exchange*, 3. Crosby's *Columbian Exchange: Biological and Cultural Consequences of 1492* is the seminal work on this subject. Crosby followed up *The Columbian Exchange* with *Ecological Imperialism* and *Germs, Seeds, and Animals.* His work has had a wide influence on later books such as William McNeill's *Plagues and Peoples*, my own *Stolen Continents*, Jared Diamond's *Guns, Germs, and Steel* and Charles C. Mann's *1491*.

39. Crosby, *Ecological Imperialism*, 200. Even fifty years later, in 1571–72, a short-lived Jesuit mission on the shores of Chesapeake Bay was wiped out, probably by the Powhatans, leaving no trace (Morison, *European Discovery of America*, 631).

40. Crosby, *Ecological Imperialism*, 201.

41. Prescott, *History of the Conquest*, 830. The rumours reached Balboa's ears as early as 1511, spurring him to become the first European to cross the Isthmus of Panama and see the Pacific, in 1513. Once he was there, the local people, who probably traded with Inca shipping, gave him more detailed information, including drawings of llamas.

42. In Heyerdahl, *Sea Routes,* 99. See also Porras Barrenechea, *Los Cronistas del Perú,* 54–55.

43. Until the nineteenth century, they continued to go as far as the Galápagos in such craft, which could tack against the wind with centreboards. In ancient times they traded with Central America and perhaps with western Mexico. See Edwards, "Possibilities"; Heyerdahl and Skjolsvold, "Archaeological Evidence"; Heyerdahl, "Guara Navigation" and *Sea Routes;* and Hosler, "Ancient West Mexican Metallurgy."

44. Pizarro, *Relación del Descubrimiento,* 50. Although we now use the word *Inca* loosely for ancient Peruvians in general, it was a title more than an ethnic term. The ruler was called *Sapa Inca*—the Inca—while members of the nobility, including commoners promoted for merit, also belonged to the Inca class.

45. It is possible that Huayna Capac had already died by then; if so, the plague had not yet reached this part of Peru, and the dynastic war between his sons had not begun. For more detail on this first plague, see Crosby, *Columbian Exchange,* 47–58, and Wright, *Stolen Continents,* 44–47, 72–83. Pizarro had briefly visited the Peruvian port of Tumbez twice in 1527, about a year after his pilot Ruiz boarded the oceangoing Inca *balsa* near the equator. However, it is unlikely that Pizarro's own men or the captive Peruvian seamen who guided him to Tumbez brought the first pandemic that killed Huayna Capac, as the chronicles make no mention of illness during the several months Pizarro spent on this first scouting of the Peruvian coast.

    In 1527 smallpox hit the native population of Panama so severely that the Spaniards began taking slaves from outlying regions (Crosby, *Columbian Exchange,* 51). It seems more likely, then, that the pestilence made its way south from Panama overland, crossing the Inca frontier in southern Colombia and sweeping through the empire shortly after Pizarro had left—late in 1527 or early in 1528.

The fullest account of the early voyages to Peru is still to be found in Prescott's classic *History of the Conquest of Peru* (1847). Hemming, in his definitive *Conquest of the Incas* (1983), gives the best modern account. The precise dating of the various incidents mentioned by the chroniclers is still uncertain. It is known that Pizarro was back in Panama by the spring of 1528 and that he arrived in Spain to plead for royal support in the middle of that year.

46. This is my own speculation, based on circumstantial evidence. Given Pizarro's wariness in 1527 and his conscious emulation of Cortés, it seems unlikely that he would have risked an invasion with his famously small army unless he had heard that a plague like Mexico's had struck Peru (at 160 soldiers, his army was only an eighth the size of Cortés's force that was beaten by the Aztecs in 1520). The rumour mill along native shipping routes could have brought this news to Panama during the three years before Pizarro set sail in December 1530.

47. The pandemic "consumed the greater part" of the Inca court, according to the chronicler Murúa. Quoted in Hemming, *Conquest of the Incas,* 28.

48. San Miguel, now the city of Piura.

49. Pizarro, *Relación del Descubrimiento,* 49–50.

50. See Cook, *Demographic Collapse,* and Lovell, "'Heavy Shadows and Black Night.'" Cook suggests 14 million Inca subjects before contact: 9 million within what is now Peru plus another 5 million elsewhere in the empire. The area with the 9 million had fallen to about 0.6 million a century later—a drop of 93 percent. Cook notes that the people of the coastal valleys were "almost completely wiped out"—a statement supported by the eyewitness chronicler Cieza de León.

51. Atahuallpa (or Atahualpa): in modern Quechua spelling, the name is usually written as Atau Wallpa.

52. Pizarro, *Relación del Descubrimiento,* 31. Hernando Pizarro (a brother of Francisco) adds that when he and the Inca met, Atahuallpa "smiled as someone who did not think much of us"

(quoted in Hemming, *Conquest of the Incas,* 35). The smile came on the first day at the Cajamarca baths, after the Inca heard boasts of Spanish valour.

53. Miguel de Estete, quoted in Hemming, *Conquest of the Incas,* 45.

54. On their first visit to Tumbes, Pizarro's men had demonstrated the arquebus (a heavy matchlock musket) by firing at a wooden target.

55. Titu Kusi Yupanki, *Relación,* 15–16. See note 59, below.

56. In Lockhart and Otte, *Letters and People,* 5–6.

57. Titu Kusi Yupanki, *Relación,* 18: *"ni tampoco tenían armas, porque no las habían traído, por el poco caso que hiçieron de los españoles."*

58. Modern writers have become too fond of portraying this moment as the beginning and end of conquest, a shocking materialization of bearded desperadoes (wrongly said to have been mistaken for gods) in the heart of an empire sealed until the very instant of its death. It wasn't so, as the first-hand accounts from both sides make clear. Presumably Atahuallpa thought that the large army he had encamped on the surrounding hills was an adequate deterrent. But his men could not counterattack without endangering the Inca's life. If not a Bible, the book may have been a breviary (a priest's prayer and hymn book) or the text of the *Requirement,* a document offering the choice of submission to Christ and king, or death. I doubt the hoary notion that Atahuallpa tossed the book away because he didn't understand writing. He knew about encoded information, having *quipus* full of statistics that were read out loud by experts as well as *qillqa* (a Quechua word now used for writing), said to have been painted historical and genealogical scenes. Surviving Incas claimed that *quipus* could also record events. The scholar Gary Urton now thinks that the system had as many distinct "signs" as Sumerian cuneiform and should be considered a form of writing (see Urton, *Signs of the Inka Khipu*). Atahuallpa's spies had almost certainly told him about the Spanish reverence for holy writ and may have sent him examples of Spanish paperwork, so he must have known that the

Bible had great religious meaning to the Spaniards. His nephew
Titu Kusi Yupanki says in his *Relación* that when Soto and others
visited the Inca on the day before the massacre, he had given
them a ceremonial drink: cups of *chicha,* which they had tipped
on the ground, fearing poison; Atahuallpa threw down the
Spanish book in return for that insult.

59. In Lockhart and Otte, *Letters and People,* 5–6. The number may be
exaggerated, but Titu Kusi Yupanki says ten thousand died, with
fewer than two hundred survivors.

60. Indigenous chronicler and illustrator Waman Puma de Ayala
shows the conversation in a drawing, though he puts the words
into the mouths of Huayna Capac and Pedro de Candía, who never
met each other. For symbolic effect, each is speaking his own language: *Kay qoritachu mikhunki? Este oro comemos!* (Waman Puma
de Ayala, *Nueva Corónica,* vol. 2, 343). Thomas (*Conquest of Mexico,*
557–58) mentions a Tarascan leader in Mexico who asked the
same question.

61. The Aztecs sometimes used gold as convertible wealth, though the
main currencies in Mesoamerica were bronze and cacao.

62. It is generally thought that gold and silver had no monetary value
to the Incas, but they seem to have been items of foreign trade:
among the thirty tons of goods on the Inca *balsa* boarded in 1526
were "small weights to weigh gold, resembling Roman workman-
ship" (Porras Barrenechea, *Los Cronistas del Perú,* 54–55).

63. Diego de Almagro arrived at Cajamarca with another 150 men in
April 1533. See Hemming, *Conquest of the Incas,* 71.

64. As a bonus for himself, Pizarro kept the Inca's palanquin, made
with 183 pounds of gold.

65. The official haul in Mexico was much less—perhaps a ton—and the
amount was disputed, many claiming that Cortés had hidden a large
hoard. An unknown quantity of gold was lost when the Spaniards
fled in 1520, its weight drowning many who fell in the city's canals.

66. See Hemming, *Conquest of the Incas,* 73, 570, and Prescott, *History
of the Conquest,* 364–65, 964–66. At Cusco there was so much fine

silver that it was worth somewhat more than the 3 tons of gold (at
the time). My rough calculation (gold only) is as follows. Total
Cajamarca and Cusco gold taken in 1533: 1,914,805 pesos de oro.
That is about 20,000 lbs., or 9,000 kg, which = 24,000 troy
pounds, or 290,000 troy ounces. And 290,000 troy ounces ×
US$1,000 = $290 million.

    Forbes magazine counted 946 billionaires in 2007, with a
combined net worth of about $3.5 trillion. Gates, at $56 billion,
was top for the thirteenth straight year; Warren Buffett was number 2 with $52 billion. In 2008, Gates fell to third place, though
his worth rose to $58 billion; Buffett made number 1 at $62 billion. The total number of billionaires rose to more than 1,100.

67. Smith, however, did not understand the historical role of the New
World civilizations, whose existence he dismissed as "in a great
measure fabulous" (Smith, *Wealth of Nations*, 308). He was speaking only of mining output and seems never to have considered
where the labour, local knowledge and infrastructure came from.

68. Prescott estimates the Cajamarca gold alone—1,326,539 pesos de
oro—at £3.5 million sterling in his day.

69. *Encyclopaedia Britannica* 1911, vol. 3, gives the reserve as
£8.5 million in 1845 and £8 million in 1865 (341). By 1906 it
was £23.5 million. In 1899, the entire output of the Klondike
goldrush at its height was £2.8 million (*Encyclopaedia Britannica*
1911, vol. 12, 194).

70. Hemming, *Conquest of the Incas*, 68. Both silver and copper
horseshoes were made by Inca smiths at Xauxa (Jauja) in 1533.
The practice continued for some years, especially as the paving
blocks on Inca roads wore out even iron shoes quickly. The
Spaniards deliberately wrecked thousands of miles of roads by
tearing up the pavement to expose the softer underlay. Metals
had been worked in Peru for three thousand years (longer than
in Japan). The Incas made extensive use of bronze but had little
iron, except perhaps from meteorites (there was a Quechua word
for iron).

71. It is often said that Peru was conquered with the overthrow of Atahuallpa in 1532. But the United Four Quarters did not go down without a fight. The empire took forty more years to die, until the last Inca stronghold fell in 1572 and Viceroy Toledo beheaded Tupa Amaru before a weeping crowd in Cusco.

    In 1780 a descendant of Tupa Amaru took the name Tupa Amaru II and tried to reinstate Inca rule. The rebellion lasted three years and may have cost two hundred thousand lives; it came close to ending Spanish rule in Peru and, by exposing both Spain's weakness and the revival of Indian strength, led first to suppression of the Inca colonial elite and then to the white and mestizo revolts that established the Latin American republics in the early nineteenth century. The name of Tupa Amaru (or Tupac Amaru) has since become a watchword for South American revolutionaries, adopted by the Tupamaro guerrillas of Uruguay, Peru's Velasco government (1968–75), the Tupac Amaru Revolutionary Movement of the 1990s and others. (It was also adopted, in part, by the late rap musician Tupac Shakur.)

72. Mancio Sierra (who is said to have gambled away a great image of the sun), writing in 1589.

73. Thompson, *Making of the English Working Class*, 12.

74. *La Misère de la philosophie* [Poverty of Philosophy, 1847], excerpted in Marx, *Karl Marx*, 137–38.

75. Croesus, a king of Lydia in Asia Minor, is credited with inventing money in the sixth century B.C., and some Greek states had coinage in early Classical times. But a general currency did not appear in Western Europe until the Roman Empire.

76. Ferdinand and Maximilian of Germany are both singled out for their insolvency in Prescott, *History of Conquest,* 365n.

77. Gunpowder, the compass, cast iron and block printing were all Chinese inventions. In his recent survey of world exploration, Felipe Fernández-Armesto writes that "an observer of the world in the fifteenth century would surely have forecast that the Chinese would precede all other peoples in the discovery of world-girdling,

transoceanic routes" (Fernández-Armesto, *Pathfinders*, 115). China and Europe went exploring at about the same time, and it's telling to compare the scale of their efforts. Columbus took ninety men in three ships, two of which carried no more freight than an Inca *balsa*—about 30 or 40 tons. The Chinese admiral Zheng He (Cheng Ho) sailed the Indian Ocean with more than 280 ships, the biggest displacing 3,000 tons. Of Zheng He's many voyages, there is independent confirmation for at least one: in 1414 a Chinese fleet got as far as the Red Sea, causing a sensation in Jeddah and Cairo. Had China continued to probe the unknown, Atahuallpa's gold might have ended up in Shanghai instead of Seville.

78. Kamen, *Spain's Road to Empire*, 88. King Charles I of Spain was also the Holy Roman Emperor, Charles V. More German than Spanish, he is famous for saying, "I speak Spanish to God, Italian to women, French to men, and German to my horse." By Charles's own calculation, he was suddenly 800,000 ducats richer with "the timely arrival of the gold from Peru and other parts" (ibid., 88). By my reckoning, based on Hemming's conversions, 800,000 ducats was about 664,000 pesos de oro and is roughly 20 percent (the king's fifth) of the Peruvian loot from 1533.

79. See Ross, ed., *Codex Mendoza*, for an example of Aztec tribute records copied by Mexican scribes for Viceroy Antonio de Mendoza (1535–50).

80. Rodrigo de Loaisa, 1586, quoted in Hemming, *Conquest of the Incas*, 372.

81. Large amounts of quicksilver were needed for the toxic but effective amalgam process of silver extraction. Potosí is 14,000 thousand feet up in the highlands of what is now Bolivia. For good summaries of labour and mining conditions, see Hemming, *Conquest of the Incas*, 404–10, and Werlich, *Peru*, 42–47. In theory, under Spanish law, the *mitayos* were to be paid a fair wage; in practice they usually received so little that they had to buy their own food and even their candles during the long periods they spent in the mines. Hemming gives details of Viceroy Toledo's

forced labour law of 1570 (declaring mining to be in the public interest of "the mother country") and of the contemporary outcry against both this legalized slavery and the inhuman mining conditions; the Archbishop of Lima, who had initially approved the law, later wrote to the king: "For the love of God, let Your Highness order [its] revocation." But the laws stayed in effect and the levies were never officially reduced, though the subject population dwindled to way below its 1570 level. The period of *mit'a* service, in fact, was lengthened to as much as one whole year in four (far higher than the Incas had ever demanded).

If we take the figure of 16,500 working at any one time (3,000 *mitayos* at Huancavelica and 13,500 at Potosí) and estimate that one in four men died per year at or from the work—probably a low guess—more than a million would have died at these two mines alone over 270 years. Hemming (*Conquest of the Incas,* 409) notes that by the mid-seventeenth century, the population of the provinces subject to the mining *mit'a* had fallen by more than three-quarters, though not all these people had died—many had fled. Wolf, *Europe,* 133–49, gives a good, brief summary of the European impact on native populations.

82. The 1533 official total was roughly 3.1 million pesos (or 1.4 billion *maravedis*) counting Cajamarca and Cusco, both gold and silver (see Hemming, *Conquest of the Incas,* 570 and 609). In the years between Potosí's discovery in 1545 and 1574, 70 million pesos were extracted, and a further 35 million between 1574 and 1585. The quicksilver mined at Huancavelica in central Peru was taken to Potosí and even to silver mines in Mexico, to be used in the amalgam refining process. Production from Potosí later rose to 7.6 million pesos yearly, accounting for more than 70 percent of all New World silver (see Kamen, *Spain's Road to Empire,* 286–87, and Richards, ed., *Precious Metals*). By the mid-seventeenth century, the boomtown of Potosí had a population of one hundred and fifty thousand—one of the largest in Christendom (Hemming, *Conquest of the Incas,* 407).

83. Smith, *Wealth of Nations*, 313–14. His numbers are 1,101,107 troy pounds of silver at 62 shillings (£3.1) a pound and 49,940 troy pounds of gold at 44.5 guineas (about £47) a pound—that is, £3.4 million in silver and £2.35 million in gold. He adds an eighth to the above for smuggled metal. These figures do not include direct exports to Asia from the Americas.

84. Cross, "South American Bullion Production," 404–5, cited in Kamen, *Spain's Road to Empire*, 286.

85. Philip boasted of Potosí that "this lofty mountain of silver could conquer the whole world" (Hemming, *Conquest of the Incas*, 407).

86. The friar was writing in 1630. Quoted in Kamen, *Spain's Road to Empire*, 286. To this end, the metal was hocked to foreign lenders before it was dug from the ground; Charles alone borrowed the equivalent of eight Inca treasures, mostly from Genoese and German bankers (ibid., 89).

87. The spirit of the conquistadors lived on for some time in the China Sea. Latter-day Pizarros boasted that a thousand Christians would be enough to conquer Siam and that six thousand could take over the Chinese Empire. But it was nothing more than talk.

88. The Eighty Years' War (1566–1648) in the Netherlands to subdue Protestant and nationalist revolts became Castile's Iraq or Vietnam. See Jamieson's article "America's Eighty Years War?"

89. Prescott, *History of the Conquest*, 967.

90. Wright, *A Short History of Progress*, 113.

91. By the 1760s about one-hundredth of the entire output of New World mines was being consumed annually by the factories of Birmingham alone (Smith, *Wealth of Nations*, 314). Smith seems to mean the literal consumption of gold and silver in Birmingham's manufactured goods, rather than the capitalization of industry in general. I have deducted about a fifth to represent Portugal's share, which Smith included in his total landed in Iberia.

92. These were condensing beam engines for pumping water (see *Encyclopaedia Britannica* 1911, vol. 28, 415). Four times more

efficient than Newcomen's old design, Watt's engine gave the
flooding tin mines of Cornwall a new lease on life.

93. Gardner, *Grendel*, 63.

94. Ponting, *A Green History*, 103.

95. As recently as 1900, there were only sixteen cities with a population of 1 million or more in the world; now there are at least four
hundred.

96. Fertilizers also played a role. Guano and nitrates, though of natural origin, were the first "industrial" fertilizers, imported mainly
from Peru, Chile and Pacific islands, beginning soon after 1800.
Guano (from the Inca word *wanu*, meaning "manure") was yet
another of Peru's gifts to the world. Manufactured chemical fertilizers became common about one hundred years ago, as natural
deposits were worked out.

97. The period lies neatly between two hefty intellectual bookends:
Newton's *Principia Mathematica* (1687) and Lyell's *Principles of
Geology* (1830–33).

98. Thomas Newcomen's atmospheric (vacuum or condensing)
steam engine of 1711 was based on a 1698 design by Thomas
Savery, with whom he shared the patent; it was used for pumping water from mines. James Watt developed a better type of
engine from this design, which he patented in 1769 and produced near Birmingham in the 1770s; he coined the word *horse-
power* and was honoured by having a unit of electrical power
named after him. Richard Arkwright patented a water-powered
spinning machine in 1769 and soon established huge cotton
mills, pioneering the modern factory system. Isambard
Kingdom Brunel built bridges, railways and ships, including the
Great Western of 1838, the first transatlantic steamship, and the
gigantic *Great Eastern* of 1858, the biggest ship afloat until the
twentieth century.

99. In the same 1972 book in which he documented the collapse
of native America from Old World germs after 1492, Alfred
Crosby also explored the role of New World crops in the modern

population boom. "The number of human beings on this planet today," he wrote, "would be a good deal smaller but for the horticultural skills of the neolithic American" (Crosby, *Columbian Exchange*, 202). In the thirty-six years since those words were written, mankind has doubled. Crosby cites the precedent of William McNeill's *The Rise of the West* (627–28) in suggesting this connection. See also McNeill's "American Food Crops."

The following English words all come from American languages: *maize, potato, tomato, squash, chocolate, quinoa, avocado, chile, manioc, guava* and *cashew.* Many other American foods— peanuts, beans, the pineapple, turkeys—came without their names, and many terms are highly distorted: *avocado,* for instance, began as the Aztec *ahuacacuahuitl,* meaning "testicle tree." Native American names that eluded English survive in other European languages—above all, Spanish. Two different species of wild peanut may have been developed independently in the Old World and the New, and the same may also be true of cotton. Long before Columbus, the sweet potato had made its way west across the Pacific on Peruvian *balsas* or Polynesian catamarans, and it is known as far away as New Zealand by its Andean name, *kumara.* Some foods were named for the way stations with which they became associated. In English these items are mainly American animals: the turkey, the guinea fowl and the guinea pig (a food, not a pet, in its South American homeland).

100. See Braudel, *Structures,* 74. Cassava was first shown to Henry VIII in about 1540 by Roger Barlow, who explained how to prepare bitter manioc, which is poisonous unless processed correctly, in his *Brief Summe of Geographie,* written about 1541. It is little eaten in cold climes today, except as tapioca pudding.

101. In 1905 the United States devoted 94 million acres to maize, yielding some 29 bushels an acre, for a total of 2.7 billion bushels; in the same year, wheat acreage was 48 million acres, half that of maize, yielding 14.5 bushels per acre for a total of 693 million

bushels (*Encyclopaedia Britannica* 1911, vol. 1, s.v. "Agriculture," 418–19).

102. A useful (if slightly dated) discussion of American crops can be found in Braudel, *Structures*, 158–71.

103. I have relied mainly on Crosby (*Columbian Exchange*, 165–207) for the above information as well as on McNeill, "American Food Crops," 42–59, and Hall, "Savoring Africa," 160–71. When Marie-Antoinette's compatriot Crèvecoeur, the self-styled American Farmer, returned to France, he was among those who championed the Inca staple. Regarded in the sixteenth century as an aphrodisiac, then feared (from its look) as a bringer of leprosy, the potato caught on first among the poor, as reflected in Van Gogh's painting *The Potato Eaters*.

104. Walter Raleigh had planted the first potatoes on his Irish estate in the 1580s, his ships bringing them from North Carolina. Two hundred years later, Frederick the Great fought a Potato War with Russia over army food supplies.

105. The quotation and numbers are from Crosby, *Columbian Exchange*, 183. He gives figures of 3.2 million Irish in 1754 rising to 8.2 million in 1845 plus a further 1.75 million who emigrated during that time. Unlike the Peruvians, who had (and have) hundreds of potato varieties, the Irish had introduced only one; indeed, it may be that all the potatoes on the island were clones of the same founder plant—and the lack of genetic variety made them uniquely vulnerable. Lundy (*Men*, 19, 143) suggests a figure of 1 million deaths from the great blight and the associated cholera. He notes that there had been severe Irish famines early in the eighteenth century, inspiring Swift's mordant 1729 satire, *A Modest Proposal*.

106. Maize may also have been introduced to Asia by Portuguese traders.

107. In Mexico and Peru, most of the decline happened in the first one hundred years; in much of North America it was more gradual but more complete, as contact with whites took about three hundred years to take its toll from sea to sea.

108. Crosby (*Columbian Exchange*, 166) gives a world population table, broken down by region, from 1650 to 1950. It took thirteen centuries for the world's inhabitants to double from about 200 million at the height of the Roman Empire to 400 million by A.D. 1500. The next doubling, by about 1775, took only a quarter of that time, despite the loss of up to 90 million in the Western Hemisphere from smallpox and the like.

109. Clean drinking water and safe sewers were not widely available, even in the most advanced countries, until late Victorian times.

110. Quoted in Thompson, *Making of the English Working Class*, 231.

111. *Poor Law Commissioners Report* of 1836, quoted in Thompson, *Making of the English Working Class*, 223.

112. *Encyclopaedia Britannica* 1911, vol. 26, 46.

113. The amount of sugar consumed by the average Briton rose fivefold between 1860 and 1890 (Manning, *Oil We Eat*, 43).

114. The term *world market* was used by Marx and others from the mid-nineteenth century to mean what we now less elegantly call "globalization."

115. Tocqueville, *Democracy in America*, 461.

Chapter 3 — Very Well Peopled and Towned

1. Wright, *Stolen Continents*, 84.

2. Baldwin, *American Quest*, 117.

3. Limerick, *Something in the Soil*, 33–34.

4. Adams, *Epic of America*, 4. The same author is credited with coining the phrase "the American Dream" (in the same book).

5. Tocqueville, *Democracy in America*, 27.

6. For a recent book devoted to this subject and covering the hemisphere, see Charles C. Mann's 2005 *Ancient Americans* (published in the United States as *1491: New Revelations of the Americas before Columbus*).

7. His birthplace is disputed. If it was not Florence itself, it may have been Lyons, France, where a colony of Florentine bankers

and merchants had settled. The name is sometimes spelled Verrazano. See Wroth, *Voyages of Verrazzano,* for a definitive study of the explorer, his voyages and writings, and the map making based on them.

8. Morison, *European Discovery of America,* 293–95. The Arcadian hill became bald long before the Wright brothers made their test flights there in the early 1900s.

9. See Wroth, *Voyages of Verrazzano,* 123–43, for both a transcription and a translation of the original Italian narrative.

10. Heavily populated is *"terra . . . molto popolata,"* and the rest, *"andavano discorrendo da l'una et l'altra parte al numero di xxx di loro barchette con infinite gente"* (see Wroth, *Voyages of Verrazzano,* 127).

11. The houses were evidently of the domed wigwam type: "14 to 15 paces across, made of bent saplings . . . covered with cleverly worked mats" (Wroth, *Voyages of Verrazzano,* 139).

12. The "league" was a maddeningly vague measure, its definitions ranging from 2.2 to 3.18 English nautical miles (see Morison, *European Discovery of America,* 288n). I am reckoning 3 leagues as about 10 land miles.

13. Wroth, *Voyages of Verrazzano,* 139. It seems remarkable that he learned so much in a couple of weeks, but it was spring, so plant-ing rituals may have been carried out while he was there. His mention of the Pleiades lends credence to the account, as this constellation was (and is) very important in both Mesoamerica and the Andes. He called the crops *legumi* and described them as "excellent and delicious." Given the earliness of the season, these were probably dried beans and corn kept from the previous year; the absence of standing crops may explain why he gives no description of the plants themselves.

14. These are the most likely candidates for the languages spoken at Quebec and Montreal, respectively. It is possible that both towns spoke Huron at this early date, though Mohawks were certainly living in the Montreal area a century or so later. The Iroquoian

family includes all six tongues of the Iroquois Confederacy as well as its great rivals, the Huron to the north and the Cherokee far to the south.

15. My translation from Cartier, *Relations*, 150–53.

16. Cartier, *Voyages of Jacques Cartier*, 61. See Morison, *European Discovery of America*, 412, for Ramusio's plan of the centre, which he calls a "city." Cartier calls Hochelaga a *ville*, which should be translated as "town," not "village" as many English versions have it. See Cartier, *Relations*, and Cartier, *Voyages en Nouvelle-France*, for the original French and a transcription in modern French, respectively. The name *Hochelaga* seems to have been a form of *Osheaga*, meaning "Great Rapids" (Cartier, *Relations*, 372, n. 299).

17. Cartier returned once more to Stadacona (Quebec City) in 1541. By that time only one of the ten Quebeckers he had taken to France was still alive, and he dared not repatriate her lest she reveal what had happened.

18. The Spanish arquebus of this period was a heavy and inaccurate weapon fired by a match-lock, or smouldering wick. It did not work well in the rain.

19. One of the chroniclers, Elvas, says as much. See Clayton et al., *De Soto Chronicles*, vol. 1, 84.

20. Beans were planted to grow up the corn stems, fix nitrogen and provide proteins lacking in the maize; the broad-leafed squash kept down the weeds. Maize is most nutritious when combined with small amounts of lime, as in *nixtamal*, the Mexican tortilla dough. New discoveries keep pushing back the origins of New World agriculture; already-domesticated maize was recently dated to 6,250 years ago (see *Science*, November 14, 2003). Domestication of beans and squash in both Mexico and South America (and of potatoes in the latter) was earlier than that of maize, starting ten thousand years ago.

21. The first corn in the area that is now the United States may have been grown as early as 3500 B.C. in New Mexico, but these early cultigens were low-yield, and the plant did not become the primary

Notes for page 54

staple until later. See Waldman, *Atlas*, 28–29, for good maps of maize use in the United States.

22. I shall use "North America" colloquially, not geographically, to mean everything north of modern Mexico. The Cahokia Mound (the biggest of 120 that once stood in the city) covers 16 acres— 3 more acres than the Great Pyramid—but is only a fourth of the latter's height. The largest ancient structure in the world is at Cholula, Mexico, being greater in volume than the Great Pyramid of Egypt, though squatter. The Maya Temple IV, built in the eighth century at the city of Tikal, Guatemala, was the tallest building in the Americas until the late nineteenth century, when it was surpassed by the Washington Capitol dome and the Flatiron Building in New York.

23. Inca Garcilaso, a cousin of Atahuallpa, was born in Cusco in 1539 to a conquistador and a niece of Huayna Capac. Of the four Soto chronicles, Garcilaso's work *La Florida del Inca*, though the best written, is thought to be the least reliable, because it was done at second hand years after the events. Romantic and colourful, it has the merit of being written by a gifted man who thought deeply about the tragic collision between America and Europe, which had produced him.

24. See James A. Robertson's 1933 notes in Clayton et al., *De Soto Chronicles*, vol. 1, 173–219, for convincing identifications and discussion of the names. Citing Mary Ross, he favours Columbia, South Carolina, rather than Augusta, as the likely site of Cofitachiqui's capital. Several mentions of the same town or chiefdom by other sixteenth- and seventeenth-century travellers are also discussed. Talimeco may well be the Creek word *Talimiko*, meaning "head town" or "capital" (ibid., 195–99). The locations and routes in the Soto chronicles are still hotly mooted. In general, I find Mooney's (*Myths of the Cherokee*) and Robertson's old identifications more plausible than recent ones such as Hudson's (*Knights of Spain*). Writing at the end of the nineteenth century, Mooney knew the country, place names, ancient remains and

native traditions intimately and wrote before modern disturbance by dams, roads, industrial farming and urban sprawl. The same is true of Robertson. It makes sense to assume that most major pre-Columbian settlements are unlikely to be found by archaeology, as they lie beneath modern ones. The spelling of Cofitachiqui and other names in the Soto chronicles varies widely.

25. Clayton et al., *De Soto Chronicles*, vol. 1, 278 (Rangel).

26. Ibid., 278–80 (Rangel).

27. Inca Garcilaso de la Vega, *La Florida*, 339–45. See also Inca Garcilaso de la Vega, *La Florida del Inca*, 220ff., and Clayton et al., *De Soto Chronicles*, vol. 2, 297–303.

28. South American metallurgists (with whose work Soto was certainly familiar) did indeed make an alloy of bronze and gold called *tumbaga;* the surface was treated with acid, which leached away the cheaper metals, leaving a golden surface that took a high polish.

29. Clayton et al., *De Soto Chronicles*, vol. 1, 85 (Elvas).

30. Ibid.

31. Guaxule (or Guasili) was probably in the Cherokee lands of northern Georgia. Some chroniclers say that the Indians didn't eat dogs themselves, but others refer to small dogs raised for food as in Mexico. There are also many references to "chickens." Some were wild turkeys, but others may have been the domesticated turkey, also of Mexican origin.

32. "Chiaha was where these Spaniards first found the towns palisaded. Chiaha gave them five hundred *tamemes* [bearers], and they consented to leave off collars and chains" (Clayton et al., *De Soto Chronicles*, vol. 1, 283 [Rangel]).

33. Either under or near the modern city of that name.

34. Hudson gives a full and lively account of the battle in *Knights of Spain*, 238–45.

35. Female rulers like the Lady of Cofitachiqui are not mentioned elsewhere. Queenship may have been the rule in her polity or she may have come to power, as Atahuallpa had in Peru, after a

pandemic of European origin swept away the established leadership.

36. Clayton et al., *De Soto Chronicles*, vol. 1, 134 (Elvas). The wit (or his chiefdom or both) was named Quigaltam, and his capital town was somewhere between Natchez and Winterville. The Natchez rulers on the Mississippi, who were still living on top of ancestral mounds when met by the French in the eighteenth century, styled themselves "Great Sun." See Hudson, *Knights of Spain*, 420.

37. Bourne, *Narratives of De Soto*, vol. 1, 66 (Elvas), and Inca Garcilaso de la Vega, *La Florida del Inca*, 220, 229.

38. See Jennings, *Invasion of America*, 30.

39. Later in life, Raleigh did go up the Orinoco River in South America, searching for El Dorado, where Columbus had sensed the breast-shaped presence of the Earthly Paradise. See Author's Foreword, n. 5.

40. In 1590 Raleigh was openly accused of atheism, which was tantamount to treason in the young days of the Church of England.

41. Morison, *European Discovery of America*, 632–33.

42. Hakluyt, quoted in Jennings, *Invasion of America*, 76. This correspondent is the elder of two cousins, both named Richard Hakluyt, who sometimes worked together on Elizabethan ventures in America. Among other distinctions, the younger Hakluyt (geographer, historian and travel writer) collected maps and documents, including the famous *Codex Mendoza*, an Aztec glyphic book of tribute records and Mexican history with a Spanish commentary, commissioned by the first Spanish viceroy of Mexico for King Charles I (a.k.a. the Emperor Charles V). Before it reached Spain, the book was taken with other booty by a French warship, later sold to Hakluyt in Paris and left by him to Samuel Purchas. It is now in the Bodleian Library at Oxford. See Ross, ed., *Codex Mendoza*.

43. Lane, quoted in Jennings, *Invasion of America*, 76.

44. Morison, *European Discovery of America*, 647.

45. Quoted in Morison, *European Discovery of America*, 624.

46. Lane and other Englishmen resorted to eating dogs while exploring the Chowan River in March 1586 (Morison, *European Discovery of America*, 646).

47. Morison, *European Discovery of America*, 642.

48. Ibid., 648–49. "Preventive war" is Morison's phrase here.

49. Descendants of the Croatoan Indians claim that their ancestors intermarried with survivors. Morison (*European Discovery of America*, 677) favours this explanation. See also Thornton, *American Indian Holocaust*, 68.

Chapter 4 — Religion and Profit Jump Together

1. Quoted in Woolley, *Savage Kingdom*, 408.

2. Melville, *Confidence Man*, 191.

3. Conrad, *Heart of Darkness*.

4. Not all empires were as nakedly exploitive as the Aztec Empire, but throughout history the list of subject peoples who have chosen to stay in an empire when they had the means for independence is a short one.

5. The Spanish installed themselves at the top of existing social pyramids and used these indigenous structures for their own purposes. This system continued until the late nineteenth century, when the Latin American republics began to encourage European immigration and agricultural exports, expropriating Indian lands and using Indian labour—often forced—to work the farms. Even today, millions of landless or land-hungry peasants survive as migrants on cotton, coffee and sugar estates, above all in Guatemala.

6. Limerick, *Something in the Soil*, 33.

7. Only about one hundred thousand Europeans are thought to have crossed the Atlantic to Spanish America in the whole of the sixteenth century. Parry, cited in Jennings, *Invasion of America*, 32.

8. Parkman, *Jesuits in North America*, 418, quoted in Jennings, *Invasion of America*, 85.

9. Limerick, *Something in the Soil*, 53.

10. The venture was organized by the London Company (later renamed the Virginia Company) under a charter from King James.

11. Woolley, *Savage Kingdom*, 24.

12. Quoted in Conn, *American Literature*, 6.

13. Robert Beverley, writing in 1705, quoted in Thornton, *American Indian Holocaust*, 68.

14. The word *tribe* as a description of American ethnic groups is highly problematic, though it is still used by the United States as an official term. In general I try to avoid it. However, the members of the Powhatan Confederacy do not seem large enough to be called nations, as estimates of their combined population range from fifteen to thirty thousand. Whatever the figure in 1607, it would have been much higher before 1520.

15. Woolley, *Savage Kingdom*, 70, 126. The site of Powhatan's Tower is uncertain, nor is it known whether the structure was natural, artificial or both. It may have been what is now Tree Hill on the outskirts of modern Richmond. If so, it is no longer steep enough to suggest a "tower."

16. Quoted in Wilson, *Earth Shall Weep*, 65.

17. Brookhiser, "America at 400," 28.

18. McLuhan, *Touch the Earth*, 66. See also Wilson, *Earth Shall Weep*, 43, 68 (modernization differs slightly).

19. George Percy, quoted in Wilson, *Earth Shall Weep*, 68 (spelling modernized).

20. Captain Butler, quoted in Jennings, *Invasion of America*, 79 (spelling modernized).

21. Refutation to Butler, quoted in Jennings, *Invasion of America*, 79, n. 66.

22. Cooke wrote the satirical poem "The Sot-weed Factor" (the tobacco merchant) in the 1700s, and in 1960 Barth took the title for his sparkling novel of colonial Maryland. Jamestown is also known for "Jimson" weed, a poisonous and psychotropic datura that was eaten by starving settlers—to their great surprise and distress.

23. Woolley, *Savage Kingdom*, 186.

24. Weatherford, *Native Roots*, 119–20. The 1619 figure (20,000 lb.) is in *Encyclopaedia Britannica* 1911, vol. 28, 122. The original Thirteen Colonies had all taken at least embryonic shape by the 1740s. In rough north-to-south order, they were New Hampshire, Massachusetts, Rhode Island and Connecticut (known together as New England), New York, New Jersey, Pennsylvania, Maryland, Delaware, Virginia, North Carolina, South Carolina and Georgia.

25. For the *White Lyon*, see Woolley, *Savage Kingdom*, 363. Jennings writes that, with tobacco, "the colonists . . . now coveted their neighbours' cleared lands more than their company" (*Invasion of America*, 78). Indentured labour was (and is) a form of thralldom based on the working off of costs and advances. Poor whites were bound to work seven years in return for their passage and board.

26. Jennings (*Invasion of America*, 78) notes that there are no surviving deeds or any other legal mechanism for alienating land from the Indians during this period. It appears that the number of whites in the colony doubled between 1618 and 1622, suggesting that land was taken by force.

27. Gilbert (1539–1583), a cultured man drawn to New World voyaging by Thomas More's *Utopia*, had fought in Ireland in 1569 with a "savagery and cruelty" notable even for his day: "The heddes of all those [Irish] which were killed [were] laied on the ground . . . so that none should come into his tente for any cause but commonly he must passe through a lane of heddes which he used *ad terrorem*" (Jennings, *Invasion of America*, 168; see also Morison, *European Discovery of America*, 565).

28. For example, Foster (*Jeffersonian America*, 40) mentions native torture and revenge cannibalism. A British envoy to the United States before 1812, Foster also makes the point that "the said species of revenge, however, is not unknown even to [European] Christians; at Naples . . . men and even women having been seen eating of the hearts and drinking the blood of their fellow creatures from . . . hatred and revenge."

29. This right of indigenous people to self-defence is amply illus-
    trated by the writings of the early sixteenth-century clerical
    scholar Bartolomé de las Casas, who witnessed the conquistadors
    in action, and by the Spaniards' curious legal fiction, devised in
    1514, of reading out the *Requirement,* a document offering foreign
    peoples the option of "voluntary" submission or conquest. See
    Wright, *Stolen Continents,* 65–66, for a partial English translation.

30. The prophet's name was Nemattanew, though he was called Jack of
    Feathers by the English (Wilson, *Earth Shall Weep,* 70). Very few
    Powhatans had followed Pocahontas's example of conversion to
    Christianity. And the colony, despite injunctions in its charter
    and the raising of funds at home for the purpose, had made little
    effort to spread the Word among the heathen.

31. He was charged with murdering a white trader, but this was prob-
    ably just a pretext for getting rid of him.

32. Wilson, *Earth Shall Weep,* 71.

33. The war of 1622 should really be called the "first" Powhatan War,
    as there was a second and final round in the 1640s.

34. Quoted in Wilson, *Earth Shall Weep,* 69.

35. Edward Waterhouse, quoted in Jennings, *Invasion of America,* 80.

36. Waterhouse went on to recommend the means: "By force, by
    surprise, by famine in burning their corn, by destroying and
    burning their boats, canoes, and houses, by breaking their fishing
    weirs . . . by pursuing and chasing them with our horses, and
    bloodhounds . . . and mastiffs to tear them" (Waterhouse 1622,
    quoted in Woolley, *Savage Kingdom,* 397).

37. Alexander Whitaker, quoted in Wilson, *Earth Shall Weep,* 66.

38. Jennings, *Invasion of America,* 80.

39. Quoted in ibid., 77.

40. Quoted in Jennings, *Invasion of America,* 80.

41. Quoted in ibid., 81–82.

42. Throughout history, nomads have seldom been acknowledged to
    have rights. They are still being persecuted by governments in
    places as diverse as Canada, India and Botswana.

43. The falsehood of this statement could be shown in sources available at the time—notably, the writings of the naturalist William Bartram. In the 1770s, for instance, he described the Cherokee ruins he saw at Keowee. See Bartram, *Travels*, 270.

44. Edward Winslow, quoted in Wilson, *Earth Shall Weep*, 78.

45. His name is also given as Tisquantum. He was from the eastern end of the Wampanoag territory, while Verrazzano's landing had been at the western end, near the border with the Wampanoag's traditional enemies, the Narragansetts. Tisquantum's story is told in greater detail by Mann, *1491*, chap. 2.

46. There is doubt as to when he was taken and by whom, and it could have been some years earlier. The captain of the 1615 slave ship was Thomas Hunt, an associate of John Smith. See Weatherford, *Native Roots*, 112, 139, and Wilson, *Earth Shall Weep*, 73.

47. Thomas Morton, quoted in Wilson, *Earth Shall Weep*, 77.

48. William Bradford, ca. 1630, quoted in Wilson, *Earth Shall Weep*, 75.

49. Quoted in Wilson, *Earth Shall Weep*, 77.

50. Andean, or "Irish," potatoes had probably reached North America in the mid-1500s, brought from Peru by the Spaniards.

51. Lauded for its virtue in the 1790s poem "Hasty Pudding" by Joel Barlow: "Come, dear bowl, / Glide o'er my palate, and inspire my soul" (quoted in Conn, *American Literature*, 98).

52. Parker, *Parker on the Iroquois*, 15. Arthur Parker (or Gawasowaneh) was a great-nephew of Lewis Henry Morgan's informant and colleague, Colonel Ely Parker. See also Parker, *History of the Seneca*.

53. Tocqueville, *Journey to America*, 343–44.

54. Quoted in Conn, *American Literature*, 26. Bradford also described how, in the spring of 1621, Squanto had shown the English the way to plant maize, with the revealing detail that it would need fish fertilizer "in these old grounds [or] it would come to nothing" (quoted in Flannery, *Eternal Frontier*, 273). The "old grounds" were obviously fields that had been in use for years—which makes his insistence that Plymouth was a wilderness all the stranger.

55. See Tocqueville, *Democracy in America*, chap. 2.

56. Many Pilgrims, though originally from Britain, had spent years
    in the Netherlands before moving on to America to escape
    assimilation and warfare between Dutch rebels and the
    Spanish Empire.

57. William Wood, writing in 1634, noted the effect of declining pop-
    ulation on the land. He said that the native women were good
    weeders, who kept their farmland "so cleare with their Clamme
    shell-hoes, as if it were a garden rather than a corne-field," adding
    that land which belonged to Indians who had died during the
    epidemics but which had not yet been taken over by whites was
    getting overgrown with "much underwood . . . because it hath not
    been burned" (quoted in Jennings, *Invasion of America,* 63, and
    Wilson, *Earth Shall Weep,* 83).

58. See Miller, *Errand into the Wilderness.*

59. Wright, *Religion and Empire,* 158. Wright ascribes this story (which
    may be apocryphal or satirical) to Milford, Connecticut. See also
    Jennings, *Invasion of America,* 83.

60. Illustrated in Jennings, *Invasion of America,* 229.

61. Alcohol, in the form of maize beer, cassava beer, *pulque* (fer-
    mented agave) and probably palm toddy and various fruit wines,
    was known in most of pre-Columbian America but apparently not
    in the North. Certainly there was nothing as strong as distilled
    spirits, which had become common in Europe only two centuries
    before 1492.

62. When Francisco de Miranda, who had acted as a Spanish agent
    supporting American independence during the Revolution, trav-
    elled in the States in 1783–84, he described the whaling fleet at Sag
    Harbor, Long Island, with its ships of 160 tons: "Their crews are in
    large part Indians, who are the most capable harpoonists and are
    generally named boat officers" (Miranda, *New Democracy in
    America,* 129–30). By the time of Melville's 1851 *Moby Dick,* the
    ships were bigger and most crews were international, but
    Tashtego, "a Gay Head Indian," plays a prominent role in the novel.

63. Wilson, *Earth Shall Weep,* 84–86.

64. See Flannery, *Eternal Frontier*, 275.

65. Quoted in Conn, *America Literature*, 34.

66. Massachusetts Bay had investor backing of £200,000, a huge sum at that time, while the Pilgrims started with only £7,000. See Wilson, *Earth Shall Weep*, 82.

67. British attorney general Seymour in 1690, quoted in Baldwin, *American Quest*, 40.

68. Jennings, *Invasion of America*, 186. When, back in England, the Wessagusset men began to talk, the Plymouth colony sent Edward Winslow to spread counterpropaganda. See also Willison, *Saints and Strangers*, chap. 15.

69. See Chapter 6. The Utah events are well told in greater detail by Krakauer, *Under the Banner*, 210–27.

70. Baldwin, *American Quest*, 41–42. Finished only three days before he died in his mid-eighties, *American Quest* was the culmination of this distinguished historian's career.

71. Bloom, *American Religion*, quoted in Krakauer, *Under the Banner*, ix.

72. Inflamed by both ideological and material grievances, the German masses rose in the bloody Peasants' War of 1525. Their grievances included land enclosures, tithes and abuses of the law. As many as one hundred thousand people may have died throughout the German states and Austria.

73. There was, for example, the thirteenth-century "crusade" against the Albigensians in the South of France.

74. This is not to say there had been no *conflict* between earthly and heavenly powers; indeed, the matter of how to divide them had lain behind much of medieval history ever since Pope Gelasius I declared the Church supreme at the end of the fifth century. The martyrdom of Thomas à Becket in 1170 is a notorious incident in this struggle. Atheism was a similar challenge to Church authority, though few were rash enough to profess it openly. The word *atheism* came into English in the late sixteenth century— just in time for Walter Raleigh to be accused of it. See Chapter 3, note 39.

75. Officially, the Holy Roman Empire existed from 936 to 1806, when it was famously described by Napoleon as "neither holy, nor Roman, nor an empire." Many historians date its beginnings from the coronation of Charles the Great (Charlemagne) in 800.

76. The sleuth was Lorenzo Valla (ca. 1407–1457), who is often hailed as a founder of textual criticism because he established that the *Donation* was written in a dialect of Latin that did not exist until four hundred years after Constantine's death.

77. Pontifex Maximus means "Great Bridge Builder" and refers to the role of the high priest (and later the pope) as the link between Heaven and Earth.

78. From *Mr. Dooley's Opinions* by Finley Dunne (1900), originally in the dialect of the character.

79. Always, according to Robertson Davies in his 1972 novel *The Manticore*.

80. Burning was the fate of Joan of Arc, the Maid of Orleans, considered a witch and heretic by the English and by some of the French Catholic hierarchy; she was rehabilitated as a saint in 1920.

81. Taxes were also rising steeply. See Cheyney, *Short History of England*, 428–29.

82. The English common law had its origins in ancient Anglo-Saxon forms of democracy. Trampled by the Norman Conquest of 1066, it had been steadily reviving ever since, a process helped (unintentionally) by the efforts of the Anglo-Norman aristocracy in 1215 to curb King John with the Magna Carta. The Magna Carta borrowed wording from Henry I's coronation charter, which had included the laws of Edward the Confessor.

83. The Court of Star Chamber (named for a room in Westminster Palace) had been set up by Henry VII. Unlike the regular law courts, it had no jury. Its use grew under the Tudors, and both James and Charles seized on it in their fights with Parliament and their efforts to rule alone. For Prynne and other cases against Puritans, see Cheyney, *Short History of England*, 422.

84. For delightfully free sketches of key players of the time, see John Aubrey's *Brief Lives,* a compendium of gossip, biography and history written in the late 1670s by a witty observer who had been a young man during the Civil War and the Commonwealth.

85. Lines spoken in a sermon by John Ball, a defrocked priest who was calling for the deaths of all lords and lawyers. He has an echo in Shakespeare's *Henry VI, Part Two:* "The first thing we do, let's kill all the lawyers." The Levellers' demands grew too strong for Cromwell, who suppressed them.

86. By that time Parliament itself had split into factions (the kangaroo court that condemned and beheaded Charles I was only a minority). The word *Commonwealth* denoted a republic. It must not be confused with the modern Commonwealth, which arose from the ashes of the British Empire.

87. Besides keeping order among Puritan factions, Cromwell expended his energies reconquering the Irish with infamous savagery while also attacking Spain and other foreign powers.

88. The new King William was Dutch, the Prince of Orange; his co-monarch, Queen Mary, was the Protestant daughter of James II (himself a Catholic).

89. According to Bailyn (*Voyagers to the West,* 25), in the thirty years from the founding of Boston in 1630 to the Restoration of 1660, a staggering 210,000 migrants left Britain for America, though many did not survive.

90. Edward Johnson, quoted in Conn, *American Literature,* 28.

91. Revelation 21:2.

92. Salem (Naumkeag) had already been founded in a small way in 1628, but Winthrop's arrival with nine hundred people on eleven ships ensured that Boston became the capital of the Massachusetts Bay Colony.

93. Baldwin, *American Quest,* 42.

94. End in both senses: terminus and goal (see Fukuyama, *End of History*). He has since distanced himself from the Republican

right, saying that he could no longer support the policy of the
Bush administration.

95. The latest political settlement in Northern Ireland seems to be
holding, with the surprising support of the former Protestant
hardliner Ian Paisley. In 2007 the British government formally
ended its military operation in the region.

96. Baldwin, *American Quest,* 50.

97. Jerry Falwell, a leading figure in the evangelical-Republican
alliance behind the Reagan and Bush electoral campaigns,
had supported the apartheid regime in South Africa. According
to a BBC report on Liberty University in 2007, creationism is
taught and global warming denied there, though some other
evangelical schools are teaching that climate change and
environmental problems must be faced (BBC World News,
May 15, 2007).

98. Psalm 2:8–9

99. Melville, *Moby Dick,* chap. 16.

100. Most of these names have variant spellings such as Mohegans,
Pequods and Pequits. There is some evidence that, during a time
within memory, the Pequots had themselves conquered this
region.

101. In the 1620s and 1630s, more than twenty thousand migrants
landed in New England, and by 1670 there were about fifty thousand of British origin living there (Flannery, *Eternal Frontier,* 274;
Jennings, *Invasion of America,* 30). The legal basis for early land
alienations and cessions of "Indian right" (or sovereignty) is
unclear; many of the deeds and documents that do exist seem to
have been written retroactively. See Jennings, *Invasion of America,*
chap. 8, "The Deed Game."

102. Quoted in Jennings, *Invasion of America,* 28, and Wilson, *Earth
Shall Weep,* 86.

103. Jennings, *Invasion of America,* 189. Stone's killers were probably
Western Niantics, who were tributaries of the Pequots (see
Jennings, *Invasion of America,* 194n). Captain John Oldham was

killed on Block Island, likely by Eastern Niantics or their over-
lords, the Narragansetts.

104. Gardiner, quoted in Jennings (*Invasion of America*, 212) and in
Wilson, *Earth Shall Weep*, 88 (spelling modernized).

105. The nine were killed at Wethersfield, Connecticut. Jennings,
Invasion of America, 217.

106. Jennings (*Invasion of America*, 220) discusses the evidence for this
assumption.

107. Captain Underhill, quoted in Wilson, *Earth Shall Weep*, 92–93.

108. This inference is backed up by the fact that some Pequots had
firearms, yet Mason's account makes no mention of any guns in
native hands at Mystic.

109. Mason, quoted in Wilson, *Earth Shall Weep*, 91.

110. Bradford and Mather, quoted in Zinn, *A People's History*, 15.

111. Quoted in Jennings, *Invasion of America*, 223. Jennings provides a
longer quotation and discusses the archaic wording of the English
translation.

112. Bradford, quoted in Zinn, *A People's History*, 15.

113. After the Mystic massacre, the English (including Boston late-
comers who hoped to share in the spoils) harried all the Pequots
they could find until the "proud Enemie" was indeed exterminated, except for captives and refugees among other groups.
William Hubbard, quoted in Jennings, *Invasion of America*, 226.

114. Waldman, *Atlas*, 91.

115. *Mystic* is a native word meaning "great tidal river." The modern
town was the scene of a vapid 1988 film, *Mystic Pizza*. A few
Pequots managed to survive; in 1774 they numbered 151 all told.
Like many tribes in the United States, their descendants have
prospered in recent years by running a casino. Ironically, their
effort to buy back some of their ancient homeland with their
earnings has drawn hostility from neighbouring whites. See
Harris, "Fortune Favours the Braves."

116. "New York was the special jurisdiction of the king's brother"
(Jennings, *Invasion of America*, 322). The Crown also threatened to

encroach on Puritan land by taking up Dutch claims to western
Connecticut and Massachusetts as well as unconquered native
land running north to Canada—the future Vermont and Maine.

117. The most notable white victory was the Great Swamp Fight in
December 1675, when about a thousand Narragansetts—most of
them noncombatants who tried to keep out of the war by withdrawing to a fort deep in the swampland between Shamrock
and West Kingston, Rhode Island—died in a Mystic-style burning. Jennings (*Invasion of America,* 312) discusses the casualty
figures on both sides, saying twenty English were killed and two
hundred wounded. (At Mystic, only two whites had died, probably from "friendly fire.") The decisive battle in King Philip's War
took place far to the west, where Metacom's main army of two
thousand men was scattered by Mohawk forces. The Mohawks,
who had their own agenda, were allied with the British colony
of New York.

118. The New England colonies recouped some of their costs by selling
prisoners at 30 shillings a head in the Caribbean, in Bermuda, and
even (like Squanto) in Spain. King Philip's wife and child were
among those sold in Bermuda, while his head was stuck on a pike
over Plymouth's main gate. See Wilson, *Earth Shall Weep,* 96–97.

119. Quoted in Jennings, *Invasion of America,* 324. The report estimated
the financial losses at £150,000—close to the entire investment
backing of the Massachusetts Bay Company (£200,000) and more
than twenty times the founding capital of Plymouth (£7,000).

Chapter 5 – White Savages

1. Smyth, ed., *Writings of Franklin,* vol. 10, 97.
2. Quoted in King and Chapman, *Sequoyah Legacy,* 51.
3. Williams, *Empire,* 79.
4. As mentioned in the notes to Chapter 4, the original thirteen,
   in rough north-to-south order, were New Hampshire,
   Massachusetts, Rhode Island and Connecticut (known together as

New England), New York, New Jersey, Pennsylvania, Maryland, Delaware, Virginia, North Carolina, South Carolina and Georgia.

5. Tocqueville, *Journey to America*, 330.

6. The foundations measure 334 feet and have been dated to the 1300s. Onondaga has become the city of Syracuse, though the Onondaga Nation still has a reservation and a League assembly hall nearby.

7. The Iroquois name for themselves, Haudenosaunee, means People of the Longhouse (the name varies slightly in the six Iroquois languages). As the implications of Mystic and other town burnings sank in, many native peoples, including the Iroquois, gave up communal living for single-family cabins, keeping long-houses only for ceremonial use. Some Indians, such as the Iroquoian Cherokee, had always lived in cabins, so it is difficult to say whether the Six Nations adopted this pattern from other native peoples or from whites. Log cabins were certainly easier to build after the introduction of steel tools.

8. The foundation date is moot. Mann (*1491*, 332) summarizes eth-nohistorical and astronomical evidence suggesting a date of 1142. Other writers favour a date around 1450. A few believe that the League was formed in response to early European impact, but that seems unlikely to me; none of the contemporary written sources, which go back to the early 1600s, suggest that it was anything less than ancient. It seems likely that the Iroquois Confederacy was founded—as its traditions say—during a time of chronic strife between related peoples. Such unrest may well have been sparked by rising numbers and competition for farmland some time after the spread of cold-tolerant maize to the Great Lakes about a thousand years ago. The decline of Cahokia's authority and trade networks, which happened shortly before Columbus, may also have been a factor. When Engels wrote that the Iroquois had "no nobles," he may have been only half right. It is possible that in ancient times the Iroquois, like the Mississippians, had had social classes that faded as the population shrank.

9. In 1760, when New France fell, it had only sixty-five thousand settlers, while there were about 1.5 million British Americans at that time (Nelles, *Little History of Canada*, 58).

10. By 1900 only a quarter million Indians would be left in the whole United States—the same as the number of whites two centuries before. The original population of North America in 1500 is not known, but well-argued estimates range between 7 and 18 million. A round number of 10 million for everywhere north of the (modern) Mexican border strikes me as reasonable. If, in 1520, the population of what became the United States was 10 million, then the nadir represents an overall decline of 97.5 percent—greater than in Mexico and Peru (about 95 percent from peak to low) but less than in the Caribbean and other coastal regions of the New World (99 to 100 percent). A decline of this order does not seem unlikely, given that the North Americans were being invaded and driven out almost continually and were unable to rebuild their numbers until the twentieth century. Thornton, *American Indian Holocaust*, 30–32, gives the nadir figure and discusses the range of estimates derived from it. He considers estimates of about 7 million for the continent north of Mexico and of 5 million for the United States to be "conservative" but says that Dobyns's 18 million figure is too high.

11. This assumption is supported by the disappearance of the St. Lawrence Iroquoians between Cartier's visits in the 1530s and Champlain's in 1603: by then the towns of Stadacona (Quebec City) and Hochelaga (Montreal) had vanished, just like Soto's Talimeco. Jennings, *Ambiguous Iroquois Empire*, 86–89, discusses Champlain's estimate of 1616 and Gabriel Sagard's of the 1620s and Iroquois numbers in the seventeenth century (ibid., 34–36). I agree with his point that archaeology cannot establish anything other than a minimum. Merrell (*Indians' New World*, 18–27, and throughout) discusses population decline and its cultural effects in the Southeast, citing the travels of John Lawson in 1700.

12. Adriaen Van der Donck, quoted in Jennings, *Invasion of America*, 24. By 1700 the Six Nations' population had fallen to less than a

fourth of its strength in 1630 (Wilson, *Earth Shall Weep*, 112). The early English traveller John Lawson, who visited the Catawbas and other peoples in the former Cofitachiqui realm in 1700, wrote that the Congarees were "a small People, having lost much of their for-mer Numbers . . . by the Small-pox, which hath often visited them." He added, "Neither do I know any Savages that have traded with the English, but what have been great losers by this Distemper. . . . there is not the sixth Savage living within two hun-dred miles of all our Settlements, as there were fifty Years ago." In some places plague "destroy'd whole Towns without leaving one Indian alive" (Lawson, *New Voyage to Carolina*, quoted in Merrell, *Indians' New World*, 19).

13. "The design of the Iroquois, as far as I can see," wrote a Jesuit missionary, "is . . . to make them both but one people" (quoted in Jennings, *Ambiguous Iroquois Empire*, 93). Tocqueville was told by a Scottish citizen of Quebec that in their heyday, the Hurons alone "could put up to 60,000 men under arms" (Tocqueville, *Journey to America*, 47). The figure may be an exaggeration but would be consistent with a pre-1520s population of several hundred thou-sand each for the Huron and Iroquois confederacies.

14. Quoted in Axtell, *European and the Indian*, 172. The captivity tale, in which a god-fearing settler (often a maidenly young woman) tells of her perils among savages, became a thriving American genre. Perhaps the best and fairest of these memoirs was the *Narrative* of Mary Jemison, who was married to a Seneca war leader for fifty years. She noted her husband's ferocity on the battlefield, yet his "kindness and attention" at home. The Iroquois were justly famous for abusing enemies in almost Aztec style, but such treatment was reserved for fighters. "Bad as these savages are," an American general allowed during the Revolutionary War, "they never violate the chastity of any woman"—which was more than he could say for his own troops (General James Clinton, quoted in Bonvillain, ed., *Studies on Iroquoian Culture*, 53).

15. Turner, *Significance of the Frontier*, 4, 17.

16. James Adair, an Irish trader who lived with the Cherokees for many years before the Revolution, praised the "equality among [them], and the just rewards they always confer on merit. . . . Their whole constitution breathes nothing but liberty" (Adair, *History of the American Indians,* 379).

17. After Lewis Henry Morgan published his 1851 *League of the Iroquois,* a cornerstone of modern anthropology, Iroquois influence also reached the wider world. Morgan's informant and colleague was the Iroquois chief Hasanoanda, better known as Ely S. Parker, the Union colonel who wrote the surrender terms at Appomattox and served under President Grant as the first Indian commissioner of Indian Affairs. Under the Iroquois constitution, known as the Great Law of Peace, fifty sachems, or "condoled chiefs" (so named because the condolence ritual for a dead chief installs his successor), hold office. These are men, but they are made—and can be unmade—by the leading women, or "clan mothers," giving a balance of power between sexes unknown in most other democracies until after the First World War. The heart of the women's suffrage movement was the Iroquois' old home of upstate New York; Harriet Maxwell Converse wrote of every woman's "gratitude to the memory of the Iroquois Indian who . . . rendered to the mothers of his people the rights maternal, political, social, civil, religious and of land!" (quoted in Wilson, *Earth Shall Weep,* 106). "This gentile constitution is wonderful!" Engels wrote in *The Origin of the Family, Private Property and the State* in 1884. "All are free and equal—including the women." See Weatherford, *Indian Givers,* 161–62.

18. Franklin's inventions include the lightning rod, bifocal eyeglasses and the Franklin stove. In 1818 the English critic Sydney Smith, writing scornfully of American literature, conceded that the new nation "may afford to live for half a century" on Franklin's fame alone. See Conn, *American Literature,* 113.

19. The linguisters were usually of mixed blood or fully bilingual, such as the powerful trader and Indian expert Conrad Weiser, adopted

by the Mohawks, who was a friend and colleague of Franklin. See Boyd, *Indian Treaties,* for an edition of Franklin's Treaties.

20. Boyd, *Indian Treaties,* 78.

21. Written in 1751. See Campbell and Campbell, "Cherokee Participation," 92–105.

22. Of course, the idea of federation was not new in either world, but successful examples were rare. The Americans needed a fresh approach to avoid repeating the failure of the United Colonies of New England. The longest-lived confederacy in Europe was Switzerland, but as Tocqueville observed, it survived mainly because of its neighbours' mutual jealousies. See Tocqueville, *Democracy in America,* 178. Tocqueville did not even mention the League as a precedent for the American Union (*Journey to America,* 330).

23. America's lexicographer, Noah Webster, lauded the choice in these words: "The Eagle is the chief of the feathered race . . . fierce, rapacious, and holding a sort of empire over the whole" (Webster 1812, quoted in Friedman, *Inventors,* vii).

24. Quoted in Brown, *Old Frontiers,* 81.

25. The Oneida chief Scarouady, quoted in Wallace, *Conrad Weiser,* 390.

26. Colonel Henry Babcock, quoted in O'Toole, *White Savage,* 104. Sir William Johnson understood the political power of Iroquois women. He set himself up like a feudal baron in the Mohawk Valley and was generally upright, though he always set the Crown's interests above those of his Iroquois kin and took over large tracts of land. The marriage was only by Six Nations law; he and Molly had eight children. See O'Toole, *White Savage,* for a recent life of Johnson and see Huey and Pulis, *Molly Brant,* for contemporary sketches of, and documents on, Molly Brant. Many Indians of this time used European names as well as their own.

27. In 1772 Governor Tryon of New York wrote to London that the Mohawks "appear to be actuated as a community by principles of rectitude, that would do honour to the most civilised nations. Indeed they are in a civilised state, and many of them good Farmers" (O'Toole, *White Savage,* 320).

28. Quoted in Wallace, *Death and Rebirth of the Seneca*, 118–21.

29. Brown, *Old Frontiers*, 119–20. In 1760–61 Amherst had pressed a punitive war against the Cherokees, and the following year, the Cherokee leader Ostenaco and two others visited King George III in London to state their case.

30. Fort Pitt, the former Fort Duquesne, is now the city of Pittsburgh. Despite many warnings from Johnson, Amherst claimed to have no idea what "can have induced these barbarians to this perfidious attempt" (quoted in O'Toole, *White Savage*, 245).

31. These events are sometimes denied but are well documented. See Bouquet to Amherst, 13 July 1763, British Manuscript Project, Library of Congress microfilm reel 34/40, item 305; Amherst to Bouquet, 16 July 1763, reel 34/41, item 114. Amherst's letter to Johnson is in O'Callaghan, ed., *Colonial History*, vol. 7, 545–46. All are quoted in O'Toole, *White Savage*, 245–46. See also Jennings, *Ambiguous Iroquois Empire*, 440–48, and Wright, *Stolen Continents*, 134–40.

32. To engineer the negotiations, Johnson went through the Board of Trade. In theory, the line ran along the divide, restricting whites to watersheds flowing directly into the Atlantic, not toward the Mississippi and the Caribbean (Turner, *Significance of the Frontier*, 6). The Proclamation also set limits on Quebec and regulated other unfinished and often contradictory business left over from the conquest of New France.

33. See Waldman, *Atlas*, 108–9, for a good summary of these events. The quotation is from Franklin's essay *A Narrative of the Late Massacres in Lancaster County of a Number of Indians, Friends of this Province, by Persons Unknown*, published in January 1764.

34. Tocqueville was told as much by retired president John Quincy Adams in 1831: "Mr. Adams [thought] that one of the greatest guarantees of order and internal security in the US was found in the movement of the population towards the West. 'Many more generations will yet pass,' he added, 'before we feel that we are overcrowded'" (Tocqueville, *Journey to America*, 62). However,

Bailyn writes that "during the decade and a half after 1760, thousands of settlers set out to find land. . . . This massive *Völkerwanderung*, this surge of innumerable farming families . . . could not be contained within the margins of the existing colonies. . . . Settlers defied all legal constraints" (Bailyn, *Voyagers to the West*, 20).

35. Steinbeck's insightful explanation of why socialism seldom took root in the United States.

36. Augustus Foster, who travelled widely in the United States two hundred years ago, remarked: "In thickly populated lands where shark meets shark . . . interests keep interests in check. But [in America] the wild unruly young adventurers of the western woods[,] especially the Democrats of the slave districts . . . and all those who are readers of nothing but newspapers or party pamphlets . . . are like dry tinder ever ready for blazing up, tho' the outlet . . . open to their excesses thro' the woods after Indians or wild beasts, serves and will long serve as a diversion" (Foster, *Jeffersonian America*, 159–60).

37. Tocqueville, *Journey to America*, 124. See also ibid., 89, where an American diplomat told Tocqueville: "The land never stays in the hands of the one who clears it. When it begins to yield a crop, the pioneer sells it and plunges again into the forest."

38. Long ago, these fertile lands had supported a branch of Mississippian civilization. The Senecas' oral history told that their ancestors had built the pyramidal earthworks, and the size of the trees on these mounds by the eighteenth century suggests that they were abandoned around the time that Old World diseases reached America. In colonial times the region was nominally under Six Nations tutelage, though settled mainly by "Western Indians"—Shawnees, Delawares, Ottawas and others—many of whom had fled there from the seaboard. French influence was strong in Ohio for a time, and the encroachment of Anglo-Americans was among the causes of the French and Indian War.

39. O'Toole, *White Savage*, 160, and Wallace, *Death and Rebirth of the Seneca*, 180, 198. Gilbert (*God Gave Us*, 64) describes George Washington's activities in Ohio in the early 1770s, when he wanted to get ten thousand acres in the heart of the Shawnee Nation or, as he wrote in a letter, "to have my lands run out on the banks of the Ohio."

40. Gilbert, *God Gave Us*, 58. See also Wright, *Stolen Continents*, 222–38, and Wilson, *Earth Shall Weep*, 98–131.

41. Crèvecoeur, *American Farmer*, 43–44. For clarity, I have reversed the order of the last two sentences in this quotation.

42. The last point is underlined by the writer elsewhere: in America "there are very few poor except the idle" (Crèvecoeur, *American Farmer*, 156–57). While many Americans abhor Darwinism for religious reasons, *social* Darwinism (the Victorian idea that the poor and weak should be left to die out by natural selection) is another matter. The phrase "the American dream" seems to have been coined by James Truslow Adams in his 1931 history *The Epic of America*.

43. Crèvecoeur, *American Farmer*, 5, 11. Apparently written on the eve of the Revolution, the collected essays were first published in 1782.

44. Crèvecoeur also used other variations on these names. His surname was Englished by the poet John Berryman as "Mr. Heartbreak" in his poem "Dream Song No. 5."

45. Crèvecoeur, *American Farmer*, 23.

46. Cunliffe, in his 1978 edition of Crèvecoeur, writes: "As Crèvecoeur saw it in 1776–78, the revolution was a squalid and murderous civil war."

47. See the good introductory essay by Marcus Cunliffe to the 1978 Folio Society edition of Crèvecoeur, though this version of Crèvecoeur's text is rather ruthlessly abridged and sometimes unreliable.

48. He continues by saying that the native way of life is "sufficiently complete to answer all the primary wants of man, and to constitute him a social being, such as he ought to be" (*American Farmer*, 211).

The term *original Americans* appears at about this time. It was used, for example, by the Seneca orator Red Jacket (and his trans-lator) when addressing George Washington at Philadelphia in 1792 (see Stone, *Red Jacket*, 170–76).

49. Crèvecoeur, *American Farmer*, 41.

50. George Washington, quoted in Turner, *Significance of the Frontier*, 18. This was one thing the young criollo republics of Latin America would have in common with their northern neighbour: around this time they became internal empires, in which small, white elites renewed a ruthless conquest of Indian communities which, under Spanish rule, had managed to retain land, culture and a degree of political autonomy.

51. "We have lost out of [our] town by death ninety," the Iroquois reported. "We, the remaining part of the Onondagas, do now inform our [British] brethren that there is no longer a council fire at the capital of the Six Nations" (Stone, *Joseph Brant*, vol. 1, 176). This outbreak seems to have been accidental.

52. He and others re-established the Confederacy on the Grand River in Ontario, with its assembly at Ohsweken.

53. James Duane, a member of the Continental Congress, quoted in Wallace, *Death and Rebirth of the Seneca*, 197. In similar circum-stances only three years earlier, the Spanish Crown tried much the same policy after the Incas' last great bid for independence in Peru. At the execution of Inca Tupa Amaru II in 1781, Spain not only abolished the Andean nobility but also tried to stamp out its culture and language, including the word *Inca*, in the hope of crushing forever "the illusory nation of the Indians" (see Wright, *Stolen Continents*, 193–99).

54. Quoted in Wallace, *Death and Rebirth of the Seneca*, 198. See also Manley, *Fort Stanwix*.

55. See Wallace, *Death and Rebirth of the Seneca*, 194–96. This number seems to include those Brant took to Canada (at first about six hundred; later, more). Iroquois numbers recovered to more than 60,000 by the end of the twentieth century.

56. In the rout by Michikinikwa (or Little Turtle) of General St. Clair's forces in western Ohio. For a vivid, detailed account of this battle and its context, see Gilbert, *God Gave Us*, chap. 7. Proportionately, "this still stands as the most one-sided defeat ever suffered by the United States army" (ibid., 152).

57. Perdue and Green, *Cherokee Removal*, 9. See Gilbert (*God Gave Us*, 133) for Knox's reckoning that it would take 2,500 men and $200,000 to fight for the Ohio Valley but only $15,000 for a "conciliatory" system of Indian subsidies and bribes.

58. Knox to Wayne, quoted in Gilbert, *God Gave Us*, 340. See also ibid., 133. Foster commented, in notes written before 1812: "These territories . . . are becoming rapidly prepared for future empire and Indiana, Illinois, Alabama, Missouri, Arkansas and Michigan have already their Representative or delegates in Congress, and claim the land as belonging to the respective settlers just as if the . . . Indian tribes were wholly extinct or had never existed" (Foster, *Jeffersonian America*, 197).

59. *Writings of Thomas Jefferson*, quoted in Weinberg, *Manifest Destiny*, 72.

60. The number of Eastern Indians at this date is uncertain. They had fallen heavily between 1760 and the 1780s and were down to about 125,000 by the 1820s.

61. The tide of this war changed with General "Mad" Anthony Wayne's defeat of the main Indian army at Fallen Timbers, near Toledo, in August 1794. In the same year, the radical Chickamauga Cherokees near Chattanooga ended their twenty-year guerrilla campaign.

62. Perdue and Green, *Cherokee Removal*, 9–10. The first act passed in 1790; the second, incorporating the civilization program, passed in 1793.

63. Peach growing (probably taken, like hogs and horses, from the Spaniards) had become so much a part of native farming that by 1700, both the Southeastern Indians and John Lawson thought the peach was an indigenous fruit. Merrell, *Indians' New World*, 16. More than a million deer hides were shipped from South Carolina

between 1700 and 1715, a staggering figure that reflects the great boom in wildlife that had followed the human decline.

64. Pocahontas was not the first North American in London, and she was by no means the last. In the eighteenth century, the Cherokees and Iroquois sent several delegations there. While Joseph Brant (Thayendanegea), a graduate of Dartmouth College, was in the city to seal the Mohawk-British alliance in 1776, he was interviewed by James Boswell, who was disappointed not to meet a real "savage."

65. Enslavement of Indian captives, often children, was common practice on British plantations throughout the seventeenth century. By 1682 any Indian brought into the Virginia colony could lawfully be enslaved. When Cadwallader Jones, who traded from his Rappahannock River plantation, listed his merchandise in 1682, the first item was "indyan children Prisoners," followed by "Deereskines and some furs" (quoted in Merrell, *Indians' New World*, 36).

66. Stone, *Red Jacket*, 169–70. Although the Five Nations became Six in the 1720s, the old usage continued for many years. The number of seats in the Iroquois parliament was unchanged, as Tuscarora interests were represented by proxy.

67. Stone, *Red Jacket*, 105.

68. The full speech is in Stone, *Red Jacket*, 170–76.

69. Red Jacket reminded the whites that their own ancestors had fled to America to enjoy religious freedom. Why shouldn't the Senecas be allowed the same right? He concluded dryly that his people might yet be open to religious conversion—but only if they could first see signs that Christianity made their white neighbours "good . . . honest, and less disposed to cheat Indians." The full exchange is in Stone, *Red Jacket*, 273–76. The speech was printed in 1811 in Canandaigua's first newspaper, which published many of Red Jacket's speeches during his lifetime. Though Red Jacket himself spoke in Seneca, many bilingual people lived in the area, so the translations may be considered especially reliable.

70. Bartram, *Travels*, 384–87; regarding Creek slavery, see ibid., 164.

71. "The Muscogulges [Creeks], the Chactaws, Chicasaws, and perhaps the Cherokees, eminently deserve the encomium of all nations, for their wisdom and virtue in resisting . . . the common enemy of mankind . . . I mean spirituous liquors" (Bartram, *Travels*, 384–87).

72. In 1730 the Cherokee Nation alone numbered thirty thousand people and held a territory the size of Britain; by 1780 it had dwindled to ten thousand and lost two-thirds of its land. Bartram (whose writings influenced Coleridge) gives a melancholy sight of Cherokee ruins, some old—"several Indian mounts or tumuli, and terraces, monuments of the ancients"—but most dating from the past twenty years of frontier war. "This fertile vale [Keowee] within the remembrance of some old traders with whom I conversed, was one continued settlement; the swelling sides of the adjoining hills were then covered with [Cherokee] habitations, and the rich level ground beneath lying on the river, was cultivated and planted: the vestiges . . . are yet visible . . . as posts or pillars of their habitations" (Bartram, *Travels*, 270–71).

73. Foster, *Jeffersonian America*, 27. "Since then however," Foster wrote in the late 1830s when organizing his old journals into book form, "they have had reason bitterly to lament the loss of his [Jefferson's] friendly and protecting influence."

74. Like their Iroquoian cousins, the Cherokee were matrilineal and democratic, but they lived in single-family dwellings in stockaded towns, not longhouses. Although the details of ancient Cherokee politics are lost, women played a strong role—which early whites called "a petticoat government" (quoted in Conley, *Cherokee Nation*, 6). Among the sixty to eighty towns in the Cherokee Nation, Chota (also known as "Echota") was considered the capital, though its authority may have been mainly a matter of prestige.

75. Their sports included games from which modern lacrosse descends. As in the great ball games of Mexico, the ancient Olympic Games and even early European football, sport was a

ritualized outlet for aggression, known as the "little brother of war." *Creek* and *Seminole* are European terms for two branches of a large Muskogean-speaking people of South Carolina, Georgia and Alabama—all probably ruled in Soto's day by the Lady of Cofitachiqui.

76. Jefferson to the Western Indians in 1808, quoted in McLoughlin, *Cherokee Renascence*, 33.

77. Among matrilineal peoples such as the Iroquoians, ancestry, and therefore nationality, was reckoned in the female line, as among the Jews. In the 1824 Cherokee Nation census, 73 white women had Cherokee husbands and 147 Cherokee women had white husbands (Mankiller and Wallis, *Mankiller*, 79).

78. John Mack Faragher writes in a recent biography of Daniel Boone: "Both [peoples] were warlike and violent . . . adherents to the ancient law of blood, and for both cultures the bloodshed was made worse by alcohol. . . . These two groups were fully acculturated into each other's ways" (Faragher, *Daniel Boone*, quoted in Grant, *Ghost Riders*, 124).

79. Quoted in Turner, *Significance of the Frontier*, 5. The frontier settler, Turner added, "shouts the war cry and takes the scalp in orthodox Indian fashion." The practice was American in origin but escalated during the colonial wars, when the French began paying a bounty for English scalps and the British did the same, justifying themselves on the usual grounds for wartime atrocities: "a barbarous method . . . introduced by the French, which we are obliged to follow in our own defence" (quoted in Brown, *Old Frontiers*, 82). White forces continued the practice into the War of 1812, the Civil War and numerous wars for the Far West. In 1776 South Carolina's legislature offered a bounty of £75 for Cherokee scalps (Perdue and Green, *Cherokee Removal*, 7).

80. François, Duc de La Rochefoucauld, quoted in McLoughlin, *Cherokee Renascence*, 49.

81. Jefferson to Harrison, 1803, quoted in Gilbert, *God Gave Us*, 200.

82. Roosevelt, quoted in Wilson, *Earth Shall Weep*, 303.

83. Senator Dawes, quoted in Hendrix, "Redbird Smith," 32.

84. At the Paris Peace Conference of 1919, Maréchal Foch turned out to be right almost to the month when he bitterly remarked: "This is not peace. It is an armistice for twenty years."

85. Turner noted how the gulf widened the further the settlers moved west: "From the time the mountains rose between the pioneer and seaboard, a new order of Americanism arose. The West and East began to get out of touch of each other. . . . The East took a narrow view of American advance, and nearly lost these men" (Turner, *Significance of the Frontier,* 14).

86. Gilbert, *God Gave Us,* 276. They also hoped to drive the Spaniards and the Seminoles from Florida.

87. The region, little of which France had ever controlled or even explored, ran westward to Mexican territory (then including Texas and surrounding lands), to the Rocky Mountains and northward to British North America, the borders of which were also undefined. At close to a million square miles, it doubled the territory claimed by the United States. Native peoples, who actually held most of it, were not considered or consulted. It was, therefore, a cession of a claim by another European power, not a transfer of land over which European sovereignty had been won by conquest or by treaty. Jefferson paid Napoleon $15 million for the whole region.

88. Decades earlier, there had been a similar split within the Cherokee Nation. When older, wiser and indeed sadder Cherokee leaders had unlawfully but pragmatically ceded much of what are now Kentucky and Tennessee to a party of land speculators led by Daniel Boone in 1775, the hawks seceded from the Cherokee Nation and waged a quixotic guerrilla war against the whites for twenty years. "You have bought a fair land," their leader, Dragging Canoe, warned Boone, "but there is a black cloud hanging over it. You will find its settlement dark and bloody" (quoted in Evans, "Notable Persons,"179). See also Gilbert, *God Gave Us,* 126.

89. The exact location of the Mobile burned by Soto isn't known, but it was likely in the same neighbourhood as Fort Mims. The militant Creeks were known as Red Sticks, from the symbolic colour of war. (Peace was white.)

90. Description from Turner, *Significance of the Frontier*, 36. The famed 1911 edition of the *Encyclopaedia Britannica* (normally tactful on its subjects' personal failings) gives details on his duelling and calls him "ignorant, violent, perverse, quarrelsome and astonishingly indiscreet . . . vigorous, brusque, uncouth, relentless, straightforward and open" (see *Encyclopaedia Britannica* 1911, vol. 15, 107–9).

91. The battle is also known as Tohopeka, the Creek word for "horseshoe."

92. For a lively and well-documented account of the Creek War, see Wilkins, *Cherokee Tragedy*, chap. 3.

93. In a battle at Talleshatchee four months earlier, Crockett and his platoon had burned a house with forty-six Creeks inside it. They had then eaten the contents of the burned-out cellar: potatoes "basted in drippings of oil from the roasted warriors" (Wilkins, *Cherokee Tragedy*, 68). Crockett later redeemed himself by helping the Cherokees fight Jackson's *Removal Act* in Washington. See Conley, *Cherokee Nation*, 66, 133–34.

94. Conley (*Cherokee Nation*, 91) says there were about three hundred women and children in addition to the thousand fighting men, though some of the civilians were taken prisoner. Wilkins, *Cherokee Tragedy*, 77, mentions that the Creek leader Menawa escaped by hiding in "a pile of dead squaws."

95. This treaty, made in August 1814, is known by two names: Horsehoe Bend and Fort Jackson.

96. McLoughlin, *Cherokee Renascence*, 193–94. Jackson's white troops also looted and terrorized the Cherokee Nation on their way home to the United States.

97. In 1788 Tennessee, which achieved statehood in 1796, was named after Tanasi, one of the Cherokees' main towns. Before that it had

been known among whites as North Carolina's Western District. It
and much of Kentucky were parts of the large, unlawful land cession to Daniel Boone and his group in 1775.

98. Tocqueville, *Journey to America,* 50.

99. Tocqueville, *Democracy in America,* 469n. His exact figure, derived
from U.S. government documents, is 271 steamboats in the ten
years after 1821. The Erie Canal opened in 1825. Tocqueville wrote
in his *Journey to America:* "America has undertaken and finished
the construction of some immense canals. It already has more railways than France; no one fails to see that the discovery of steam has
incredibly increased the power and prosperity of the Union" (271).

100. Vann's house, built about 1803, is now a state museum.

101. Some wealthy Indians even had white sharecroppers working
their cotton fields. A milder form of slavery had existed in native
culture before Europeans arrived. Traditionally, in America (as in
Africa), slaves were prisoners of war; if not killed in revenge for
other killings, they were assigned menial tasks and eventually
adopted, and their children became free. A commercial element
began with the early white demand for labour: Indians (like
Africans) began trafficking in captives to white planters. When
"civilized" Indians became owners of black slaves, the rule of
freeing a slave's children was usually applied. Henry Bibb, a slave
owned by a Cherokee in Oklahoma, said, "If I must be a slave, I
had by far, rather be a slave to an Indian, than to a white man"
(quoted in King, ed., *Cherokee Indian Nation,* 125).

102. Named after Chota (or Echota), the Cherokees' ancient "Mother
Town" on the Little Tennessee River. Chota was abandoned in the
late eighteenth century after the cession of what is now Tennessee
to the whites.

103. The syllabic script was invented independently by Sequoyah, who
was not literate in English. He was among a small number of
Cherokee who had moved to Arkansas, and his invention caught
on quickly among monolingual Cherokees who wanted to write
home to their kin. By 1825 the majority of Cherokee adults were

literate, a higher proportion than in the United States. Special type was cast to print newspaper articles and other documents in Sequoyan at the Cherokee national press.

104. Elias Boudinot (a full-blood or nearly so) was editor and publisher of the *Cherokee Phoenix*.

105. Differences were seen as differences of "manners"—what we now call *culture* in the anthropological sense.

106. Quoted in Mankiller and Wallis, *Mankiller*, 52.

107. Miranda, *New Democracy in America*, 130, 165.

108. Quoted in Wilkins, *Cherokee Tragedy*, 3. John Ridge was the son of Major Ridge, who fought in the Creek War. Foster says that the witty and eccentric John Randolph (U.S. senator for Virginia from 1825 to 1827) claimed descent from Pocahontas (Foster, *Jeffersonian America*, 153).

109. The Age of Reason gave way to the Age of Romanticism. See, for example, McLoughlin, *Cherokee Renascence*, 448.

110. Friedman, *Inventors*, xviii, and Tocqueville, *Journey to America*, 329. See also Tocqueville, *Democracy in America* (2000 [1835]), 456: "The inhabitants of the United States [are convinced] that they constitute the only religious, enlightened, and free people . . . they conceive an overweening opinion of their superiority, and they are not very remote from believing themselves to belong to a distinct race of mankind." Thousands of black Americans were shipped back to Africa, partly for philanthropic reasons but also to reduce the number of free (and potentially free) blacks.

111. Quoted in Perdue and Green, *Cherokee Removal*, 15.

112. James Farnham, 1839, quoted in Delbanco, *Melville*, 48.

113. Jackson, message to U.S. Congress, December 3, 1833, quoted in McLoughlin, *Cherokee Renascence*, 449. Jackson added: "Established in the midst of another and superior race . . . they must necessarily yield." On his travels, Tocqueville saw "a cold selfishness and complete insensibility. . . . This world here belongs to us, [Americans] tell themselves every day: the Indian race is destined for final destruction . . . it is necessary that they

die. . . . I will have their lands and will be innocent of their death"
(Tocqueville, *Journey to America,* 200–201).

114. See McLoughlin, *Cherokee Renascence,* 432–33; he describes the
Georgia Guard as "essentially a private security force under militia officers. . . . the state accepted no responsibility for the actions
of the Guard."

115. The Americans of that part of the Union [the South] look with
jealousy upon the aborigines," wrote Tocqueville. Well aware of
this envy, the Cherokees described their borders in their constitution and banned any further cessions, except by their elected
government, on pain of death.

116. Quoted in Perdue and Green, *Cherokee Removal.*

117. $1.25 million plus other undertakings (Perdue and Green,
Cherokee Removal, 71).

118. See Perdue and Green, *Cherokee Removal,* 71–76.

119. Cotton is a heavy feeder that soon exhausts the soil. In the days
before chemical fertilizers, cotton planters needed a steady supply of new land to stay in business. The white method of corn
growing was also harder on the land than the old Indian techniques. Ploughs caused more erosion than the native hoes. And
the Indians had usually sown corn together with beans, which are
nitrogen fixers, and squash, which kept down weeds.

120. Mooney, *Myths of the Cherokee,* 117. Removal was probably at the
top of Jackson's personal agenda, but in other areas he was a pop-
ulist front man, playing to the frontier gallery and chosen and
manipulated by abler politicians behind the scenes, especially
Martin Van Buren.

121. Quoted in Zinn, *People's History,* 130. Zinn notes that modern books
on the Jacksonian period often fail even to mention his Indian
policy. The popular vote for Jackson's re-election in 1832 was
687,000 for Jackson and 530,000 for Henry Clay. At that time only
about 2 million of the United States' 13 million people had the vote.

122. "The rapacity of the settlers," Tocqueville wrote, was "backed by
the tyranny of the government" (Tocqueville, *Democracy in*

America, 404). The actions of Alabama and Mississippi are summarized in his footnotes on pages 404–5.

123. Quoted in Perdue and Green, *Cherokee Removal*, 75. Georgia's legislation called on "the United States [to] redeem her pledged honor" and threatened dire consequences "if the Indians continue to turn a deaf ear to the voice of reason and friendship."

124. Tocqueville, *Democracy in America*, 405.

125. Jeremiah Evarts writing as "William Penn," quoted in Perdue and Green, *Cherokee Removal*, 109. See also Tocqueville, *Democracy in America*, 405n, who noted that France then had 162 to the square mile—more than twenty times Georgia's density.

126. The whole 1827 Cherokee Constitution is in Perdue and Green, *Cherokee Removal*, 60–70.

127. See Tocqueville, *Democracy in America*, 472–81, for his analysis of Jackson's politics, "nullification," a brief but perceptive comment on the Indian Removal, and the bank issue. Like many of Jackson's policies, his attack on South Carolina had a strong personal element, as he had fallen out with his former vice-president, John C. Calhoun, over personal matters and Calhoun's denunciation of Jackson's behaviour in the 1818 Seminole War.

128. Quoted in Conley, *Cherokee Nation*, 134. In the Senate the bill passed 28 to 19, but in the House it passed by only 102 to 97 (Perdue and Green, *Cherokee Removal*, 122).

129. Quoted in Brown, *Old Frontiers*, 495.

130. "May a gracious Providence," wrote one essayist, "avert from this country the awful calamity of exposing ourselves to the wrath of heaven [for this] cruelty and oppression"(Jeremiah Evarts, November 1829, writing as "William Penn" in *A Brief View of the Present Relations between the Government . . . and the Indians*, quoted in Perdue and Green, *Cherokee Removal*, 105 10). See also Prucha, ed., *Cherokee Removal*. In a Christmas newsletter to her women's movement, Catharine Beecher explained that the Cherokees were about to be driven to "final annihilation, unless the feelings of a humane and Christian nation shall be aroused to

prevent the unhallowed sacrifice" (Catharine Beecher, *Circular Addressed to Benevolent Ladies of the U. States, December 25, 1829,* quoted in Perdue and Green, *Cherokee Removal,* 111–14).

131. Trollope, *Domestic Manners,* 220–21, quoted in Wilkins, *Cherokee Tragedy,* 174.

132. Quoted in Parker, *Melville,* 529.

133. Recently, white apologists claimed that the enigmatic nine-thousand-year-old skeleton of Kennewick Man, unearthed in 1996, belonged to a "European" killed by Indians. The issue has been clouded by disputes over the ownership of the bones and the wish of native groups to have them laid to rest as an ancestor. The racial features of the skull are said by some to be unclear—but many human remains of such an early date do not correspond closely to modern racial features. Even if arguments such as Jackson's had any basis in fact, it is difficult to see how they would justify extermination by "civilized" Europeans.

134. Quoted in Perdue and Green, *Cherokee Removal,* 127–28.

135. Jackson's remark is quoted in Carter, *Cherokee Sunset,* 83.

136. Jackson directed that the treaty money no longer be paid to the nation but to each individual. In fact it wasn't paid at all for many years, and if it had been, it would have amounted to only 42 cents a head each year (Mooney, *Myths of the Cherokee,* 119). Mooney gives a good account of this period, with many quotations and details.

137. *Georgia House of Representatives* (journal), 1830, quoted in Weinberg, *Manifest Destiny,* 83. George Gilmer was governor in the crucial years of 1829 to 1831.

138. This law was aimed mainly at the missionaries in the nation who supported Cherokee rights. One of them, Samuel Austin Worcester, was among several who were arrested in 1831 and sentenced to hard labour; his is the case on which Chief Justice John Marshall ruled in 1832.

139. This case was inconclusive. The court declined to rule, on the grounds that the Cherokees, being a foreign nation, had no legal

standing before the United States. But it left the door open for a U.S. citizen to bring a similar suit—and that is why the second case was brought before it.

140. Quoted in Perdue and Green, *Cherokee Removal,* 81–84. These authors note how the Marshall decision has become a cornerstone of modern federal Indian law and how the "key element [in Marshall] is the doctrine of retained sovereignty—the idea that a nation retains all those attributes of sovereignty it does not voluntarily surrender."

141. Both quoted in Woodward, *Cherokees,* 171. Jackson's remark (attributed, not written, but widely known in living memory) differs slightly in Mooney, *Myths of the Cherokee,* 120: "John Marshall has made his decision, now let him enforce it." John Marshall died, at eighty, in July 1835. Ominously, the great Liberty Bell cracked while tolling for his death.

142. Friedman, for example, describes Jackson's Indian policy as genocidal (*Inventors,* 68).

143. The exact number is not known. The widely accepted estimate is four thousand Cherokee deaths or more, about half in the camps and half on the road; some scholars believe the number may have been higher. A census of the Cherokee Nation in 1835 showed the total in the East to be 16,542, not including 1,592 black slaves and 201 whites married to Cherokees. At that time the Cherokee Nation held about 20,000 square miles, covering parts of four states: some 9,000 Cherokees lived within what is now Georgia; 3,600 in North Carolina; 2,500 in Tennessee; and 1,400 in Alabama. See Mooney, *Myths of the Cherokee,* 125.

144. See Zinn, *People's History,* 138–45.

145. John Ross to the Senecas, April 14, 1834, in Ross, *The Papers,* vol. 1, 284–87.

146. A U.S. officer, Major W.M. Davis, sent to enroll the Cherokees for removal, wrote in disgust to the secretary of war: "Sir, that paper . . . called a treaty, is no treaty at all." If put to a vote, "it would be instantly rejected by nine-tenths of them" (quoted in

Mooney, *Myths of the Cherokee*, 126). Some who put their names to the document may have been bribed (an old treaty-making tactic), but Boudinot, the Ridges and others believed they were doing the best they could for their people in impossible circumstances. They also knew that the treaty was illegal under the Cherokee Constitution and that their actions carried the death penalty. "I have signed my death warrant," said Major Ridge prophetically. Boudinot said: "We can die but the great Cherokee Nation will be saved." After the Trail of Tears, they and others who had signed the Echota Treaty were killed, and the nation split into virtual civil war for the first decade in its new home.

147. Quoted in Mooney, *Myths of the Cherokee*, 127.

148. Quoted in ibid., 127–28.

149. An alternative form of the name is Gulkalaski. See Mankiller and Wallis, *Mankiller*, 88.

150. Quoted in King and Evans, eds., "Trail of Tears," 183. Later the Cherokee veteran said: "If I had known that Jackson would drive us from our homes, I would have killed him that day at the Horseshoe" (quoted in Mooney, *Myths of the Cherokee*, 164).

151. Quoted in King and Chapman, *Sequoyah Legacy*, 51.

152. Emerson, April 1838 (my emphasis), quoted in Zinn, *People's History*, 147. See also Conley, *Cherokee Nation*, 148, and Ehle, *Trail of Tears*, 303, for quotations from Emerson's letter.

153. Concentration camps in the pre-Nazi sense. The word seems to have been coined by the British in their roundups of civilians during the Boer War. The British also set a precedent for ethnic cleansing in America: during the French and Indian War, they deported eight thousand Acadians by ship from maritime New France. See Nelles, *Little History of Canada*, 58–61.

154. Quoted in Mankiller and Wallis, *Mankiller*, 93 (the wording differs slightly in other sources).

155. A few had left voluntarily in the 1820s: first to Arkansas and then to Oklahoma when Arkansas was overrun by whites.

156. Several hundred Cherokees in North Carolina, and others who hid out in the Smoky Mountains, managed to stay in North Carolina to become what is now called the Eastern Band. With the help of William Thomas, a white lawyer and businessman who had been raised by a Cherokee family, these people were able to secure a reservation at Qualla that their descendants still hold. About five thousand Seminoles held out in Florida, waging a guerrilla resistance in the Everglades that went on for many years, costing $20 million and 1,500 American lives (Zinn, *People's History*, 144–46). Tocqueville may not have known the full extent of the evil, but he commented acidly on its "philanthropic" justifications: "It is impossible to destroy men with more respect for the laws of humanity." An 1870 editor of his *Democracy in America* noted that in much of the East, "the race is extinct; and the predictions of M. de Tocqueville are fulfilled." See Tocqueville, *Democracy in America*, 410–11.

157. Black Hoof, Shawnee, to John Johnston, 1830 (when Black Hoof was more than one hundred years old), quoted in Gilbert, *God Gave Us*, 331.

Chapter 6 – Manifest Destiny

1. "The Oregon Question" (lecture, Boston, January 1845), quoted in Van Alstyne, *Rising American Empire*, 112.
2. Quoted in Baldwin, *American Quest*, 155.
3. Melville, *Moby Dick*, chap. 93.
4. Oakes Shaw (Lemuel's son), quoted in Parker, *Melville*, 176.
5. Tocqueville, *Journey to America*, 134, 337. From Detroit, Tocqueville and his friend, with two Indian guides, followed the road into the woods as far as Saginaw. "You can go forward without fear," a trader told him. "I should sleep more soundly surrounded by Indians than by whites." In the opening scenes of *Moby Dick*, Ishmael makes a similar remark: "Better sleep with a sober cannibal than a drunken Christian."

6. On the Fourth of July 1832, when Tocqueville was in St. Louis, he jotted in his notebook that the neighbouring Indians "have just crossed into American territory, putting everything to fire and sword" (Tocqueville, *Journey to America*, 123–24). The Cahokia platform has a bigger footprint than Egypt's Great Pyramid, which covers 13 acres.

7. Tocqueville, *Democracy in America*, 307. Ralph Waldo Emerson agreed: "We have yet had no genius in America," he wrote in an essay titled "The Poet" in 1844. "Our fisheries, our Negroes, and Indians, our boasts . . . and the pusillanimity of honest men . . . are yet unsung." Quoted in Conn, *American Literature*, 170.

8. For an analysis of this tradition, see Hofstadter, *Anti-intellectualism*.

9. In the 1860s this intellectual conquest would be put aside while the internal nature of the American experiment was settled on the battlefield, to be resumed with less euphoria as the country digested certain truths after the Civil War.

10. Published in 1848 and 1851, respectively, as *Ancient Monuments of the Mississippi Valley* and *Aboriginal Monuments of the State of New York*.

11. The account of the first expedition was published as *Incidents of Travel in Central America, Chiapas, and Yucatan*. The English artist Frederick Catherwood travelled with Stephens and produced superb illustrations, using a combination of fine draughtsmanship and early photographic techniques. Their more detailed *Incidents of Travel in Yucatan* came out in 1843. Both works were published by Harper and Brothers and are available in modern reprints, complete with the fine engravings. The quotation is from a "Biographical Notice" by Catherwood in a later edition after Stephens's early death in 1852. See Stephens, *Travel in Central America*, vol. 1, v–vi.

12. Stephens, *Travel in Central America*, vol. 2, 124. One of the sculptured stelae is thought to be the biggest stone ever quarried by the Maya—35 feet long and weighing 65 tons. Inscriptions (deciphered

long after Stephens's day) show it was erected in A D. 771. Not far from Quiriguá is the much larger ancient city of Copan, which Stephens bought (on paper) for $50. Stephens also had business interests in the region, promoting steamships and the Panama Railway—the safest and quickest way to California in those days.

13. Squier also shared Stephens's political and commercial interest in Central America, believing Nicaragua to be the best gateway through the isthmus to Asia: "To us is given, in this modern time, the ability of acquiring the rule of the East [by] transferring into our unarmed hands that passage for which Columbus strove in vain. . . . The fortune of war [with Mexico] has planted our eagles on the Pacific: across the entire continent . . . our Republic is supreme" (quoted in Van Alstyne, *Rising American Empire*, 159).

14. Stephens, *Travel in Central America*, vol. 2, 442.

15. Prescott's *Mexico* was published in 1843, his *Peru* in 1847. John Hemming's 1970 *Conquest of the Incas* is the latter work's outstanding modern successor, including new information from Inca and Spanish sources that was not available to Prescott.

16. Squier, *Peru*, 543.

17. Melville, *Moby Dick*, chap. 24. Melville puts these words in the mouth of his narrator, Ishmael, one of the most autobiographical characters in American fiction.

18. Based closely on his desertion from the *Acushnet*, the book takes the form of a captivity narrative—those breathless tales of life among Indians written by close-kneed Yankee maidens. But Melville turns the genre on its head: he flees *to* the savages from tyranny aboard the whaler, which, like other ships in his work, is a microcosm of the United States.

19. Castigated for indecency and atheism by pious reviewers, *Typee* was lauded by Hawthorne, Whitman and Irving. Melville avoids romanticizing the islanders as noble savages (he fears, with some reason, that they may be cannibals) or himself as a noble civilizer (he wields a knife during his escape).

20. The first British edition (published shortly before the American for copyright reasons) was called *The Whale*. Some later editions keep both titles. Cooper, author of *Last of the Mohicans* and other frontier yarns, died in 1851, the year *Moby Dick* was published; Irving, best known for his *Sketch Book*, died in 1859.

21. Lawrence, *Selected Essays*, 258.

22. Miranda, *New Democracy in America*, 129–30. See *Moby Dick*, chap. 81, for the antiquity of whales and native whaling. No one knows how long sperm whales can live, but some authorities believe it may be centuries: "A lance-head of stone being found in him [an old whale], the flesh perfectly firm about it. Who had darted that stone lance? And when? It might have been darted by some Nor' West Indian long before America was discovered" (Melville, *Moby Dick*, chap. 81).

23. Delbanco calls whaling "the first international industry dominated by the United States" (Delbanco, *Melville*, 40). The estimate in *Moby Dick* (chap. 24) that "we whalemen of American now outnumber all the rest [with] upward of seven hundred vessels; manned by eighteen thousand men" was accurate enough. No other nation came close. The first commercial oil well in the United States began production near Titusville, Pennsylvania, in 1859. Until 1948, wells on American soil produced half or more of the world's total; since that year, the United States has been a net importer. See Williams, *Empire*, 209–10.

24. Melville, *Moby Dick*, chap. 105.

25. See the Jefferson quote at the head of Chapter 1. Melville, however, may not have thought that God was just. In *Melville's Quarrel with God*, Lawrence Thompson argues that as Melville lost his faith, he fell into the old Ophitic heresy that the world being what it is, God must be evil or mad. See Thompson, *Melville's Quarrel*.

26. Among them James Farnham, the Vermont lawyer, quoted in my Chapter 5 and Delbanco, *Melville*, 48.

27. Melville, *Moby Dick*, chap. 37.

28. The boiling down of blubber in a stormy night becomes a scene from hell: "The rushing *Pequod*, freighted with savages, and laden with fire, and burning a corpse, and plunging into that blackness . . . seemed the material counterpart of her monomaniac commander's soul" (Melville, *Moby Dick*, chap. 96, "The Try-Works").

29. *Moby Dick*, chap. 135. The ramming and sinking of the ship was no wild fancy. Several whaleships were sunk by large bull sperm whales (which could weigh up to a hundred tons)—notably, the *Essex* in 1820, referred to by Melville, and the *Ann Alexander*, which by an extraordinary coincidence was sunk by a whale just weeks before *Moby Dick* came out. "Ye Gods!" wrote Melville when he heard the news. "What a commentator is this Ann Alexander whale. . . . Crash! comes Moby Dick himself." The victorious whale was caught and killed three years later, identified by harpoons and wreckage in its head. See Parker, *Melville*, 194–96, 877–78.

30. For Inca mythology and statecraft, Prescott drew heavily on the writer Garcilaso de la Vega (1539–1616), who had been born in Cusco, Peru, to an Inca princess and a conquistador. Besides his bestselling *Comentarios Reales de los Incas* [Royal Commentaries of the Incas] (1609), Inca Garcilaso wrote a history of Soto's campaigns in the Southeastern United States, *La Florida del Inca* [The Inca's Florida] (1606). See my Chapter 2.

31. America is a "confidence culture . . . of land boomers and poets, prophets and profiteers" (Lindberg, *Confidence Man*, quoted in Tony Tanner's introduction to Melville, *Confidence Man*, xviii).

32. Quoted in Miller, *Nature's Nation*, 83. The camp meeting, at Cane Ridge, went on for weeks. Estimates of the crowd vary from twenty to thirty thousand.

33. Baldwin, *American Quest*, 134–35.

34. The spiritual heirs of Transcendentalism include the Beats, the Hippies, the Peace Movement and various quasi-Oriental cults and communes.

35. Turner, *Significance of the Frontier*, 5–6, 22 (see also Flannery, *Eternal Frontier*, 288–89). In later essays, Turner, who came from Wisconsin, took a rosier view of the frontiersmen and barely mentioned the indigenous influence.

36. Quoted in Grant, *Ghost Riders*, 127. See also Gilbert, *Westering Man*.

37. Dominionists are best described as Christian Taliban, wanting to run America on extreme theocratic lines. To quote from one recent blog: "Our job is to reclaim America for Christ, whatever the cost. As the vice regents of God, we are to exercise godly dominion and influence over . . . every aspect and institution of human society." One frontier vigilante group, the Minuteman Civil Defense Corps, has even built its own border fence in Arizona. These groups also descend from white "nativist" movements of the 1840s: the Native American Party, the Know-Nothings and other bigots who attacked Catholics, blacks and immigrants— especially those bringing "un-American" ideas from Europe. The Know-Nothings were so called because their standard answer to any question was "I know nothing" (like the Spanish waiter in *Fawlty Towers*). Variants of these movements included the American Republicans, the American Party, the Order of United Americans and the Order of the Star-Spangled Banner.

38. William Miller foretold the Second Coming for 1843; then, on its no-show, for 1844. When he failed to deliver the second time, Miller was able to persuade his more gullible followers that Christ *had* come back to Earth but, for reasons best known to Himself, was keeping out of sight. The sect survives, in various forms, as the Adventists. See Baldwin, *American Quest*, 139.

39. More than a century ago, Count Leo Tolstoy called the Mormons "the American religion." His remark was made in 1892 to Andrew White, the U.S. foreign minister to Russia. Harold Bloom took the phrase "the American religion" for the title of his 1992 book on American belief. Most recently, Jon Krakauer has written that Mormonism "is now widely considered to be the quintessential American religion" (Krakauer, *Under the Banner*, 7).

40. The English in the *Book of Mormon* is a pastiche of the style of the 1611 King James Bible (with some unfortunate slips of pseudo-archaic grammar).

41. James Adair, in his *History of the American Indians,* published in 1775, thought along these lines. In James Fenimore Cooper's 1848 tale *The Oak Openings,* the character Amer believes that the Bible has directed him to lead the Indians—the Lost Tribes—back to Palestine.

42. Champollion was a gifted linguist. After learning Coptic (the descendant of ancient Egyptian), he was able to unravel the mystery by using the Rosetta Stone, which gave two Egyptian versions of a text also in Greek.

43. Moroni himself (the angel who purportedly led Smith to the gold sheets) discusses the script in the part of the *Book of Mormon* also called the Book of Mormon, chap. 9, 32–34.

44. *Book of Mormon,* 2 Nephi, chap. 5, 24.

45. Krakauer, *Under the Banner,* 70.

46. Mormonism breathed new life into the "inverted conquest" story in American mythology, one in which the winners escape guilt by casting themselves as victims. See Limerick, *Something in the Soil,* 79–87, for her discussion of "inverted conquest" and the use of the frontier metaphor in modern politics.

47. Krakauer, *Under the Banner,* 98.

48. Mormonism also manages to blend both low- and high-church elements. The leadership is a Vatican like theocracy, yet every Mormon man (not woman) can be a lesser prophet, open to instructions from heaven.

49. *Book of Mormon,* Jacob 2:27–28. The "delighteth" has been corrected in some later editions. The word normally used is *polygamy,* but that can apply to multiple marriage by either sex. *Polygyny* is the correct term for a system where men may have many wives, but women may have only one husband. *Plural marriage* was the term most favoured by Mormons.

50. From Fawn Brodie's *No Man Knows My History,* 1995, quoted in Krakauer, *Under the Banner.*

51. Smith, quoted in Krakauer, *Under the Banner,* 102.

52. Quoted in Krakauer, *Under the Banner,* 104.

53. The Sauk, Fox and other native groups were driven out after the Black Hawk War in 1832.

54. For a few years in the early 1840s, Nauvoo became a boom town rivalling Chicago. Mormon converts came from as far away as Europe, and there was the usual influx of unruly backwoods characters. At its height in 1845, the town had about twelve thousand citizens (not all Mormons), with a similar number in the surrounding country. Today Nauvoo is a backwater, with about one thousand residents.

55. He ran a serious campaign, but too many non-Mormons distrusted him, fearing, with good reason, that if elected he might make himself Priest and King of the United States. Whether or not Smith suffered from epilepsy (which has been correlated with intense religious feelings), his running mate and fellow Mormon, Sidney Rigdon, certainly did.

56. Among other things, Smith wrecked his opponents' newspaper and printing press.

57. Young had been away in Massachusetts, campaigning for Smith's run at the presidency, but once he heard of the murder, he made a hasty return to Nauvoo. He won the succession as Prophet after giving an extraordinary speech, during which he seemed to those present to *become* Joseph Smith before their eyes. The metamorphosis did not last long, but was enough.

58. Smith claimed to have received well over a hundred revelations from the Almighty; Young had only one—about organizing wagon trains to Utah. Young's attitude toward the Bible was equally pragmatic: parts of it, he said, were "baby stories." Quoted in Metzger and Coogan, *Oxford Companion to the Bible,* 527–28.

59. Quoted in Baldwin, *American Quest,* 140. See also Krakauer, *Under the Banner,* chap. 17.

60. In 1819 Spain resigned her claims north of the forty-second parallel, the northern boundary of California. The British and the

Americans argued over ownership of the "Oregon" region between there and the Russian colonies in Alaska until 1845, when they agreed on the forty-ninth parallel as the border. See Van Alstyne, *Rising American Empire*, 105–118.

61. See Van Alstyne, *Rising American Empire*, 136.

62. In 1680 about 400 Spaniards were killed and 2,500 settlers driven out. The Spaniards abandoned Santa Fe to the Pueblo leader, Pope, and withdrew to El Paso. They did not return until 1692 and never regained full control. Most of the surviving native towns of the Southwest are thought to have been founded about eight hundred years ago, when the Pueblo peoples moved to their present locations after a crisis in the Anasazi culture, from which they are descended. Only Cusco, Mexico, and a few other Mesoamerican and Peruvian cities have a comparable record of unbroken occupancy. There are much older buildings in the Americas, some dating back more than five thousand years, but these have not been in continuous use.

63. The non-Indian population of Texas rose from about four thousand in 1821 to one hundred thousand by 1845.

64. Jackson's description is surely as Orwellian a phrase as his "true philanthropy" toward Indians. Quoted in Williams, *Empire*, 84.

65. Quoted in Van Alstyne, *Rising American Empire*, 107.

66. Quoted in ibid., 143.

67. Quoted in Williams, *Empire*, 89.

68. Whitman, writing in the *Brooklyn Eagle,* quoted in Williams, *Empire,* and Zinn, *People's History,* 154.

69. Quoted in Zinn, *People's History,* 155. The population of Mexico at the time was about 7 million, half of whom were ethnic Indians and the rest whites (criollos) and mestizos, with the criollos in charge.

70. His name is spelled Moctezuma in Mexico. The National (and Viceregal) Palace stands on the site of his palace, forming one side of the great square at the heart of the city, which was an island in a shallow lake in Aztec times. Chapultepec, where the

Aztec emperor also had a residence, is a fortified rock outcrop on the mainland a few miles to the west.

71. This relationship was later challenged by Mexico several times, notably during the Mexican Revolution and the presidency of the left-leaning nationalist Lázaro Cárdenas in the 1930s. The "domestic dependent" Indian nations and some small countries such as Hawaii were also arguably client states at this time.

72. Quoted in Van Alstyne, *Rising American Empire*, 152.

73. The first known use of "manifest destiny" is in an editorial by John O'Sullivan in the *New York Morning News*, December 27, 1845.

74. Weinberg, *Manifest Destiny*, 41. He also called it "such a creature as Frankenstein fashioned. Gaining control over the doctrine of natural right, it in effect changed the impartial law of nature into the unique code favorable to the rights of one nation."

75. Quoted in Krakauer, *Under the Banner*, 205–7.

76. Taney applied his ruling even to the descendants of slaves. The case overthrew the Missouri Compromise, thereby reopening the whole question of the power balance between North and South.

77. Advice to Buchanan from Robert Tyler, the son of former president John Tyler. Quoted in Krakauer, *Under the Banner*, 210.

78. The motive for the killing seems to have been a combination of plunder and paranoia. See Krakauer, *Under the Banner*, chap. 18.

79. Rice, *Francis Burton*, 336.

80. Tocqueville, *Journey to America*, 340.

81. In 1830 the Northern states had only a tiny population of African descent: about 1 percent in Massachusetts and 2 percent in New York (see Tocqueville, *Democracy in America* [2000 (1835)], 428). Cotton production rose from 1,000 tons in 1790 to 1 million tons in 1860. Over the same period, the slave population grew from 0.5 million to 4 million.

82. Ancient thralldom was a complex institution, and it had withered with the Roman Empire. Slaves had filled many social roles: most were domestic servants; some were trusted retainers, even teachers; and a few became wealthy enough to buy their freedom. Only

the unluckier ones were worked to death in galleys, mines and quarries. Slavery began making a comeback with the revival of Europe's economy in the late Middle Ages. As early as the twelfth century, slaves were being used to work mines and sugar estates in Sicily and Cyprus (Wolf, *Europe,* 195). As noted in Chapter 2, overseas plantations in Madeira, the Canaries and the Azores shortly before 1492 became the prototype for slavery in the Caribbean and mainland Americas.

83. Tocqueville, *Democracy in America* (2000 [1835]), 440.

84. Columbus, Vespucci and many others had taken New World slaves to Europe. Eventually the pope, after much debate, declared American Indians to be human beings. The Spaniards then resorted to various forms of "paid," yet forced, labour in mines and on estates (see Chapter 2). New forms of de facto slavery appeared in Amazonia during the rubber boom of the early twentieth century.

85. The laws banning the trade were passed in 1807–8 but took some time to have effect. Slaveholding was abolished by the British in 1833. Slavery had been abolished by most of Latin America (except Brazil and Cuba) in the 1820s.

86. See Wolf (*Europe,* chap. 7) for these conservative estimates and Crosby, *Columbian Exchange,* 188, for a total figure of 12 million. Besides those who died on the way, many others soon died from exploitation. Once established in America, the black population grew strongly and mixed with both Indians and whites. Today more than 100 million people throughout the Americas have visible African ancestry.

87. Tocqueville, *Journey to America,* 97.

88. Tocqueville, *Journey to America,* 99.

89. There are countless works on the subject; among the best for non-specialists are Robert Penn Warren's *Legacy of the Civil War* (1961), Shelby Foote's multivolume history and Ken Burns's outstanding television series. David Blight's *Race and Reunion* (2001) is a penetrating analysis of the cultural aftermath.

90. Blight (*Race and Reunion*, 64) gives a total of 620,000, more than in all the other American wars together through Korea. In 1914–18 Britain lost 750,000 men from a population of 43 million (see Clarke, *Hope and Glory*, 8, 80, and MacMillan, *Paris 1919*, xxvi). German and French losses per capita in the First World War were even higher. About two-thirds of the men lost in the American Civil War died from sickness. In the First World War, the United States lost about 54,000 and in the Second World War, about 292,000. Japan's losses in the Second World War were about 1.2 million. See Hobsbawm, *Age of Extremes*, 28, and Keegan, *Second World War*, 591.

91. Warren, *Legacy of the Civil War*, 4 (my emphasis).

92. Quoted in Lindqvist, *Exterminate*, 54. The young Churchill was in Sudan as what is now called an "embedded" correspondent. The poetry of Rudyard Kipling illustrates the transformation from imperial jingoism to home slaughter. In 1898 he had written of "Lesser breeds without the Law" and in 1899 of "the White Man's burden" (referring to the Philippines). After losing a son in the Great War, however, he was less sanguine: "If any question why we died / Tell them, because our fathers lied" (quoted in Clarke, *Hope and Glory*, 83).

93. Waldman, *Atlas*, 119.

94. Brown, *Bury My Heart*, 5.

95. Williams, *Empire*, 91.

96. Douglass, "Our Work Is Not Done" (speech to the American Antislavery Society, Philadelphia, Penn., December 3–4, 1863), quoted in Blight, *Race and Reunion*, 16.

97. Carpetbaggers were Northerners who went to the South to profit from Reconstruction. Southerners who collaborated with the North were known as scalawags, and Northerners with Southern sympathies were called copperheads (after a venomous breed of snake).

98. Despite the Fifteenth Amendment of 1870, which extended the franchise to all adult men, the Southern states kept passing

racially discriminatory laws. When the Supreme Court ruled that such laws were constitutional in 1896, it encouraged further entrenchment of America's apartheid. Some Northern states had allowed free blacks to vote long before the Civil War, but white intimidation often prevented them from doing so. American Indians were not granted U.S. citizenship and voting rights until 1924.

99. Whitman's preface to the first edition of *Leaves of Grass* (my emphasis).

100. About 180,000 African Americans served (under white officers) in the Union Army and Navy; one in five of them died (Blight, *Race and Reunion*, 64).

101. See Chapter 5.

102. In accordance with Cherokee law, Elias Boudinot had paid with his life (in 1839) for having signed the Treaty of New Echota, which had led to the Cherokee Removal (see Chapter 5). Under the Iroquois name of Hasanoanda, Ely Parker was an elected sachem of the Six Nations, which had managed to regroup somewhat on both sides of the U.S.-Canada border. Prevented by race discrimination from going into law, Parker had trained as a civil engineer. Today both he and Morgan are considered co-founders of modern American anthropology. Parker was Indian Affairs commissioner under President Ulysses S. Grant from 1869 to 1871. See Parker, *Ely S. Parker*, for a biography written by his nephew.

103. It was estimated at the time that the federal government had spent $3.4 billion on the war; by 1879 the total cost, including pensions and other long-term outlays, was reckoned at more than $6 billion—staggering figures in those days (*Encyclopaedia Britannica* 1911, vol.1, 827).

104. Quoted in Brown, *Bury My Heart*, 166. Under Sheridan's command was George A. Custer, who would die at the Battle of the Little Bighorn in 1876.

105. The animal is more properly known as the American bison (*Bison bison*).

106. This image was also popularized in Europe by the bestselling German novelist Karl May. To this day there are people in Germany who go from their banking jobs to a weekend in a tipi village, dressing in buckskins and war bonnets with obsessive authenticity.

107. The first post-Columbian horses in North America may well have been an unintended gift of Hernando de Soto. Ironically, a horse native to America had been among the early victims of the Ice Age hunters. Indeed, horses were very nearly driven to extinction in the Old World as well at that time. The horse seems to have been adopted on most of the Plains and Canadian Prairies by the 1770s.

108. About 20 million immigrated in these seventy years, though the rest of the growth was natural increase. Herman Melville's life spans this growth of the United States from migrant outpost to world power. When he was born in 1819, Manhattan had barely 100,000 people; when he died in 1891, it held more than 3 million (Delbanco, *Melville*, 3).

109. In 1903 Horatio Nelson Jackson drove from San Francisco to New York City in a gasoline-powered Winton car, following railway service tracks and wagon trails. The 5,600-mile trip took sixty-three days.

110. The first machine gun in general use was the Gatling. A later type, the Hotchkiss, was used at Wounded Knee and elsewhere. As Frederick W. Turner observed of the crushing of the Ghost Dance: "In this clash between visions and Hotchkiss guns, the latter won" (Turner, ed., *Indian Reader*, 1974, 15). See also Lazarus, *Black Hills*, 114–16.

111. The U.S. Army killed about six thousand Plains Indians in the twenty-five years after the Civil War. That alone was not enough for victory, and it was said that the cost was a million dollars a head by the 1870s (Flannery, *Eternal Frontier*, 310).

112. The army also shot buffalo on sight, to starve the Indians. Six million hides were exported to Europe in this decade—only a small fraction of the animals killed. See Flannery, *Eternal Frontier*, 321,

and Walton, "Were Bison Victims?" for a report on a new study by the economist M. Scott Taylor.

113. Some estimates go as high as 60 million bison (buffalo) in the early 1800s; eyewitnesses saw herds so big they made a sea of hairy backs from foreground to horizon (see Flannery, *Eternal Frontier*, 312–24). Canada also took part in the slaughter. At one point the total number of bison alive in the world may have been only two or three hundred. They have since recovered to about a quarter million.

114. For more historical background and the modern aftermath involving the American Indian Movement, the Sioux and the FBI, see Matthiessen, *Crazy Horse*, and Lazarus, *Black Hills*.

115. Quoted in Brown, *Bury My Heart*, 85, and Wilson, *Earth Shall Weep*, 273. Chivington attacked at dawn with about six hundred Colorado militiamen, many of whom were drunk. Estimates of the dead run from 105 to 200.

116. Also called the *Severalty Act*, it was passed in 1887. The irony of the *Dawes Act* is that it began as a response to Helen Hunt Jackson's searing condemnation of her country's treatment of Indians, *A Century of Dishonor* (1881).

117. Flannery, *Eternal Frontier*, 310.

118. The words of Waterhouse after the Powhatan War. See Chapter 3.

119. In 1874 the United States produced 5 tons of barbed wire; in 1890, 125,000 tons (*Encyclopaedia Britannica* 1911, vol. 3, 384–85).

120. Gatling invented his steam plough in 1857. In 1911 a Montana farmer turned photographer, Evelyn Cameron, wrote to her brother: "The range country that you knew so well is about all gone now & the prairie swarms with farmers who plough up the land with steam and gasoline engines" (quoted in Raban, *Bad Land*, 83).

121. Daniels, *Horse Trader*, 16.

122. Quoted in Turner, ed., *Indian Reader*, 255.

Chapter 7 — A Sort of Empire

1. Webster 1812, quoted in Friedman, *Inventors*, vii.
2. F.D. Roosevelt to Colonel Edward Mandell House, 21 November 1933.
3. Beuve-Méry was the founder of the French newspaper *Le Monde*. He said this in 1944, shortly before the D-Day landings. See Justin Webb, *Death to America: Anti-Americanism Examined*, BBC Radio Four series, April 2007, and article by Webb on BBC World News website, April 12, 2007.
4. Zinn, *People's History*, 301.
5. Weinberg, *Manifest Destiny*, 71.
6. LaFeber, *New Empire*, 12.
7. William Shakespeare, *Henry IV, Part Two*, act 4, scene 5.
8. Americans had been freebooting in the Pacific for some time. As early as the War of 1812, an American captain, David Porter, had tried to seize the remote Marquesan island of Nuku Hiva (where Melville jumped ship years later), naming its great volcanic haven "Massachusetts Bay." But the United States did not follow up. After the Civil War, when cotton prices were sky high, unrecon-structed Southerners, joined by Britons of like mind, set up a chapter of the Ku Klux Klan in Fiji and tried to overthrow the local king, whom they lampooned as "an old nigger" (quoted in Scarr, *Majesty of Colour*, 193).
9. In 1832 there were 130,000 Hawaiians; by 1900 their number had dropped to fewer than 30,000 (*Encyclopaedia Britannica* 1911, vol. 13, 88–89). Disease was by no means the only factor; white settler encroachment prevented recovery. On Polynesian islands where the land stayed in native hands, the population was able to rebuild—just as Cherokee numbers began to rise when the settler tide was halted for several decades before the Removal. The Fiji islands, for example, are about the same size as the Hawaiian group and, before contact, had a similar number of people. After Britain took over Fiji in 1874, land alienation

was halted; today about 83 percent of the land is still owned communally by native clans, and more than half the population is indigenous Fijian. In Hawaii, by contrast, only 1 percent of the population is indigenous Hawaiian, and about 15 percent are of mixed ancestry.

10. Welcomed as equals at the British court, the Hawaiian royals were not always so well treated in America: on one occasion two princes were thrown off a Pullman car in Philadelphia for being "niggers" (Allen, *Betrayal of Liliuokalani,* 73).

11. Quoted in Allen, *Betrayal of Liliuokalani,* 401.

12. Quoted in Van Alstyne, *Rising American Empire,* 177.

13. The parallel with Texas—the likelihood of American migrants overwhelming the sovereignty of their host—was widely noted by 1875. Van Alstyne, *Rising American Empire,* 177. The queen told her side of the story eloquently in her autobiography, published in 1898. See Liliuokalani, *Hawaii's Queen.*

14. Dole was a cousin of the pineapple czar. The term *Gospel Republic* was coined by his opponents.

15. Ironically, the territory would not be given statehood until 1959, mainly because of fears that the non-white population, which included many Asians, might take charge if they were allowed too much democracy. For similar reasons, Puerto Rico, taken from Spain in 1898, still remains in political limbo.

16. See Van Alstyne, *Rising American Empire,* 184–86. Roosevelt, quoted in Zinn, *People's History,* 297, 300.

17. Roosevelt gave the order on February 25 to Admiral Dewey, who was at Hong Kong. The bombardment of the Spanish fleet at Manila began on May 1.

18. Roosevelt to Henry Cabot Lodge, September 1897. Quoted in Van Alstyne, *Rising American Empire,* 185.

19. Cuban sovereignty was curtailed by the Platt Amendment of 1901, which reserved an American right to intervene in several areas of the island's life, including the protection of property. In 1901 General Leonard Wood, in charge of U.S. forces on the island,

reported to President Roosevelt: "There is, of course, little or no independence left in Cuba" (quoted in Zinn, *People's History,* 311–12). In 1921 President Warren Harding (Republican) made Wood governor general of the Philippines.

20. For example, see Luzviminda Francisco's 1973 paper "The First Vietnam: The Philippine-American War, 1899–1902."

21. The 1903 census (after war losses from fighting and disease) gave a figure of nearly 8 million. By 2000 the population was some 80 million—a tenfold rise in one century, or more than twice the world average. Yearly income in 2006 was US$1,300 per head.

22. Quoted in Weinberg, *Manifest Destiny,* 287.

23. Quoted in ibid., 292, and Zinn, *People's History,* 313. For a kinder view of McKinley, see LaFeber, *New Empire.*

24. See Dennett, *Eastern Asia,* 629. In January 1899 Senator Augustus Bacon of Georgia introduced a resolution that would have satisfied Filipino and American interests, promising to return the islands to their people "when a stable and independent government shall have been duly erected therein." The vote was tied, and Vice-President Garret Hobart killed the Bacon resolution. Aguinaldo is quoted in Weinberg, *Manifest Destiny,* 299.

25. Weinberg, Manifest Destiny, 308–9.

26. "In Support of an American Empire," 56th Cong., 1st sess., *Congressional Record* (January 9, 1900): 704–12.

27. Zinn, *People's History,* 300.

28. Weinberg, *Manifest Destiny,* 297.

29. The phrase "the new imperialism, the imperialism of liberty" was coined by Lyman Abbott in his article "The New Monroe Doctrine," *Outlook* 59 (1898): 1006. Quoted in Weinberg, *Manifest Destiny,* 290.

30. Dennett, *Eastern Asia,* 629.

31. James, quoted in Zinn, *People's History,* 314.

32. Quoted in Zinn, *People's History,* 315. White troops called the Filipinos "niggers," and a number of black American troops deserted and went over to the native side. Caloocan is now a suburb of greater Manila.

33. Weinberg (*Manifest Destiny,* 315) called it "the painful 'water cure' for Filipino patriotism." Berman (*Dark Ages,* 8) calls it "near drowning of suspects . . . a technique long used in Latin American dictatorships." At his Senate confirmation hearings in November 2007, Michael Mukasey, Bush's new attorney general, claimed that he did not know enough about waterboarding to be sure whether it was torture or not. Speaking to Congress in February 2008, CIA director Michael Hayden admitted to the use of waterboarding on a few al Qaeda suspects (BBC World News, February 5, 2008).

34. *Ledger* (Philadelphia), 1901, quoted in Zinn, *People's History,* 315.

35. Root, quoted in Zinn, *People's History,* 316.

36. Rumsfeld, quoted in the *Boston Globe,* March 26, 2003: "The care that goes into it, the humanity that goes into it, to see that military targets are destroyed . . . every single target has been analyzed, and the weapon has been carefully selected. . . . It is an enormously impressive effort, a humane effort."

37. Tocqueville, *Democracy in America,* 467. In his inaugural address of 1801, Thomas Jefferson had said that America had "room enough for our descendants to the thousandth and thousandth generation."

38. Senator James R. Doolittle of Wisconsin, 1860, quoted in Williams, *Empire,* 95: "I sustain this [homestead] measure . . . because its benign operation will postpone for centuries, if it will not forever, all serious conflict between capital and labor in the older free States, withdrawing their surplus population to create in greater abundance the means of subsistence."

39. John Hay, mid-1880s, quoted in LaFeber, *New Empire,* 17.

40. See Zinn, *People's History,* chap. 13, for the sources and quotations in this section.

41. Jack London, the bestselling novelist and adventurer, wrote in 1906 that "modern man lives more wretchedly than the caveman," while his producing power was "a thousand times greater." The conclusion was obvious to anyone who gave it thought: capital was once again enslaving human beings regardless of race, age

or sex—though non-whites, women, and children certainly had it
the worst.

42. A Wobbly-led general strike at Seattle in 1919 was described by
the city's mayor as "an attempted revolution . . . for the overthrow
of the industrial system" (Zinn, *People's History,* 379). Eighty years
later, Seattle became the scene of the biggest antiglobalization
protest in North America.

43. The tribunal, intended to avoid war by binding arbitration of
international disputes, was founded on the initiative of the
Russian czar in 1899 and strengthened, with American support,
in 1907. It is sorrowfully ironic to read the optimism of the 1911
Britannica, three years before the assassination at Sarajevo:
"Although religious animosities between Christian nations have
died out, although dynasties may now rise and fall without raising
half Europe to arms, the springs of warlike enterprise are still to
be found in commercial jealousies, in imperialistic ambitions
and in the doctrine of survival of the fittest which lends scientific
support to both. These must one and all be cleared away before
we can enter on that era of universal peace" (*Encyclopaedia
Britannica* 1911, vol. 2, 331).

44. Of course, the Victorian Age nominally ended with Queen
Victoria's death in 1901, but I follow the view of historian Eric
Hobsbawm that the "long" nineteenth century lasted through the
Edwardian Period and until the First World War.

45. *The Secret Agent* was first published in serial form in 1906 and as a
book in 1907.

46. The vehicle became known as Buda's Waggon (see Davis, *Buda's
Waggon*). In January 2008 ex–prime minister Tony Blair accepted
a lucrative part-time directorship at J.P. Morgan.

47. The assassin, Gavrilo Princip, was acting for a Serbian nationalist
group called Union or Death. The motive was the repressive
Balkan policy of Austria-Hungary, the Middle European empire.
Both the archduke and his pregnant wife were killed.

48. For example, the British *Dreadnought,* launched in 1906.

49. Keegan, *Second World War,* 24.

50. Theodore Roosevelt thought him a cold-blooded opportunist, but that was nonsense. "Kindly, sincere, straightforward" was how British prime minister Lloyd George later summed up Wilson's character, adding "tactless, obstinate and vain" (MacMillan, *Paris 1919,* 6–7).

51. Under Wilson, Filipinos were given limited self-rule. Progress in this direction was later halted by the Republicans but resumed in the 1930s. Wilson's promise was at last fulfilled after the Second World War, though the United States kept several naval bases on the islands.

52. The main allies were Britain, France and Czarist Russia, also known as the Triple Alliance.

53. Known as the Zimmerman Telegram, Germany's offer to Mexico was decoded by the British and published by the White House in March 1917. However, without America's clumsy interventions in the Mexican Revolution after 1910, the madcap scheme might never have occurred to Berlin.

54. See Hobsbawm, *Age of Extremes,* 25–35, for this argument. Hobsbawm suggests that the war took as long as it did because both sides knew that the only conclusive result, as in the American Civil War, would be unconditional surrender; anything less would lead to further war—which is, of course, what happened. Because Germany surrendered with her armies undefeated on the battle-field, the result was soon seen by many Germans as illegitimate and inconclusive—a belief skilfully exploited by the Nazi Party.

55. About fifty-four thousand Americans died in battle—a fourteenth of Britain's losses, or only a fortieth if adjusted for population.

56. Dos Passos, *Nineteen Nineteen,* 199. Dick, or perhaps Dos Passos, forgets that all apes (unlike monkeys) are tailless.

57. He was the first U.S. president to leave American soil while in office.

58. The war had made Russia into a Bolshevik dictatorship, shattered Austria-Hungary beyond repair, driven Turkey from the Middle East and strengthened Japan.

59. MacMillan lists all Fourteen Points (*Paris 1919,* 495–96). They were written early in 1918 and later accepted by Germany as the basis of the Armistice of November 11 that year.

60. Tennyson, "Locksley Hall," 1842.

61. Although the "blitz" is thought of as a feature of the Second World War, many destructive bombing raids were carried out over England by German planes and zeppelins during the Great War. ·

62. The bylaw was passed in 1916. Another option, taken by some architects, was to keep vertical sides but use only part of the site. After seeing Mexico in 1921, British architect Alfred C. Bossom, who practised widely in the United States, explicitly used pre-Columbian motifs in his art deco skyscrapers (see Braun, *Pre-Columbian Art,* 167–74). Apart from buildings, art deco was used mainly in mass-produced consumer durables, but Mesoamerican influence was also strong in the work of artists such as Henry Moore.

63. Tikal Temple IV, built about A.D. 740, held the record until the 268-foot Washington Capitol dome was completed after the Civil War. The temple's existing height is 230 feet, but the weathered stonework of the roof comb was originally somewhat higher. Temple IV and its neighbouring towers are solid masses of stone and concrete rising in tiers, with single-flight stairways to the shrines at the top—a look imitated by the central inset of many art deco skyscrapers.

64. See Chapter 5. Wilson had almost certainly read *League of the Iroquois* (1851), written by Lewis Henry Morgan and his Seneca colleague Ely Parker, who later became head of Indian Affairs under Ulysses Grant. The influence of the Iroquois League on Wilson's thinking at the end of the Great War was noted at the time. Several papers of Wilson's secretary of state Robert Lansing, who was a colleague at the Paris Peace Conference, mention the link. See, for example, "The Iroquois League of Nations," dated 1921, kept in Princeton University's Seeley G. Mudd Manuscript Library.

65. The treaty had to pass the Senate by a two-thirds vote. Even so, if Wilson had made some compromises, he might have succeeded.

There is some evidence that his judgment was impaired by over-work or stroke He died in 1924.

66. Tocqueville, *Journey to America*, 85. In his *Democracy* he put it this way: "In the conduct of foreign relations . . . democratic govern-ments appear to me to be decidedly inferior to governments car-ried on upon different principles" (see Tocqueville, *Democracy in America*, 270).

67. MacMillan, *Paris 1919*, 493. Among the League of Nations' achievements was the International Labour Organization, offer-ing, it was hoped, a moderate alternative to the Wobblies and other radicals worldwide.

68. A.J.P. Taylor, quoted in Keegan, *Second World War*, 10.

69. Germany was forced to admit "war guilt" and to pay the winners back for the cost of the war, a sum fixed at $33 billion in 1921. Hitler's propaganda replaced history with a myth that the Germans had not really lost at all but had been sold out by traitors and Jews.

70. See Raban, *Bad Land*, especially page 26, where the expert F. Walden is quoted: "It seems to be a matter of common observa-tion that rainfall in a new country increases with settlement [and] cultivation."

71. Raban, *Bad Land*, 232.

72. Steinbeck, *Grapes of Wrath*, 34.

73. Steffens said and wrote this on several occasions and in slightly different forms. His trip to Russia was in 1919. See Kaplan, *Lincoln Steffens*, chap. 13.

74. Hitler's father's surname was originally Schicklgrüber; Stalin means "Man of Steel."

75. Hobsbawm, *Age of Extremes*, 96.

76. Klein, *Shock Doctrine*, 301.

77. Hoover had also started to address the slump with dams and with emergency camps for "Okies"—known as Hoovervilles.

78. These reforms later came under attack during the anticommu-nist hysteria of the 1950s. Several tribes were "terminated"— their legal existence (and therefore their treaty rights and land

claims) abolished in the name of free enterprise and advancement. Most Indians strongly resisted termination, so the policy
was withdrawn, and some lands were restored in the 1970s. See
Waldman, *Atlas,* chap. 7, for a good overview of modern Indian
policy in the United States and Canada until the Reagan years,
when reservation-based casinos were promoted as the "new
buffalo." A recent *Guardian* article by Paul Harris ("Fortune
Favours the Braves") describes some consequences of the
casino policy, especially as it affects the Pequots and Oglala
Sioux today.

79. The coming war delayed Philippine independence; it also eased
President Cárdenas's bold nationalization of Mexico's oil.

80. Hitler was made chancellor on January 30, 1933. The Reichstag
building was empty when it was firebombed a month later. A
communist faction or the Nazis themselves are the prime suspects, but Hitler immediately said he did "not doubt" the bombing was the work of communists, and he used the attack to
suppress the left and round up opponents. Scheduled elections
went ahead the following week, with freedom of speech and other
civil liberties suspended. The Nazis and their allies won a bare
majority, and Communist deputies were banned from taking
their seats. On March 23 the House passed the *Enabling Act,* giving
Hitler dictatorial powers. See Haffner, *Defying Hitler,* 98–102, for
a contemporary view.

81. Mann to the dean of Bonn University, 1 January 1937, quoted in
Eksteins, *Rites of Spring,* 311. Hitler, quoted in Eksteins, *Rites of
Spring,* 314.

82. Haffner, *Defying Hitler,* 236. Haffner's extraordinary memoir,
which has warnings for our own time, was written about 1939,
after the author fled to England and before the war began. The
manuscript was forgotten until Haffner's son found it after his
father's death in 1999.

83. After the opening of Japan to American trade in the 1850s,
the Japanese, who had followed a policy of isolation since the

sixteenth century—even banning the technology of firearms—embarked on a headlong policy of modernization. Japan was big enough and remote enough that it could fulfill the old dream of the Cherokees: by acquiring the tools of western civilization on its own terms, it guaranteed its national independence.

84. On a single night, the United States burned more than eighty thousand people in a napalm attack on Tokyo; in the Dresden "firestorm," more than one hundred thousand died. See Williams, *Empire*, 171–72.

85. Weller, *First into Nagasaki*, 43. George Weller's dispatches from Nagasaki were discovered by his son, the author Anthony Weller, and published for the first time in 2006.

86. Burchett, quoted in Weller, *First into Nagasaki*, 254.

87. The figure of 12 million for the Great War may well be too low, and it does not include the 20 to 40 million who died in the subsequent flu epidemic, which may have incubated in the trenches, camps and field hospitals and then been spread around the world by returning soldiers. Fewer soldiers and many more civilians died in the Second World War. The 50 million includes the Jews and others who died in the Nazi and Soviet camps (see Keegan, *Second World War*, 590–95). A third of the dead (military and civilian) were in the Soviet Union: without Stalin's dictatorship, Hitler's might not have been stopped.

88. Levi, quoted in Clendinnen, *Reading the Holocaust*, 52.

Chapter 8 – The Winds of Fear

---

1. Williams, *Empire*, 96.

2. John Adams to Thomas Jefferson, 1813, referring to the Philadelphia riots. Coined during the mob terror of the French Revolution, the word *terrorism* is nearly as old as the United States.

3. MacMillan, *Paris 1919*, 181.

4. Nixon was quoted as saying, "We are all Keynesians now" (see Klein, *Shock Doctrine*, 158). However, Berman argues that Nixon's

1971 devaluation of the dollar began the right-wing project to "repeal" Bretton Woods. Berman, *Dark Ages,* 50–58.

5. Both men, born only a year apart, would soon be dead: Roosevelt in 1945 and Keynes in 1946.

6. The war economy was epitomized by the massive Ford plant at Ypsilanti, Michigan, which had been turning out a new Flying Fortress bomber every hour. When peace came, surplus aluminum production was sold to the public as boats, gadgets and above all the aluminum siding that spread in a pastel plague over the houses of North America.

7. See Clarke, *Hope and Glory,* 209, and Berman, *Dark Ages,* 53.

8. Britain had traded away many bases, airfields and other assets to cover its war debt under the Lend-Lease scheme.

9. Like Iron Curtain, "special relationship" seems to have been another Churchill coinage, first said by him in 1946.

10. The first atomic bombs were equivalent to some twenty thousand tons of TNT; the hydrogen bomb can have an explosive force reckoned in millions of tons. With the help of ex-Nazi scientists, great missiles were developed to lob the bombs overseas. The Space Race of the 1950s and 1960s was essentially a threatening display of rocket science.

11. MacArthur (speech, Lansing, Michigan, May 15, 1951).

12. The film was released in January 1964, with Peter Sellers, Sterling Hayden and George C. Scott in leading roles (Sellers played three characters). The crisp black-and-white cinematography is matched by a sparkling script, written by Kubrick, Terry Southern and Peter George—an ex-RAF intelligence officer and author of the 1958 novel *Red Alert* (called *Two Hours to Doom* and published under Peter George's pen name, Peter Bryant, in Britain), on which the film was based. Southern wrote that because of lax security standards in Britain, "George had been able to reveal details . . . that, in the spy-crazy USA of the Cold War era, would have been downright treasonous. Thus the entire complicated technology of nuclear deterrence in *Dr. Strangelove*

was based on a bedrock of authenticity." In Southern, "Strangelove Outtake," 64.

13. Fluoride occurs naturally in some water; if not, it is added to protect children's teeth against decay.

14. Hofstadter, *Paranoid Style,* 5–6. First given at Oxford as the Herbert Spencer Lecture in November 1963, the text was published in shorter form in *Harper's Magazine* a year later. The full text is in Hofstadter, ibid., 3–40.

15. Bageant, *Deer Hunting,* 201. See also Lieven, *America,* for more on this important strain in American culture.

16. Quoted in Hofstadter, *Paranoid Style,* 110, in his essay "Goldwater and Pseudo-Conservative Politics." Barry Goldwater had made this statement in December 1961, and it was used by opponents in the 1964 campaign. To his credit, Goldwater opposed the extreme religious right and later called Richard Nixon "the most dishonest individual I have ever met in my life."

17. I have put the earlier first. The target of the 1798 sermon was the worldwide "conspiracy" of Freemasonry, which had played a part in both the American and the French revolutions. The ellipsis in the second passage (McCarthy's speech) is mine, so as not to give the game away. The missing words are "high in this government."

18. In his farewell speech to the nation in 1960, Eisenhower said: "In the councils of government, we must guard against the acquisition of unwarranted influence, whether sought or unsought, by the military-industrial complex. The potential for the disastrous rise of misplaced power exists and will persist." He went on to warn of the influence of the complex on universities, where "a government contract becomes virtually a substitute for intellectual curiosity." Presumably, such warnings led to the extremist charge that Eisenhower was a communist.

19. Rev. Richard Cizik, vice-president of the National Association of Evangelicals, quoted in the *New York Times,* May 27, 2003. See Kaplan, *God on Their Side,* 13.

20. As George Orwell foresaw in *Nineteen Eighty-Four* (1949). Kurt Vonnegut wrote in his novel *Galápagos* (146): "All the killing that had been going on since the end of the Second World War . . . was surely 'World War Three.'"

21. It was estimated that during the Nixon/Kissinger carpet bombing of Cambodia, more explosive power was unleashed on jungles and peasants than in the whole of the Second World War. Large amounts of Agent Orange, a herbicide rife with carcinogens, were used to expose the enemy by wiping out vegetation in Korea, Vietnam and Cambodia. In the aftermath of the bombing of Cambodia, the fanatical Khmer Rouge took power, led by Pol Pot (later ousted, ironically, by Vietnam).

22. American output had reached a third of world production by 1913 but lost ground during the 1930s (see Hobsbawn, *Age of Extremes*, 97, and Keegan, *Second World War*, 594–95). The United States' share of world production was just above half in 1945; today it is about a quarter, reflecting the recovery of old economies and the rise of new ones.

23. Keegan, *Second World War*, 592–95. America's only civilian deaths were 68 killed at Pearl Harbor. Britain lost 60,000 civilians to aerial bombing and 244,000 men in battle (equivalent to about three times more if compared by population to the United States). Japan's battle deaths were 1.2 million and Germany's 4 million. Until 1989, when Keegan's *Second World War* was published, the two significant American wars after 1945 were Korea and Vietnam. Since then, of course, the Gulf War, the Afghan War and the Iraq War must be added. The only major Soviet war was in Afghanistan, where losses were only a fourth of the losses suffered by the United States in Vietnam. Since the fall of communism, Russia has also fought a war against secession in Chechnya. Japan has had no army, and Germany no troops in battle, since 1945. (Keegan was among the supporters of the Iraq War.)

24. This number includes American support staff and those missing in action. Fifteen other countries, including Britain, Canada and

Australia, fought with the "United Nations" in Korea. On the communist side, huge numbers of Chinese ground troops were engaged, while Soviet and American fighters—the first jet fighters in action—battled in the sky. *The Hunters*, a remarkable 1956 novel by James Salter, who was a fighter pilot in Korea, gives an insider's view of the air war. The Americans made heavy use of napalm—seventy thousand gallons daily in 1952—and civilian casualties were very high.

25. Quoted in Blum, *Rogue State*, 174.

26. This is generally true, though there were anomalies. Egypt, Sudan, Sarawak and Tonga, for example, were under various forms of British overlordship but not formally British possessions.

27. The United States had already, under the Monroe Doctrine, developed the makings of a hegemonic system in Latin America. Cuba, Haiti, Nicaragua, the Dominican Republic and Mexico had all felt the American lash at one time or another before the Second World War. The economies of many Latin American countries were dominated by U.S. corporations such as Standard Oil and United Fruit (with its "banana republics"). In the early 1900s Theodore Roosevelt had twisted off part of Colombia to create the Republic of Panama as a haven for the American-built and -owned Panama Canal. This period was an apprenticeship in running a tribute empire.

28. On December 20, 1983, Donald Rumsfeld paid a cordial visit to Saddam Hussein in Baghdad. At that time Iraq was being supplied and encouraged as a bulwark of secularism against fundamentalist Iran.

29. Kennedy, quoted in Williams, *Empire*, 198–99.

30. See Kinzer, *Overthrow*, for a general history of American-sponsored coups, and Schlesinger and Kinzer, *Bitter Fruit*, for a good analysis of the Guatemalan case. See Klein, *Shock Doctrine*, for other examples, especially Chile. The attack on Guatemala was orchestrated by the Dulles brothers, one of whom was CIA director and the other secretary of state. They both had close ties to

United Fruit, by far the largest foreign company in Guatemala. Arbenz, whose stated aim was to turn Guatemala "from a dependent nation with a semi-colonial economy . . . into a modern capitalist state," had begun a land reform that included the expropriation of idle lands with due compensation. The coup against Chile, in which President Allende died, was orchestrated by Henry Kissinger. After Allende's electoral victory, Kissinger had said: "I don't see why we should stand by and permit a country to go Communist due to the irresponsibility of its own people" (quoted in Williams, *Empire*, x).

31. Quoted in Zinn, *People's History*, 557. Other Harris Poll numbers are also given here.

32. Somoza and his father (also Anastasio) had dominated Nicaragua since the 1930s. He was overthrown in 1979 by the leftist Sandinistas after the Americans realized the extent of popular support for the rebels and abandoned him.

33. Irving Kristol, quoted in Williams, *Empire*, 220.

34. Satirized in the film *Wall Street:* "Greed is good; greed is right; greed works; greed clarifies; greed will save the United States" (quoted in Levy, *American Vertigo*, 241).

35. The quotation is from www.cia.gov/library/publications/the-world-factbook, January 2008. Income ratios are from "The Great CEO Pay Heist," *Fortune*, June 11, 2001, quoted in Singer, *President of Good and Evil*, 28. The figures were drawn from the Top One Hundred corporations.

36. Thatcher, speech to the United Nations, November 8, 1989.

37. See Ehrenreich, *Nickel and Dimed*, for a powerful undercover exposé of what it is to live in America with low-paying jobs.

38. The *Glass-Steagall Act* of 1933, intended to prevent a recurrence of the 1929 crash, was repealed in 1999. Further deregulation followed under George W. Bush. See Janszen, "The Next Bubble," 39–45.

39. Franzen, *Corrections*, 441

40. See Johnson, "Republic or Empire," for a discussion of military Keynesianism and the U.S. military budget.

41. Klein, *Shock Doctrine*, 548.

42. Vidal, *Perpetual War*, 158.

43. *Financial Times*, May 23, 2003, quoted in Singer, *President of Good and Evil*, 15. By November 2007 official funding requests to Congress for the wars in Iraq and Afghanistan had reached $804 billion. According to a report released by Democrats in Congress at that time, the true costs had reached about $1.5 trillion when things such as oil prices were included—more than $20,000 for every American family in total to late 2007. "Hidden Costs Raise U.S. War Price," BBC World News, November 13, 2007.

44. In their 1986 book *Right Turn*, Thomas Ferguson and Joel Rogers suggested that excessive weapons spending under Reagan was intended to "create powerful pressures to cut federal spending, and thus, perhaps, enable the administration to accomplish its goal of rolling back the New Deal."

45. Flannery, *Eternal Frontier*, 292.

46. Tocqueville, *Journey to America*, 111.

47. Steinbeck, *Travels with Charley*, 26, 28.

48. LaFeber, *New Empire*, xxiv (from the author's preface to the 1998 edition of his 1963 *New Empire*).

49. See Stiglitz, *Globalization*, for a searing critique of globalization. Stiglitz, a Nobel Prize-winning economist and New Keynesian, is credited with coining the term "free market fundamentalism," as is the financier George Soros at about the same time.

50. Not forgetting Ralph Nader's intervention as a spoiler, an example of the Puritanism that would rather starve self-righteously than settle for half a loaf.

51. In a 2004 study of Bush's ethics (insofar as they can be deduced from his words), the Princeton philosopher Peter Singer points out that during the president's first few months in power, he sounded moderate and compassionate. In his inaugural address, given on January 20, 2001, Bush said: "While many of our citizens prosper, others doubt the promise—even the justice—of our own

country. . . . This is my solemn pledge: I will work to build a single nation of justice and opportunity" (quoted in Singer, *President of Good and Evil*, 11).

52. In the 1990s the Pentagon's yearly budget was about $310 billion (see Berman, *Dark Ages*, 143–44). Contributors to the 1992 Defense Planning Guidance paper included Paul Wolfowitz, Secretary of Defense Dick Cheney and General Colin Powell. All distanced themselves from the paper when it was leaked to the *New York Times*—except Powell, who said, "I want to be the bully on the block" (see ibid., 148–49).

53. Despite twenty years of development and more than $100 billion, the system does not work and is not likely to. (Even if it did, counter measures would not be hard to devise.) During his last year in office Bush was still insisting that it was "urgent" to install the system in Poland and the Czech Republic, despite the dangers of alarming Russia and setting off a new arms race.

54. Both these documents are quoted in Singer, *President of Good and Evil*, 222–23.

55. Cheney resigned as a CEO of Halliburton to become Bush's running mate but retained large holdings in the company; Rice had been a policy executive at Chevron, which was allied to the Saudi firm Arab American Oil, or Aramco. When Wolf Blitzer of CNN confronted Perle, then chairman of the Defense Policy Board, with journalist Seymour Hersh's charge that he had "set up a company that may gain from a war," Perle (of Trireme and Halliburton) accused Hersh of being "the closest thing American journalism has to a terrorist." See Klein, *Shock Doctrine*, 373–88.

56. The death toll was comparable to the number of civilians killed by terrorists in Northern Ireland (and far fewer if adjusted for population). The difference—that the victims all died at once rather than over some thirty years—evoked the shock of Pearl Harbor. The dead in the Twin Towers included many foreigners—British, Canadian, French and others.

57. Quoted in Singer, *President of Good and Evil*, 192.

58. The evidence that Iraq was buying "yellow cake" uranium from Niger was a crude forgery. So was the British government's intelligence document publicly praised by Powell: most of it was lifted from an out-of-date thesis available on the Internet.

59. After the Gulf War, Iraq had been allowed to keep its locally made Soviet-designed Scud missiles as long as their range did not exceed 72 miles. A few were found that could go slightly further, and they were all being systematically destroyed by the United Nations team headed by Blix before the war began. After the overthrow of Saddam Hussein, no other illegal weapons were ever found, nor was any evidence uncovered of a link to al Qaeda. However, as Jimmy Carter told the BBC News in October 2007, Dick Cheney, the hardliner who may have had the strongest influence on Bush, never abandoned either of these claims.

60. It is also known that Donald Rumsfeld began recommending an attack on Iraq—and not Afghanistan—by mid-afternoon on September 11, 2001. See Berman, *Dark Ages*, 203.

61. This took place in October 1990. President George H. Bush repeated the story many times, using it to attack opponents of the war. Doctors who worked at Kuwait's hospitals at the time of the alleged atrocity confirmed after the war that nothing of the sort had happened. See "Deception on Capitol Hill," *New York Times*, January 15, 1992, and Berman, *Dark Ages*, 184.

62. Federal Reserve chairman Alan Greenspan, in his memoir *The Age of Turbulence: Adventures in a New World*, reported by ABC News, September 16, 2007. In response to Greenspan, Donald Rumsfeld's successor as defence secretary, Robert Gates, said on ABC television: "I know the same allegation was made about the Gulf War in 1991, and I just don't believe it's true. . . . It's really about rogue regimes trying to develop weapons of mass destruction." But on June 3, 2003, Paul Wolfowitz had given a speech in Singapore in which he admitted that the real goal of the war was oil; the next day Cheney told Republican senators to block any investigation into the evidentiary basis of the war (see Berman,

Dark Ages, 211). Immediately after the fall of Baghdad, the only government building protected by the United States was the Oil Ministry. In 2007 a new Iraqi oil law was drawn up, giving foreign companies almost unlimited access and minimal taxation.

63. In January 2008, the Iraqi government and the World Health Organization announced an estimate of 151,000 civilian deaths from 2003 to 2006 (BBC World News, January 10, 2008). Other estimates range from a high of 655,000 by the medical journal *The Lancet* to a low of 30,000 by George W. Bush (see Gilbert Burnham, Riyadh Lafta, Shannon Doocy and Les Roberts, "Mortality after the 2003 Invasion of Iraq: A Cross-Sectional Cluster Sample Survey," *The Lancet* 368, no. 9545 [1 October 2006]: 1421–28). The independent Iraq Body Count, which reckons only confirmed deaths and chooses to err on the low side, published a total of more than 80,000 by the end of 2007.

64. Most Allied prisoners of war were generally allowed to receive Red Cross parcels, and German prison camps met international standards—at least until late in the war. The Nazi treatment of enemy fighting men should not be confused with that given to political prisoners, spies, Jews, Slavs, Gypsies and other groups—treatment that violated all standards of humanity.

65. It is not under Cuban jurisdiction either, having been taken and then "leased" from Cuba by the United States after the Spanish-American War of 1898.

66. Berman, *Dark Ages,* 218, 231.

Chapter 9 — The World's Best Hope

———————

1. Jefferson (inaugural address, March 1801).

2. Lincoln to Colonel William F. Elkins, 21 November 1864.

3. Okri, "New Dark Age." The full essay, which highlights the looting of Iraq's national museum after the American victory, can be read online at http://education.guardian.co.uk. Okri won the 1991 Booker Prize for his novel *The Famished Road.*

4. Tocqueville, *Democracy*, 183.

5. John McCain, Mitt Romney, Mike Huckabee and Ron Paul, respectively. Rudolph Giuliani, former mayor of New York, dropped out early after his antiterrorist drumbeat drew few to his banner. On the Democratic side, the early casualty was John Edwards, perhaps further to the traditional left than his rivals Hillary Clinton and Barack Obama. Born to a Kenyan father and a Kansan mother, Obama is literally African American.

6. See Lieven, "Why We Should Fear."

7. Berman, *Dark Ages*, 226.

8. Reported in *Newsweek* (July 19, 2004), the *Guardian* (July 13, 2004) and elsewhere. See Berman, *Dark Ages*, 226, 359 n.36.

9. Berman, *Dark Ages*, 298.

10. Harris, interviewed by the *Florida Baptist Witness* (August 24, 2006) during her bid for the Senate that year. Though she lost her senatorial bid, she had been elected to the House of Representatives in 2002. During the 2000 elections, she was Florida's secretary of state and was widely accused of a conflict of interest because she had worked on the campaign of G.W. Bush, whose brother, Jeb Bush, was then governor. She was also instrumental in removing thousands of voters, mainly blacks, from the electoral roll, and had already attacked the separation of church and state. The whole 2006 interview can be read at *USA Today* online, posted August 28, 2006. Congresswoman Harris added that if "godly men" are not elected, "we're going to have a nation of secular laws. That's not what our founding fathers intended and that certainly isn't what God intended."

11. Singer, *President of Good and Evil*, 5, 53–54. This total exceeded that of any other state governor in modern times.

12. Britain, the highest in Europe, jails about 1 person in 750, less than one-fifth of the American rate. A study published early in 2008 found that incarceration in the United States has reached an all-time high: 2.3 million people—one in every ninety-nine

adult Americans—are now behind bars. See "U.S. Jail Numbers at All-time High," BBC World News, February 29, 2008.

13. In 1996, for example, Republicans in Congress weakened an antiterrorism bill because the National Rifle Association opposed it. See Jerry Gray, "Republicans Weaken Bill on Combating Terrorism," *New York Times,* August 3, 1996.

14. In 2003 some 45 million Americans (nearly 16 percent of the population) had no health insurance at all (Berman, *Dark Ages,* 61). By the 2008 presidential primaries, the figure had reached 47 million.

15. "In Maryland and . . . throughout the south . . . the people refused to be educated, so as not to have to pay the tax for the schools" (Tocqueville, *Journey,* 220). There is also some federal funding nowadays, though under George W. Bush this contribution has been directed as much as possible to private (especially "faith-based") schools. See Naomi Klein's comments on the Friedmanite privatization policy in New Orleans in the wake of Hurricane Katrina (Klein, *Shock Doctrine,* 3–6).

16. Conducted by sampling two thousand Canadians and published by CBC News, February 4, 2008. Top choice for the "most important issue or problem facing the world today" was the environment, with warfare in second place. Only 3 percent of those polled chose terrorism, the same number who answered "don't know."

17. At the time of writing, Senator John McCain was being attacked by his rivals as not a "true conservative" because he favours dealing with climate change.

18. See the *Millennium Ecosystem Assessment Report* and its summary, "Living Beyond Our Means," released in 2005. The work of more than 1,300 scientists from 95 countries, including the United States, and organizations such as the United Nations and the World Bank, the report was designed to assess the level of human development that the Earth can support. It concluded that more than 60 percent of "ecosystem services" (fisheries, forests and

farmland, to name but three) were seriously degraded and being used unsustainably. The reports can be read online. For a layman's overview, see Andrew C. Revkin, "Report Tallies Hidden Costs of Human Assault on Nature," *New York Times*, April 5, 2005.

19. Hobsbawm, *Age of Extremes*, 585.

20. Perhaps the nearest historical precedent for China's blend of post-socialist state power, ethnic nationalism and a semi-private economic boom is the "German miracle" of the 1930s. China seems to have been immunized by Mao against the attractions of another Führer, but it does share prewar Germany's longing for the imprimatur of the Olympic Games.

21. Europe has about a twelfth of the world's population and a third of its economic output; the United States has about a twentieth and a fourth, respectively.

22. Some of this greater efficiency is due to higher population densities and urban patterns established before the motor car.

23. Schapiro, "Toxic Inaction," 79.

24. These cuts are from 1990 levels. The EU plan offers to raise the cuts to 30 percent with a worldwide deal (see "EU Reveals Energy Plan of Action," BBC World News, January 23, 2008). At the Paris climate change conference held in April 2008, the best offer from the United States was merely to halt the *growth* in its emissions by 2025. See "Major Emitters Cool to Bush Climate Strategy," *Globe and Mail*, April 18, 2008.

25. The notion that humans might escape the limitations of this planet by colonizing others is a non-starter. Even if there was a good place to go, we would have to fire 70 million people into space every year just to stop the Earth's population from growing.

Afterword

1. Adams, speech before the House of Representatives, July 4, 1821.

2. Obama, Preface to *Dreams from My Father*, 2004 edition.

Bibliography

Adair, James. *The History of the American Indians*. New York: Johnson, 1968 [1775].

Adams, James Truslow. *The Epic of America*. Boston: Little, Brown, 1931.

Agee, James, and Walker Evans. *Let Us Now Praise Famous Men*. Boston: Mariner, 2001 [1939].

Allen, Helena G. *The Betrayal of Liliuokalani, Last Queen of Hawaii*. Honolulu: Mutual Publishing, 1982.

Araníbar, Carlos, et al., *Nueva Historia General del Perú*. Lima: Mosca Azul Editores, 1979.

Arendt, Hannah. *Responsibility and Judgement*. New York: Schocken Books, 2003.

Armstrong, Virginia I., ed. *I Have Spoken: American History Through the Voices of the Indians*. Chicago: Swallow Press, 1971.

Aubrey, John. *Brief Lives*. Edited by Richard Barber. London: Folio Society, 1975 [1680].

Axtell, James. *The European and the Indian*. Oxford: Oxford University Press, 1981.

Bacevich, Andrew J. *The New American Militarism: How Americans Are Seduced by War*. Oxford: Oxford University Press, 2005.

Bageant, Joe. *Deer Hunting with Jesus: Dispatches from America's Class War*. New York: Crown, 2007.

Bailyn, Bernard. *Voyagers to the West: A Passage in the Peopling of America on the Eve of the Revolution*. New York: Knopf, 1986.

Baldwin, Leland D. *The American Quest for the City of God*. Macon, Ga.: Mercer University Press, 1981.

Barber, Benjamin R. *Consumed: How Markets Corrupt Children, Infantilize Adults, and Swallow Citizens Whole*. New York: Norton, 2007.

Bartram, William. *Travels of William Bartram*. Edited by Mark van Doren. New York: Dover, 1955 [1791].

Bautista, Veltisezar. *The Filipino Americans from 1763 to the Present: Their History, Culture and Traditions*. Farmington Hills, Mich.: Bookhaus Publishers, 1998.

Berman, Morris. *Dark Ages America: The Final Phase of Empire*. New York: Norton, 2006.

Beverley, Robert. *The History and Present State of Virginia*. Edited by Lewis B. Wright. Chapel Hill: University of North Carolina Press, 1947 [1705].

Black, Maggie. *The No-Nonsense Guide to International Development*. Oxford: New Internationalist Publications, 2002.

Blight, David W. *Race and Reunion: The Civil War in American Memory*. Cambridge, Mass.: Harvard University Press, 2001.

Bloom, Harold. *The American Religion: The Emergence of the Post-Christian Nation*. New York: Simon & Schuster, 1992.

Blum, William. *Rogue State: A Guide to the World's Only Superpower*. 3rd ed. Monroe, Me.: Common Courage Press, 2005.

Bonvillain, Nancy, ed. *Studies on Iroquoian Culture*. Occasional Publications in Northeastern Anthropology, no. 6. Albany: State University of New York, n.d.

Boorstin, Daniel J. *The Americans: The Colonial Experience*. London: Cardinal, 1991 [1953].

———. *The Genius of American Politics*. Chicago: University of Chicago Press, 1953.

Borah, Woodrow, and Sherburne Cook. "Conquest and Population: A Demographic Approach to Mexican History." *Proceedings of the American Philosophical Society* 113 (1969): 177–83.

Bourne, Edward Gaylord, ed. and trans. *Narratives of De Soto*. 2 vols. New York: A.S. Barnes, 1904.

Boyd, Julian P., ed. *Indian Treaties Printed by Benjamin Franklin 1736–1762*. Philadelphia: Historical Society of Pennsylvania, 1938.

Brady, Joan. *Theory of War*. London: André Deutsch, 1993.

Braudel, Fernand. *The Structures of Everyday Life*. New York: Harper & Row, 1981.

———. *The Wheels of Commerce*. New York: Harper & Row, 1982.

Braun, Barbara. *Pre-Columbian Art and the Post-Columbian World: Ancient American Sources of Modern Art*. New York: Abrams, 1993.

Bromwich, David. *Politics by Other Means*. New Haven: Yale University Press, 1992.

Brookhiser, Richard. "America at 400: How the English Colony at Jamestown Laid the Foundations for a Nation's Triumph and Tragedies." *Time*, May 2007, 28–38.

Brown, Dee. *Bury My Heart at Wounded Knee*. New York: Washington Square/Simon & Schuster, 1981 [1970].

Brown, John P. *Old Frontiers*. Kinsport, Tenn.: Southern Publishers, 1938.

Buckman, Greg. *Globalization: Tame It or Scrap It?* London: Zed Books, 2004.

Campbell, Janet, and David G. Campbell. "Cherokee Participation in the Political Impact of the North American Indian." *Journal of Cherokee Studies* 6 (Fall 1981): 92–105.

Carter, Samuel. *Cherokee Sunset*. New York: Doubleday, 1976.

Cartier, Jacques. *Relations*. Édition critique by Michel Bideaux. Montreal: Université de Montréal, 1986. [texts in original spelling]

———. *Voyages en Nouvelle-France*. Edited and introduction by Robert Lahaise and Marie Couturier. Montreal: Éditions Hurtubise, 1977. [in modern spelling]

———. *The Voyages of Jacques Cartier*. Edited and introduction by Ramsay Cook. Toronto: University of Toronto Press, 1993.

Cheyney, Edward P. *A Short History of England*. Boston: Ginn & Co., 1904.

Chomsky, Noam. *Failed States: The Abuse of Power and the Assault on Democracy*. New York: Holt, 2006.

———. *Hegemony or Survival: America's Quest for Global Dominance*. New York: Owl/Holt, 2004.

Cieza de León, Pedro de. *Crónica del Perú*. 2 vols. Edited by Franklin Pease and Francesca Cantú. Lima: Universidad Católica, 1986.

Clarke, Peter. *Hope and Glory: Britain 1900–1990*. London: Penguin, 1996.

———. *The Keynesian Revolution in the Making, 1925–36*. Oxford: Oxford University Press, 1988.

Clayton, Lawrence, Vernon James Knight and Edward Moore, eds. *The De Soto Chronicles*. 2 vols. Tuscaloosa: University of Alabama Press, 1993.

Clendinnen, Inga. *Aztecs: An Interpretation*. Cambridge: Cambridge University Press, 1991.

———. "The History Question: Who Owns the Past?" In *Quarterly Essay* 23, 1–73. Melbourne: Schwartz Publishing, 2006.

———. *Reading the Holocaust*. Melbourne: Text, 1998.

Cocker, Mark. *Rivers of Blood, Rivers of Gold: Europe's Conflict with Tribal Peoples*. London: Cape, 1998.

Coetzee, J. M. *Waiting for the Barbarians*. London: Penguin, 1980.

Conley, Robert J. *The Cherokee Nation: A History*. Albuquerque: University of New Mexico Press, 2005.

Conn, Peter. *The Cambridge Illustrated History of American Literature*. Cambridge: Cambridge University Press, 1990.

Conrad, Barnaby. *Ghost Hunting in Montana: A Search for Roots in the Old West*. New York: Harper Collins, 1994.

Cook, Noble David. *Demographic Collapse: Indian Peru, 1520–1620*. Cambridge: Cambridge University Press, 1981.

Cook, Noble David, and W. George Lovell. *"Secret Judgements of God": Old World Disease in Colonial Spanish America*. Norman: University of Oklahoma Press, 1992.

Cook, S.F., and W. Borah. *Essays in Population History*. Vol. 1. Berkeley: University of California Press, 1971.

Crèvecoeur, Hector St. John de. *The Divided Loyalist: Crèvecoeur's America*. Introduction by Marcus Cunliffe. London· Folio Society, 1978 [1782].

———. *Letters from an American Farmer*. Everyman's Library. Edited and introduction by Warren Barton Blake. London and New York: Dent and Dutton, 1926 [1782].

Crosby, Alfred W. *The Columbian Exchange: Biological and Cultural Consequences of 1492*. Westport, Conn.: Greenwood Press, 1972.

———. *Ecological Imperialism: The Biological Expansion of Europe, 900–1900*. 2nd ed. Cambridge: Cambridge University Press, 2004 [1986].

———. *Germs, Seeds, and Animals*. Armonk, N.Y.: M.E. Sharpe, 1994.

Cross, Harry. "South American Bullion Production and Export 1550–1750." In *Precious Metals in the Later Mediaeval and Early Modern Worlds*. Edited by J.F. Richards. Durham: University of North Carolina Press, 1983.

Daniels, Leroy Judson. *Tales of an Old Horse Trader*. Manchester: Carcanet, 1987.

Davis, Mike. *Buda's Waggon: A Brief History of the Car Bomb*. London: Verso, 2007.

Debo, Angie. *A History of the Indians of the United States*. Norman: University of Oklahoma Press, 1989 [1970].

De Grazia, Victoria. *Irresistible Empire: America's Advance Through Twentieth-Century Europe*. Cambridge, Mass.: Harvard University Press, 2005.

Delbanco, Andrew. *Melville: His World and Work*. New York: Knopf, 2005.

Denevan, W.M., ed. *The Native Population of the Americas in 1492*. Madison: University of Wisconsin Press, 1976.

Dennett, Tyler. *Americans in Eastern Asia*. New York: Barnes & Noble, 1963 [1922].

Díaz, Bernal. *The Conquest of New Spain*. Translated by J.M. Cohen. London: Penguin, 1963.

Domhoff, G. William, and Hoyt B. Ballard, eds. *C. Wright Mills and the Power Elite*. Boston: Beacon Press, 1968.

Dos Passos, John. *Nineteen Nineteen*. New York: New American Library, 1969 [1932].

Drinnon, Richard. *Violence in the American Experience: Winning the West*. New York: New American Library, 1979.

Dyer, Gwynne. *The Mess They Made: The Middle East after Iraq*. Toronto: McClelland & Stewart, 2007.

Edwards, Clinton R. "Possibilities of Pre-Columbian Maritime Contacts among New World Civilization." In *Pre-Columbian Contact Within Nuclear America*, edited by J.C. Kelley and C.L. Riley. Carbondale: University of Illinois Press, 1969.

Ehle, John. *Trail of Tears: The Rise and Fall of the Cherokee Nation*. New York: Doubleday, 1988.

Ehrenreich, Barbara. *Nickel and Dimed*. New York: Holt, 2001.

Ehrman, John. *The Rise of Neoconservatism, 1945–1994*. New Haven: Yale University Press, 1995.

Eksteins, Modris. *Rites of Spring: The Great War and the Birth of the Modern Age*. Toronto: Lester & Orpen Dennys, 1989.

Ellis, Joseph. *After the Revolution: Profiles of Early American Culture*. New York: Norton, 1979.

Espinoza Soriano, Waldemar. "La sociedad andina colonial y republicana (siglos XVI–XIX)." In *Nueva Historia General del Perú*, by Carlos Araníbar et al., 195–230. Lima: Mosca Azul Editores, 1979.

Evans, E. Raymond. "Notable Persons in Cherokee History: Dragging Canoe." *Journal of Cherokee Studies* 2, no. 1 (1977): 176–89.

Evans, Harold. *The American Century*. New York: Knopf, 1998.

Faragher, John Mack. *Daniel Boone: The Life and Legend of an American Pioneer*. New York: Holt, 1993.

Ferguson, Thomas, and Joel Rogers. *Right Turn*. New York: Hill & Wang, 1986.

Fernández-Armesto, Felipe. *The Americas: The History of a Hemisphere*. London: Weidenfeld & Nicolson, 2003.

———. *Amerigo: The Man Who Gave His Name to America*. London: Weidenfeld & Nicolson, 2006.

———. *Pathfinders: A Global History of Exploration*. Oxford: Oxford University Press, 2006.

Flannery, Tim. *The Eternal Frontier: An Ecological History of North America and Its Peoples*. Melbourne: Text, 2001.

———. *The Future Eaters: An Ecological History of the Australasian Lands and People*. New York: Braziller, 1995.

Foote, Shelby. *The Civil War: A Narrative*. 3 vols. New York: Vintage, 1986.

Forbes, Jack D. *Black Africans and Native Americans*. Oxford: Blackwell, 1988.

Foreman, Grant. *The Five Civilized Tribes*. Norman: University of Oklahoma Press, 1989 [1934].

———. *Indian Removal*. Norman: University of Oklahoma Press, 1972.

Foster, Sir Augustus. *Jeffersonian America: Notes on the United States of America Collected in the Years 1805–6–7 and 11–12 by Sir Augustus John Foster, Bart*. Edited by Richard Beale Davis. San Marino, Calif.: Huntington Library, 1954 [ca. 1835].

Francisco, Luzviminda. "The First Vietnam: The Philippine-American War, 1899–1902." *Bulletin of Concerned Asian Scholars* 5, no. 4 (December 1973): 2–16.

Franzen, Jonathan. *The Corrections*. New York: Picador USA, 2001.

Friedman, Lawrence J. *Inventors of the Promised Land*. New York: Knopf, 1975.

Fukuyama, Francis. *The End of History and the Last Man*. New York: Free Press, 1992.

Fussell, Paul. *The Great War and Modern Memory*. Oxford: Oxford University Press, 1975.

Galeano, Eduardo. *Memory of Fire*. 3 vols. Translated by Cedric Belfrage. London: Quartet Books, 1985–88.

Garcilaso de la Vega, El Inca. *Comentarios Reales de los Incas* [Royal Commentaries of the Incas]. Edited by Aurelio Miró Quesada. 2 vols. Caracas: Biblioteca Ayacucho, 1976 [1609].

———. *La Florida*. Introduction by Carmen de Mora. Madrid: Alianza, 1988 [1605].

———. *La Florida del Inca* [The Inca's Florida]. Mexico D.F.: Fondo de Cultura Económica, 1965 [1605].

Gardner, John. *Grendel*. New York: Knopf, 1971.

Gilbert, Bil. *God Gave Us This Country*. New York: Atheneum, 1989.

———. *Westering Man: The Life of Joseph Walker*. Norman: University of Oklahoma Press, 1983.

Gore, Al. *The Assault on Reason*. New York: Penguin, 2007.

Gott, Richard. "Brave New World." *The Liberal* 2 (February–March 2005): 8–10.

———. *Guerrilla Movements in Latin America*. London: Nelson, 1970.

Graeber, David. "Army of Altruists: On the Alienated Right to Do Good." *Harper's Magazine*, January 2007, 31–38.

Grant, Richard. *Ghost Riders: Travels with American Nomads*. London: Little, Brown, 2003.

Haffner, Sebastian. *Defying Hitler: A Memoir*. London: Weidenfeld & Nicolson, 2002.

Hall, Robert L. "Savoring Africa in the New World." In *Seeds of Change: Five Hundred Years since Columbus,* edited by Herman J. Viola and Carolyn Margolis, 160–71. Washington, D.C.: Smithsonian, 1991.

Hamor, Ralphe. *A True Discourse of the Present Estate of Virginia*. Amsterdam: Da Capo Press, 1971 [1615].

Harris, Paul. "Fortune Favours the Braves." *The Guardian*, August 19, 2007. guardian.co.uk.

Hedges, Chris. *American Fascists: The Christian Right and the War on America*. New York: Free Press, 2007.

Hemming, John. *The Conquest of the Incas*. London: Penguin, 1983 [1970].

Hendrix, Janey B. "Redbird Smith and the Nighthawk Keetoowahs." *Journal of Cherokee Studies* 8, no. 1 (Spring 1983): 22–39.

Heyerdahl, Thor. "Guara Navigation: Indigenous Sailing off the Andean
　　Coast." *Southwestern Journal of Anthropology* 13, no.2 (1957).
——— . *Sea Routes to Polynesia*. London: Futura, 1974 [1968].
Heyerdahl, Thor, and Arne Skjolsvold. "Archaeological Evidence of Pre-
　　Spanish Visits to the Galápagos Islands." *Memoirs of the Society for
　　American Archaeology* 12 (1956).
Hobsbawm, Eric. *Age of Extremes: The Short Twentieth Century 1914–1991*.
　　London: Michael Joseph, 1994.
Hofstadter, Richard. *Anti-intellectualism in American Life*. New York: Knopf,
　　1963.
———. *The Paranoid Style in American Politics and Other Essays*. New York:
　　Knopf, 1966.
———. *Social Darwinism in American Thought*. New York: Braziller, 1959
　　[1944].
Hosler, Dorothy. "Ancient West Mexican Metallurgy: South and Central
　　American Origins and West Mexican Transformations." *American
　　Anthropologist* 90, no. 4 (1988): 832–55.
Hudson, Charles. *Knights of Spain, Warriors of the Sun: Hernando de Soto and
　　the South's Ancient Chiefdoms*. Athens: University of Georgia Press,
　　1997.
Huey, Lois M., and Bonnie Pulis. *Molly Brant: A Legacy of Her Own*.
　　Youngstown, N.Y.: Old Fort Niagara Association, 1997.
Hulme, Peter, and Neil Whitehead, eds. *Wild Majesty: Encounters with Caribs
　　from Columbus to the Present Day*. Oxford: Clarendon Press, 1992.
Jackson, Helen Hunt. *A Century of Dishonor*. New York: Harper & Bros., 1881.
Jamieson, Alan. "America's Eighty Years War?" *Globe and Mail*, January 15,
　　2007.
Janszen, Eric. "The Next Bubble: Priming the Markets for Tomorrow's Big
　　Crash." *Harper's Magazine*, February 2008, 39–45.
Jefferson, Thomas. *Notes on the State of Virginia*. Paris: privately printed, 1784.
Jennings, Francis. *The Ambiguous Iroquois Empire*. New York: Norton, 1984.

———. *The Invasion of America: Indians, Colonialism, and the Cant of Conquest.* New York: Norton, 1975.

Johansen, Bruce. *Forgotten Founders: How the American Indian Helped Shape Democracy.* Ipswich, Mass.: Gambit, 1982.

———. "Native American Societies and the Evolution of Democracy in America, 1600–1800." *Ethnohistory* 37, no. 3 (1990): 279–90.

Johnson, Chalmers. "Republic or Empire: A National Intelligence Estimate on the United States." *Harper's Magazine*, January 2007, 63–69.

Jones, Dorothy V. *License for Empire: Colonialism by Treaty in Early America.* Chicago: University of Chicago Press, 1982.

Kagan, Robert. *Dangerous Nation: America and the World, 1600–1898.* New York: Atlantic, 2006.

Kamen, Henry. *Spain's Road to Empire: The Making of a World Power 1492–1763.* London: Penguin, 2002.

Kaplan, Esther. *With God on Their Side: George W. Bush and the Christian Right.* New York: New Press, 2005.

Keegan, John. *The Second World War.* New York: Penguin, 1989.

Kendall, Ann. *Everyday Life of the Incas.* New York: Putnam's, 1973.

King, Duane, ed. *The Cherokee Indian Nation.* Knoxville: University of Tennessee Press, 1979.

King, Duane, and Jefferson Chapman. *The Sequoyah Legacy.* Vonore, Tenn.: Sequoyah Birthplace Museum, 1998.

King, Duane H., and E. Raymond Evans, eds. "The Trail of Tears: Primary Documents of the Cherokee Removal." *Journal of Cherokee Studies* 3, no. 3 (Summer 1978): 129–90.

Kinzer, Stephen. *Overthrow: America's History of Regime Change from Hawaii to Iraq.* New York: Times Books, 2007.

Klein, Naomi. *The Shock Doctrine: The Rise of Disaster Capitalism.* Toronto: Knopf, 2007.

Krakauer, Jon. *Under the Banner of Heaven.* Rev. ed. New York: Anchor, 2004.

LaFeber, Walter. *The New Empire: An Interpretation of American Expansion*. Ithaca, N.Y.: Cornell University Press, 1998 [1963].

Lapham, Lewis. "Terror Alerts." *Harper's Magazine*, March 2007, 9–11.

Lawrence, D.H. *Selected Essays*. London: Penguin, 1950.

———. *Studies in Classic American Literature*. New York: Penguin USA, 1964 [1923].

Lawson, John. *A New Voyage to Carolina*. Edited by Hugh Talmage Lefler. Chapel Hill: University of North Carolina Press, 1967 [1700].

Lazarus, Edward. *Black Hills, White Justice: The Sioux Nation Versus the United States, 1775 to the Present*. New York: Harper Collins, 1991.

Levy, Bernard-Henri. *American Vertigo: Traveling America in the Footsteps of Tocqueville*. Translated by Charlotte Mandell. New York: Random House, 2006.

Lieven, Anatol. *America Right or Wrong*. New York: HarperCollins, 2005.

———. "Why We Should Fear a McCain Presidency." *Financial Times* (London), March 24, 2008.

Liliuokalani, Queen. *Hawaii's Story by Hawaii's Queen*. Honolulu: Mutual Publishing, 1990 [1898].

Limerick, Patricia Nelson. *The Legacy of Conquest: The Unbroken Past of the American West*. New York: Norton, 1987.

———. *Something in the Soil: Legacies and Reckonings in the New West*. New York: Norton, 2000.

Lindberg, Gary. *The Confidence Man in American Literature*. Oxford: Oxford University Press, 1982.

Lindqvist, Sven. *Exterminate All the Brutes*. Translated by Joan Tate. London: Granta Books, 1996 [1992].

Lockhart, James, and Enrique Otte. *Letters and People of the Spanish Indies*. Cambridge: Cambridge University Press, 1976.

Lovell, W. George. "'Heavy Shadows and Black Night': Disease and Depopulation in Colonial Spanish America." *Annals of the Association of American Geographers* 82, no. 3 (September 1992): 426–43.

Lovell, W. George, and Christopher H. Lutz. *Demography and Empire: A Guide to the Population History of Spanish Central America, 1500–1821*. Boulder, Col.: Westview Press, 1995.

Lundy, Derek. *The Men That God Made Mad*. London: Cape, 2006 (published in North America as *The Bloody Red Hand*).

Luttwak, Edward N. *The Grand Strategy of the Roman Empire from the First Century A.D. to the Third*. Baltimore, Md.: Johns Hopkins University Press, 1976.

MacMillan, Margaret. *Paris 1919: Six Months That Changed the World*. New York: Random House, 2001.

Mankiller, Wilma, and Michael Wallis. *Mankiller: A Chief and Her People*. New York: St. Martin's Press, 1993.

Manley, Henry S. *The Treaty of Fort Stanwix, 1784*, Rome, N.Y.: Rome Sentinel, 1932.

Mann, Charles C. *1491: New Revelations of the Americas before Columbus*. New York: Knopf, 2005.

Mann, Michael. *The Dark Side of Democracy: Explaining Ethnic Cleansing*. Cambridge: Cambridge University Press, 2007.

Manning, Richard. "The Oil We Eat: Following the Food Chain Back to Iraq." *Harper's Magazine*, February 2004, 37–45.

Marx, Karl. *Karl Marx: Selected Writings in Sociology and Social Philosophy*. Edited by T.B. Bottomore and Maximilien Rubel. London: Penguin, 1961.

Marx, Karl, and Frederick Engels. *Manifesto of the Communist Party*. Peking: Foreign Languages Press, 1965 [1838].

Matthiessen, Peter. *In the Spirit of Crazy Horse*. New York: Penguin, 1992.

McDowell, William L., Jr. *Colonial Records of South Carolina: Documents Relating to Indian Affairs, 1754–65*. Columbia: University of South Carolina Press, 1970.

McLoughlin, William G. *Cherokee Renascence in the New Republic*. Princeton, N.J.: Princeton University Press, 1986.

McLuhan, T.C. *Touch the Earth: A Self-Portrait of Indian Existence.* New York: Simon & Schuster, 1971.

McNeill, William H. "American Food Crops in the Old World." In *Seeds of Change: Five Hundred Years since Columbus*, edited by Herman J. Viola and Carolyn Margolis, 42–59. Washington, D.C.: Smithsonian, 1991.

———. *Plagues and Peoples.* New York: Anchor, 1976.

Melville, Herman. *The Confidence Man.* Oxford: Oxford University Press, 1989 [1857].

———. *Moby Dick.* Oxford: Oxford University Press, 1988 [1851].

Merrell, James H. *The Indians' New World: Catawbas and Their Neighbors from European Contact through the Era of Removal.* Chapel Hill: University of North Carolina Press, 1989.

Miller, Perry. *Errand into the Wilderness.* Cambridge, Mass.: Harvard University Press, 1956.

———. *Nature's Nation.* Cambridge, Mass.: Harvard University Press, 1967.

Millones, Luis. "The Time of the Inca: The Colonial Indians' Quest." *Antiquity* 66 (1992): 204–16.

Mills, C. Wright. *The Power Elite.* Oxford: Oxford University Press, 1960.

Miranda, Francisco de. *The New Democracy in America: Travels of Francisco de Miranda in the United States, 1783–84.* Edited by John S. Ezell. Translated by Judson P. Wood. Norman: University of Oklahoma Press, 1963 [ca. 1784].

Mooney, James. *Myths of the Cherokee and Sacred Formulas of the Cherokee.* Cherokee, N.C.: Cherokee Heritage Books, 1982 [1900].

More, Thomas. *Utopia.* Translated by Ralph Robinson (1551). Introduction by Richard Marius. London: Dent, 1985 [1516].

Morgan, Lewis Henry. *League of the Iroquois.* Secaucus, N.J.: Citadel Press, 1972 [1851].

Morison, Samuel Eliot. *The European Discovery of America: The Northern Voyages, A.D. 500–1600*. New York: Oxford University Press, 1971.

Moulton, Gary E. *John Ross, Cherokee Chief*. Athens: University of Georgia Press, 1978.

Mowat, Farley. *Westviking: The Ancient Norse in Greenland and North America*. Boston: Little, Brown, 1965.

Mumford, Lewis. *The Myth of the Machine*. Vol. 2, *The Pentagon of Power*. New York: Harcourt Brace Jovanovich, 1970.

National Research Council. *Lost Crops of the Incas*. Washington, D.C.: National Academy Press, 1989.

Nelles, Henry Vivian. *A Little History of Canada*. Toronto and Oxford: Oxford University Press, 2004.

Norton, Anne. *Leo Strauss and the Politics of American Empire*. New Haven, Conn.: Yale University Press, 2005.

Obama, Barack. *Dreams from My Father*. New York: Three Rivers Press, 2004.

O'Callaghan, E.B., et al., eds. *Documents Relative to the Colonial History of the State of New York*. 15 vols. Albany, N.Y.: Weed, Parsons, 1853–1887 [1969 reprint by AMS Press].

Okri, Ben. "The New Dark Age." *The Guardian*, April 19, 2003.

O'Toole, Fintan. *White Savage: William Johnson and the Invention of America*. London: Faber & Faber, 2005.

Pagden, Anthony. *Hernán Cortés: Letters from Mexico*. New Haven, Conn.: Yale University Press, 1986.

Parker, Arthur C. *The History of the Seneca Indians*. Port Washington, N.Y.: Ira J. Friedman, 1967 [1926].

———. *The Life of General Ely S. Parker*. Buffalo, N.Y.: Buffalo Historical Society, 1919.

———. *Parker on the Iroquois*. Edited by William Fenton. Syracuse, N.Y.: Syracuse University Press, 1968.

Parker, Hershel. *Herman Melville: A Biography.* Vol. 1, *1819–1851.* Baltimore, Md.: Johns Hopkins University Press, 1996

Parkman, Francis. *The Conspiracy of Pontiac, and the Indian War after the Conquest of Canada.* Boston: New Library, 1909 [1851].

———. *The Jesuits in North America in the Seventeenth Century.* Boston: New Library, 1909 [1867].

Parry, J.H. *The Spanish Seaborne Empire.* Berkeley: University of California Press, 1990 [1966].

Patten, Chris. *Cousins and Strangers: America, Britain and Europe in a New Century.* New York: Times Books, 2006.

Perdue, Theda, and Michael D. Green. *The Cherokee Removal: A Brief History with Documents.* New York: Bedford/St. Martin's, 2005.

Pizarro, Pedro. *Relación del Descubrimiento y Conquista de los Reinos del Perú.* Edited by Guillermo Lohmann Villena. Lima: Universidad Católica, 1986 [1571].

Ponting, Clive. *A Green History of the World: The Environment and the Collapse of Great Civilizations.* London: Sinclair Stevenson, 1991.

Porras Barrenechea, Raúl. *Colección de Documentos Inéditos para la Historia del Perú.* Vol. 3, *Cartas del Perú (1524–1543).* Lima: Sociedad de Bibliófilos Peruanos, 1959.

———. *Los Cronistas del Perú.* Lima: Banco de Crédito del Perú, 1986.

———. *Las Relaciones Primitivas de la Conquista del Perú.* Paris: Les Presses Modernes, 1937.

Prescott, William H. *History of the Conquest of Mexico and History of the Conquest of Peru.* New York: Random House Modern Library, n.d. [1843, 1847].

Prucha, Francis Paul, ed. *Cherokee Removal: The "William Penn" Essays and Other Writing.* Knoxville: University of Tennessee Press, 1981.

Raban, Jonathan. *Bad Land: An American Romance.* London: Picador, 1996.

Rapley, Robert. *Witch Hunts: From Salem to Guantánamo Bay.* Montreal: McGill University Press, 2007.

Remini, Robert. *Andrew Jackson*. 3 vols. New York: Harper & Row, 1977–84.

———. *The Legacy of Andrew Jackson: Essays on Democracy, Indian Removal, and Slavery*. Baton Rouge: Louisiana State University Press, 1988.

Rice, Edward. *Captain Sir Richard Francis Burton*. New York: Scribner's, 1990.

Richards, J.F., ed. *Precious Metals in the Later Mediaeval and Early Modern Worlds*. Durham: University of North Carolina Press, 1983.

Rifkin, Jeremy. "Continentalism of a Different Stripe." *The Walrus*, March 2005, 37–41.

———. *The European Dream: How Europe's Vision of the Future Is Quietly Eclipsing the American Dream*. Toronto: Penguin, 2004.

Rogin, Michael. *Fathers and Children: Andrew Jackson and the Subjugation of the American Indian*. New York: Knopf, 1975.

Roosevelt, Theodore. *African Game Trails: An Account of the African Wanderings of an American Hunter-Naturalist*. New York: Syndicate Publishing, 1910.

———. *The Winning of the West*. New York: Best Books, 1989 [1894].

Ross, Chief John Kooweskoowee. *The Papers of Chief John Ross*. Edited by Gary Moulton. 2 vols. Norman: University of Oklahoma Press, 1985.

Ross, Kurt, ed. *Codex Mendoza, Aztec Manuscript*. Fribourg, Switzerland: Miller Graphics, 1978 [ca. 1540].

Rowland, Wade. *Greed, Inc.: Why Corporations Rule Our World and How We Let It Happen*. Toronto: Thomas Allen, 2005.

Salter, James. *The Hunters*. London: Harvill, 1998 [1956].

Scarr, Deryck. *The Majesty of Colour: A Life of Sir John Bates Thurston*. Canberra: Australian National University Press, 1973.

Schapiro, Mark. "Toxic Inaction: Why Poisonous, Unregulated Chemicals End Up in Our Blood." *Harper's Magazine*, October 2007, 78–83.

Schlesinger, Stephen, and Stephen Kinzer. *Bitter Fruit: The Untold Story of the American Coup in Guatemala*. New York: Doubleday, 1983.

Seaver, James, ed. *A Narrative of the Life of Mary Jemison, the White Woman of the Genessee*. New York: New York Scenic and Historic

Preservation Society, 1932 [1824].

Sheehan, B.W. *The Seeds of Extinction: Jeffersonian Philanthropy and the American Indian*. Chapel Hill: University of North Carolina Press, 1973.

Singer, Peter. *The President of Good and Evil: The Ethics of George W. Bush*. Melbourne: Text, 2004.

Smith, Adam. *The Wealth of Nations*. London: Penguin, 1982 [1776].

Smyth, Albert Henry, ed. *The Writings of Benjamin Franklin*. 10 vols. New York: Macmillan, 1905–7.

Snow, Dean R. *The Iroquois*. Cambridge, Mass.: Blackwell, 1994.

Squier, Ephraim George. *Aboriginal Monuments of the State of New York*. New York: Sourcebook, 1984 [1851].

———. *Peru: Incidents of Travel and Exploration in the Land of the Incas*. New York: Peabody/AMS, 1973 [1877].

Squier, Ephraim George, and Edwin H. Davis. *Ancient Monuments of the Mississippi Valley*. Washington D.C.: Smithsonian Contributions to Knowledge 1, 1848.

Stegner, Wallace. *Mormon Country*. Lincoln: University of Nebraska Press, 1981.

Steinbeck, John. *The Grapes of Wrath*. New York: Penguin, 1980 [1939].

———. *Travels with Charley*. New York: Penguin, 1980 [1962].

Stephens, John Lloyd. *Incidents of Travel in Central America, Chiapas, and Yucatan*. Illustrated by Frederick Catherwood. 2 vols. New York: Dover reprint, 1969 [1841].

———. *Incidents of Travel in Yucatan*. 2 vols. New York: Dover reprint, 1963 [1843].

Stiglitz, Joseph E. "The Economic Consequences of Mr. Bush." *Vanity Fair*, December 2007, 312–15, 375–76.

———. *Globalization and Its Discontents*. New York: Norton, 2002.

Stone, William L. *The Life and Times of Sa-go-ye-wat-ha, or Red Jacket*. New York: Munsell, 1866.

————. *Life of Joseph Brant*. 2 vols. New York: Kraus, 1969 [1838].

Strachan, Hew. *The First World War*. Single-volume edition. London: Penguin, 2005.

Strachey, Lytton. *Eminent Victorians*. London: Chatto & Windus, 1918.

Taylor, Charles. *The Malaise of Modernity*. Toronto: Anansi, 1991.

Temperley, Howard. *Britain and America since Independence*. New York: Palgrave, 2002.

Thomas, Hugh. *The Conquest of Mexico*. London: Hutchinson/Random House, 1993.

Thompson, E.P. *The Making of the English Working Class*. London: Victor Gollancz, 1963.

Thompson, Lawrance. *Melville's Quarrel with God*. Princeton, N.J.: Princeton University Press, 1952.

Thoreau, Henry David. *Walden or, Life in the Woods and On the Duty of Civil Disobedience*. Afterword by Perry Miller. New York: New American Library, 1960 [1854, 1849].

Thornton, Russell. *American Indian Holocaust and Survival*. Norman: University of Oklahoma Press, 1987.

————. *We Shall Live Again*. Cambridge: Cambridge University Press, 1986.

Titu Kusi Yupanki (Titu Cusi Yupanqui). *Relación de la Conquista del Perú*. Lima: Biblioteca Universitaria, 1973 [1570].

Tocqueville, Alexis de. *Democracy in America*. Translated by Henry Reeve. Introduction by John Stuart Mill. 2 vols. New York: Schocken Books, 1961 [1835].

————. *Democracy in America*. Translated by Henry Reeve. Introduction by Joseph Epstein. New York: Bantam, 2000 [1835].

————. *Journey to America*. Edited by J.P. Mayer. Translated by George Lawrence. London: Faber, 1959 [1831–32].

Trollope, Anthony. *The Way We Live Now*. London: Penguin, 1993 [1875].

Trollope, Frances. *The Domestic Manners of the Americans*. New York:

Penguin Classics, 1997 [1832].

Turner, Frederick Jackson. *The Significance of the Frontier in American History: The Turner Thesis*. Edited and introduction by George Rogers Taylor. Lexington, Mass.: Heath, 1972 [1893].

Turner, Frederick W., III, ed. *North American Indian Reader*. New York: Viking, 1974.

Twain, Mark. *Adventures of Huckleberry Finn*. New York: Signet, 1997 [1885].

Urton, Gary. *Signs of the Inka Khipu: Binary Coding in the Andean Knotted-String Records*. Austin: University of Texas Press, 2003.

Van Alstyne, R.W. *The Rising American Empire*. Oxford: Blackwell, 1960.

Vidal, Gore. *Perpetual War for Perpetual Peace*. New York: Nation Books, 2002.

Viola, Herman J., and Carolyn Margolis, eds. *Seeds of Change: Five Hundred Years since Columbus*. Washington, D.C.: Smithsonian, 1991.

Vonnegut, Kurt. *Galápagos*. New York: Doubleday, 1985.

———. *Slaughterhouse Five*. London: Cape, 1969.

Waldman, Carl. *Atlas of the North American Indian*. New York: Facts on File, 1985.

Wallace, Anthony F.C. *The Death and Rebirth of the Seneca*. New York: Random House, 1969.

Wallace, Paul. *Conrad Weiser: Friend of Colonist and Mohawk*. Philadelphia: University of Pennsylvania Press, 1945.

Walton, Dawn. "Were Bison One of Globalization's First Victims?" *Globe and Mail*, July 31, 2007.

Waman Puma de Ayala, Felipe (Guaman Poma de Ayala). *El Primer Nueva Corónica y Buen Gobierno*. Edited by John Murra, Rolena Adorno and Jorge Urioste. 3 vols. Mexico: Siglo Veintiuno, 1980 [ca. 1615].

Warren, Robert Penn. *The Legacy of the Civil War*. Cambridge, Mass.: Harvard University Press, 1961.

Wearne, Phillip. *Return of the Indian: Conquest and Revival in the Americas*. Foreword by Rigoberta Menchú. London: Cassell, 1996.

Weatherford, Jack. *Indian Givers*. New York: Crown, 1988.

———. *Native Roots*. New York: Crown, 1991.

Weber, Max. *The Protestant Ethic and the Spirit of Capitalism*. London: Routledge, 2001 [1920].

Weinberg, Albert K. *Manifest Destiny: A Study of Nationalist Expansionism in American History*. Gloucester, Mass.: Peter Smith, 1935.

Weller, George. *First into Nagasaki: The Censored Eyewitness Dispatches on Post-Atomic Japan and Its Prisoners of War*. Edited by Anthony Weller. Foreword by Walter Cronkite. New York: Crown, 2006.

Werlich, David P. *Peru: A Short History*. Carbondale: Southern Illinois University Press, 1978.

White, Lynn. "The Historical Roots of Our Ecologic Crisis." *Science* 155, no. 3767 (March 1967): 1203–7.

Wilkins, Thurman. *Cherokee Tragedy*. London: Macmillan, 1970.

Williams, William Appleman. *Empire as a Way of Life: An Essay on the Causes and Character of America's Present Predicament along with a Few Thoughts about an Alternative*. Oxford: Oxford University Press, 1980.

———. *The Tragedy of American Diplomacy*. New York: Dell, 1959.

Willison, George F. *Saints and Strangers, Being the Lives of the Pilgrim Fathers and Their Families*. New York: Parnassus, 1983 [1945].

Wilson, Edmund. *Apologies to the Iroquois*. London: W.H. Allen, 1960.

Wilson, James. *The Earth Shall Weep: A History of Native America*. New York: Grove, 1998.

Wolf, Eric R. *Europe and the People Without History*. Berkeley: University of California Press, 1982.

Woodward, Grace Steele. *The Cherokees*. Norman: University of Oklahoma Press, 1963.

Woolley, Benjamin. *Savage Kingdom: Virginia and the Founding of English America*. London: HarperCollins, 2007.

Wright, Louis B. *Religion and Empire: The Alliance Between Piety and Commerce in English Expansion, 1558–1625*. Chapel Hill: University of North Carolina Press, 1965 [1943].

Wright, Ronald. *A Short History of Progress*, Toronto: Anansi, 2004.

———. *Stolen Continents: 500 Years of Conquest and Resistance in the Americas*. Boston: Houghton Mifflin/Mariner, 2005 [1992].

Wrobel, David M. *The End of American Exceptionalism: Frontier Anxiety from the Old West to the New Deal*. Lawrence: Kansas University Press, 1993.

———. *Promised Lands: Promotion, Memory, and the Creation of the American West*. Lawrence: Kansas University Press, 2002.

Wroth, Lawrence C. *The Voyages of Giovanni da Verrazzano 1524–1528*. New Haven: Yale University Press, 1970.

York, Geoffrey, and Loreen Pindera. *People of the Pines: The Warriors and the Legacy of Oka*. Toronto: Little, Brown, 1991.

Zinn, Howard. *A People's History of the United States, 1492–Present*. New York: Harper Perennial, 2003.

Acknowledgments

My thanks to Louise Dennys, Rosemary Shipton, Michael Heyward, Penny Hueston and William Strachan for their skilful editing and many helpful suggestions; also to copyeditor Kathryn Dean and to my agents Bella Pomer, Antony Harwood and Henry Dunow; to Diane Barlee for her kindness in reading the manuscript and for her good advice; and to all those who helped with sources, suggestions and conversations, especially Michael Baldwin, Devon Blean, Brian Brett, Michael Childs, Inga Clendinnen, Charles Foran, Rona Gilbertson, Peter Hulme, David Kendall, Derek Lundy, Margaret MacMillan, Alberto Manguel, Claire Mowat, Farley Mowat, Cassandra Pybus, Henri Theureau, Sarah Tidbury, Nancy Van Patten, Michael Wall, Anthony Weller, Anthony Robin Wilkinson, Pam Wilkinson and Eric Wredenhagen.

Index

Dennett, Tyler, 176
depression (economic)
    of 1929, 187
    of 1983, 170
deregulation, 207
de Soto, Hernando. *See* Soto,
    Hernando de
de Tocqueville, Alexis. *See*
    Tocqueville, Alexis de
Detroit Michigan, 73
Dewey, Admiral George, 315
Díaz, Bernal, 245
discrimination, racial, 310–13,
    315
Disraeli, Benjamin, 228
Dole, Sanford, 172, 315
Dominionists, 141, 304
Donation of Constantine, 80, 272
Dos Passos, John, 182
Douglass, Frederick, 160
Drake, Sir Francis, 60
Drayton, William Henry, 9, 237
Dreams from My Father (book), 228
Dred Scott decision, 154
Dubcek, Alexander, 201
Dulles, Alan, 327
Dulles, John Foster, 327
Dunne, Finley (creator of Mr.
    Dooley), 81, 272
Dutch presence in early America,
    45, 89–90, 92–93, 96

economic stability (world), potential
    collapse of, 222–23
Edwards, John, 333
Edward the Confessor, 272
Egypt, 22, 142
Eisenhower, Dwight D., 195, 198, 325
Eldorado, 1–2
Emerson, Ralph Waldo, 131–32,
    139, 150–51, 300

emigration
    to America, 42, 62, 65, 97,
        265, 273–74
    dangers of, 65
empires. *See primarily specific
    exemplars, e.g.* Britain, the
    empire of; Spain, the
    empire of
    exploitative natures of, 62,
        265
Engels, Friedrich, 98
the Enlightenment
    in America, 110, 121, 204,
        230, 234–36
    in Europe, 87, 183.
    See also America, "backwoods"
    of
the environment
    degradation of, 190, 204, 207,
        209, 217, 222–23, 225,
        274, 334
    potential collapse of, 334–35
Episcopalians, 141
erosion, the dust bowl and, 186–87
European Union, 185, 214,
    224–25
Evarts, Jeremiah, 295
evolution (Darwinian), 16
expansion into new frontiers. *See*
    growth

Falwell, Jerry, 16, 88, 239, 274
Faragher, John Mack, 289
farming, as a support for industry,
    39–40, 43, 256
Farming Revolution, 22–23
Farnham, James, 302
federation of the thirteen colonies,
    99–100, 281
Ferdinand, Archduke Franz, 180
the Five Civilized Tribes, 71, 113